THINKING
DRINKERS

THINKING DRINKERS

BEN McFARLAND and TOM SANDHAM

jacqui small

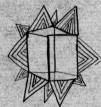

Dedication
To Thinking Drinkers Everywhere

First published in 2014 by
Jacqui Small LLP
an imprint of Aurum Press
74–77 White Lion Street
London N1 9PF

ISBN 978 1 909342 62 0

A catalogue record for this book is available from
the British Library.

Publisher Jacqui Small
Senior Commissioning Editor Fritha Saunders
Managing Editor Lydia Halliday
Project Editor Joanna Copestick
Senior Designer Rachel Cross
Picture Researcher Alexandra Labbe Thompson
Production Maeve Healy
Illustrators
  Chapter Openers: Andrew Bannecker/www.ba-reps.com
  Timelines: Nicholas Saunders/folioart.co.uk
  Distinguished Drinkers: Martin Haake/www.centralillustration.com

2016 2015 2014
10 9 8 7 6 5 4 3 2 1

Printed in China

CONTENTS

THINKING DRINKERS

Alcohol. One minute a soul mate, the next a psychopath. It pulls at the loose threads of life with one hand yet weaves joy through it with the other. A fickle fellow, flipping from faithful friend to fearsome foe in the space of a few small sips, the pin loosening from the social grenade with every pour.

On occasions when it is consumed in excess, it shoves a stick in the spokes of the central nervous system, decelerates brain activity, makes a mockery of your motor function and makes essential items such as keys, money and mobile phones to disappear.

After an initial euphoria, alcohol increases anxiety, slurs speech, aggravates any anger you may have, exaggerates irritation and it can also cause memory loss. It can also cause memory loss.

Mistreat it and it will mess you up, dropping you to your knees with nonchalant indifference. Consistent and constant abuse leads to all manner of horrible things: liver disease, diabetes, cancer and other ailments that no-one wants to have to deal with.

But compared with water, booze is a mere drop in the bucket of disease and death. Water has been spreading soluble sickness all over the world for centuries. Cholera, dysentery, salmonella, typhoid, Legionnaires' disease and, lest we forget, the Bubonic Plague, are just some of the lurgies that have happily lived in that most lethal of liquids. Don't say you haven't been warned.

Alcohol, meanwhile, has been the antidote to all of this. From the herbal wines of Hippocrates, the father of modern medicine, to modern-day alcoholic hand gels (please don't drink alcoholic hand gel, even if you're really ill), the 'water of life' has been giving the Grim Reaper the runaround for centuries.

It has also shaped the world as we know it. Not content with sowing the seeds of early civilisation, drink kept explorers alive during the Age of Discovery, and as any of history's most prestigious leaders will tell you, from Alexander the Great to Winston Churchill, there's no better weapon in war than alcohol (not including bombs, enormous guns and suchlike).

Alcohol has been instrumental in shaping the world's religious landscape. Europe, for a start, could well have been an Islamic continent, were it not for drink. A distinct lack of booze impaired Islam's advances into Europe during the 10th century when Vladimir of Kiev, the Russian ruler, was in the market for a religion to give to his hitherto Pagan empire.

Kicking the tyres of the various faiths, Vlad was intrigued by many aspects of Islam but simply couldn't stomach its strict no-booze policy. So he threw his considerable military might behind Christianity instead, Islam was ushered out of Europe and the West sidestepped a future of sobriety.

'Drinking,' exclaimed Vladimir, 'is the joy of all Russia - we cannot exist without that pleasure.' As the beleaguered dancing bear who he mercilessly poked with a stick will no doubt testify, Vlad had a point.

Afforded the requisite level of reverence and respect, alcohol peddles more pleasure than it does pain. Think of all the great things that have happened in your life and, chances are, a drink has played at least a cameo role.

Alcohol unleashes your entire array of emotions - from virtuous indignation to unabashed joy to sobbing snot-bubble sadness - often within the same evening. It's not drink that disguises us and veils our inner selves, it is sobriety; drink peels away the layers of self-consciousness and kindly drops them in your top pocket, where you can find them in the morning.

With each gentle bend of the elbow, drink rounds off the jagged edges of unease and liberally applies a unique afterglow to everything around you. Drink catalyses camaraderie. It makes music sound better, companions more compelling, conversations more absorbing, and it even steadies our cue hand too.

As one glass blends into another, it sharpens our subconscious and it coaxes out courage, confidence and creativity; it awakens our imagination and lights a fire under the rocking chair of unadventurous ideas.

As Friedrich Nietzsche, a first-class clever clogs, said: 'For art to exist, for any sort of aesthetic activity to exist, a certain physiological precondition is indispensable: intoxication.'

From Plato and Homer to André the Giant, Ernest Hemingway, Vincent van Gogh and, of course, Norm Peterson from 'Cheers', abstinence would have deprived us some of history's greatest minds.

Yet, still, the shadow forces of temperance swirl around us, demonising drink as a dark, malevolent force of questionable morality. Such crass condemnation actively encourages bad behaviour. How else are we to behave after ingesting the demon drink?

As numerous anthropological studies have proven, different cultures and societies react entirely differently to drink. What shapes drunken behaviour is not the alcohol itself but rather society's expectations. It is in those societies where drink is deemed as diabolical, where consumption is controlled and where drunkenness is almost expected, that bad behaviour tends to thrive.

The more we know about alcohol, the more we appreciate its potential for both pain and pleasure. The more society deems it daft to be antisocial while intoxicated, the less likely we are to abuse it. It's not the drink that dictates our behaviour, be it good or bad, it's what we think.

What we mustn't forget either, is that the first people to make alcohol on a commercial scale were monks and, as everyone knows, there's nothing nicer or more sensible than rosy-cheeked monks. It's their job. And their boss is God and so if it's alright with him then, well, it should be alright with everyone else.

So go on, have a drink. In fact, why not have a couple? If you drink discerningly, then there's absolutely nothing to be ashamed about. Show drink its due respect and, rest assured, drink will respect you back.

Drink Less. Drink Better.

Hope you enjoy the book.

Cheers,

The Thinking Drinkers

BEER & CIDER
Hops & Apples

Beer and Cider are the sacred essences of human endeavour. While we can thank the Big Bang / Big Guy in the Sky for furnishing the world with fermentable fruit that turns itself into wine, both these beverages were first hewn from the hardworking hands of humankind.

Mother Nature granted us the ingredients with which to make beer and cider but, the capricious tease that she is, she failed to include the instructions.

HISTORY & CULTURE

It was as if Mother Nature herself had created some kind of cruel corporate team-building exercise sent to test the human race. Barley needed malting and the apples needed crushing and, with a clipboard in hand and a stopwatch in the other, God watched and waited until we worked this out for ourselves.

Turns out, it took us a while. Armed with that all-important opposable digit, it was Neolithic Man who first cracked the code for beer. Somewhere in and around Iraq or Iran (Mesopotamia, in old money), he soaked some barley in water, it germinated and, with the help of some enzymes, barley became malt, malt became beer and, all of a sudden, after centuries of gallivanting, gathering and hunting on the hoof, man awoke to the wonders of an existence based almost entirely on an outdoor life of agriculture and the growing of all-important grain.

Man also grew apple and pear trees. And just as barley was used for bread, apples were mainly consumed in unfermented form. Boffins reckon it was Kazakhstan where the modern apple first emerged but, unlike citrus fruits and grapes, apples didn't turn alcoholic all on their own. They first needed to be smashed to smithereens before juice could be squeezed from them and, to be done on any kind of scale, this required some pretty hefty equipment.

Step forward, in typically orderly fashion, the Romans. Having invaded Britain in AD 43, the Romans discovered the Celts were already getting tight on cider made from pears and apples but, being Celts, they were not making it in a particularly organised manner.

The Romans, appalled to see such a slapdash approach to cider-making, changed all that. Not only did they introduce olive oil presses to crush the hard apples, they also introduced an intricate system that organised the different apple varieties into specific classified groups. Say what you want about the Romans, but those crazy guys sure knew how to kick loose and have a party.

If the Romans were around now, pesky pedants that they were, they'd no doubt point out that cider should really be included in the wine chapter as it has more in common with the grape than the grain. In some ways, they're absolutely correct because the cider-making process is almost identical to that used to produce wine – simply swap the grape juice for apple juice and you've pretty much nailed it.

What is more, both wine and cider are acidic, they're both fruit-based and both use a blend of different apple/grape varieties. And that's not all. Both wine and cider boast flavours that can range from dry to sweet and both can be still as well as sparkling.

So, you may well ask, why has cider been paired with beer and not wine in this informative and entertaining tome on which your inquisitive eyes are currently feasting?

For a start, it's none of your business. We're writing this, not you. Do we come into your office and tell you what to do?

Course not. We don't even know where your office is. So back off. But, if you must know, we ran out of room in the wine chapter.

Another, and more important, reason we've put beer and cider together is that they share a few things in common. Both deserve more respect than they tend to receive, and both are ripe for rediscovery, having lived in the shadow of wine for far too long.

Peek into the little book of drinking clichés and you'll discover wine looking dapper in its best bib and tucker. Cider, meanwhile, is stood in a stain-strewn smock and pointing at planes, while beer, so often deemed the doofus of drinks, impatiently pulls at the strings on his novelty hat – giggling gormlessly as the felt hands atop clap together.

But that's just a whole load of doodleflap. Both beer and cider are beverages of grand, understated and often undervalued excellence. Both beer and cider are just as complex in their aromas and flavours as wine, and both boast a rich and remarkable past.

Cider was once the preserve of the privileged and, known as 'English Champagne', it was treated with a level of reverence that would make wine blush. In fact, the professed *méthode champenoise* was perfected by English perry makers around a hundred years before the French used it in Champagne and declared it their own. Hear that sommeliers? How do you like them apples huh?

Beer, meanwhile, is the most popular alcoholic drink on the planet and consumed in vast quantities by billions worldwide (surely that many people can't be wrong, can they?). In the rinsing hands of bankers, a lot of beer has become a huge industrial commodity not worthy of the name.

But in the reverential hands of a genteel craft brewing revolution, now global in its reach, beer is now quietly reminding a new generation of

Producing cider is not for the weak and feeble. This 1920s cider press from Cornwall calls for some serious arm action to get the apple smashing process underway.

discerning drinkers how and why it achieved such greatness in the past.

Beer, lest we forget, is the world's oldest recipe, first scribbled on a clay tablet by the Ancient Sumerians. It sustained early civilization; it helped build the Pyramids; it oiled the wheels of the Industrial Revolution in Britain; it stoked the fires of discontent that sparked the American one; it's what Elizabeth I had for breakfast; it's what Winston Churchill drank regardless of the time of day; it was the heartbeat of the British Empire; it started wars and it finished them; it was the drink of Henry VIII and Homer Simpson; and it is, as Jack Nicholson so succinctly pointed out, "the best damn drink in the world."

And the best thing is (since we're Brits), both beer and cider were invented in Britain. So pat yourself on the back for choosing well and grab yourself a cold one. You deserve it.

The story of beer and cider has been shaped by all sorts:
Neolithic man, the Normans, Ninkasi, some naughty nuns, nerds with microscopes and, of course, the odd monk or two.

1664 JOHN EVELYN WRITES: 'GENERALLY ALL STRONG AND PLEASANT CIDER EXCITES AND CLEANSES THE STOMACH, STRENGTHENS DIGESTION, AND INFALLIBLY FREES THE KIDNEYS AND BLADDER FROM BREEDING THE GRAVEL STONE.'

13000 BC MEMBERS OF THE NATUFIAN CULTURE BEGIN CULTIVATING CEREALS IN THE EASTERN MEDITERRANEAN REGION KNOWN AS THE LEVANT.

1066 THE NORMANS INVADE ENGLAND AND ENCOURAGE CIDER DRINKING. NEW VARIETIES OF APPLES ARE INTRODUCED, CIDER-APPLE ORCHARDS ARE DEVELOPED AND CIDER BEGINS TO BE TAXED.

1150–60 HILDEGARD OF BINGEN WRITES ABOUT HOPS IN BREWING AND THE HEALTH BENEFITS OF DRINKING BEER.

6500 BC EARLIEST ARCHAEOLOGICAL EVIDENCE OF APPLES DATES BACK TO AROUND THIS TIME.

1040 WEIHENSTEPHAN, THE WORLD'S OLDEST BREWERY, IS FOUNDED IN A BENEDICTINE ABBEY IN BAVARIA.

1300 WIDESPREAD REFERENCES TO CIDER PRODUCTION ALL OVER BRITAIN – FROM KENT AND ESSEX TO DEVON AND SUSSEX; BUCKING-HAMSHIRE AND GLOUCESTERSHIRE TO HEREFORDSHIRE AND YORKSHIRE.

1606 A GUILD OF CIDER (CALVADOS) DISTILLING IS FORMED IN NORMANDY.

3000 BC NEOLITHIC FARMERS IN ORKNEY BREW BEER WITH INGREDIENTS THAT INCLUDE HEMLOCK, DEADLY NIGHTSHADE AND COW DUNG.

600 AD ST BENEDICT FOUNDS THE BENEDICTINE MOVEMENT – KNOWN FOR ITS DEDICATION TO BREW-ING AND DISTILLING.

1300 HOPS ARE WIDELY USED IN EUROPEAN BREWING, OVERTAKING GRUIT AS THE KEY FLAVOURING. BUT BRITAIN DOESN'T BREW HOPPED BEER UNTIL THE EARLY 15TH CENTURY.

1550S IN NORMANDY, BIG STRIDES ARE MADE TO IMPROVE CIDERMAKING THANKS TO GUILLAUME DURSUS, A PIONEER FROM THE BASQUE COUNTRY.

1800 BC 'HYMN TO NINKASI', THE GODDESS OF BEER, IS WRITTEN DOWN ON A CLAY TABLET BY THE SUMERIANS IN MESOPOTAMIA. IT IS CONSIDERED THE WORLD'S OLDEST WRITTEN RECIPE.

79 AD PLINY THE ELDER MENTIONS CIDER AND PERRY FOR THE FIRST TIME IN A TREATISE ON 'ARTIFICIAL WINE.'.

1516 IN BAVARIA, A BREWING PURITY LAW IS INTRODUCED CALLED THE REINHEITSGEBOT. INITIALLY, IT ONLY PERMITS BREWERS TO USE BARLEY, HOPS AND WATER. BUT NOT YEAST AS NO-ONE KNEW WHAT IT WAS.

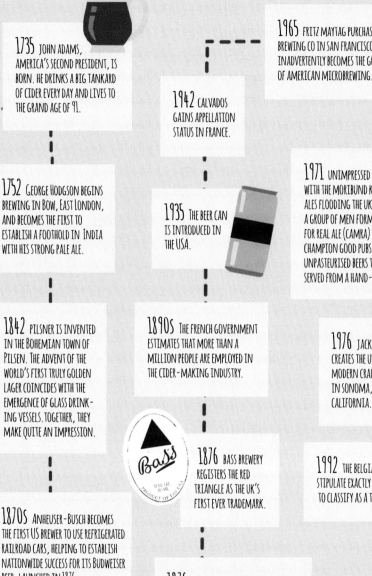

1735 JOHN ADAMS, AMERICA'S SECOND PRESIDENT, IS BORN. HE DRINKS A BIG TANKARD OF CIDER EVERY DAY AND LIVES TO THE GRAND AGE OF 91.

1752 GEORGE HODGSON BEGINS BREWING IN BOW, EAST LONDON, AND BECOMES THE FIRST TO ESTABLISH A FOOTHOLD IN INDIA WITH HIS STRONG PALE ALE.

1842 PILSNER IS INVENTED IN THE BOHEMIAN TOWN OF PILSEN. THE ADVENT OF THE WORLD'S FIRST TRULY GOLDEN LAGER COINCIDES WITH THE EMERGENCE OF GLASS DRINKING VESSELS. TOGETHER, THEY MAKE QUITE AN IMPRESSION.

1870S ANHEUSER-BUSCH BECOMES THE FIRST US BREWER TO USE REFRIGERATED RAILROAD CARS, HELPING TO ESTABLISH NATIONWIDE SUCCESS FOR ITS BUDWEISER BEER, LAUNCHED IN 1876.

1942 CALVADOS GAINS APPELLATION STATUS IN FRANCE.

1935 THE BEER CAN IS INTRODUCED IN THE USA.

1890S THE FRENCH GOVERNMENT ESTIMATES THAT MORE THAN A MILLION PEOPLE ARE EMPLOYED IN THE CIDER-MAKING INDUSTRY.

1876 BASS BREWERY REGISTERS THE RED TRIANGLE AS THE UK'S FIRST EVER TRADEMARK.

1876 LOUIS PASTEUR UNEARTHS THE SECRETS OF YEAST IN THE FERMENTATION PROCESS AND ALSO DEVELOPS PASTEURISATION WHICH HELPS BEER BECOME MORE STABLE – MORE THAN 20 YEARS BEFORE THE SAME PROCESS IS APPLIED TO MILK.

1965 FRITZ MAYTAG PURCHASES ANCHOR BREWING CO IN SAN FRANCISCO AND INADVERTENTLY BECOMES THE GODFATHER OF AMERICAN MICROBREWING.

1971 UNIMPRESSED WITH THE MORIBUND KEG ALES FLOODING THE UK MARKET, A GROUP OF MEN FORM THE CAMPAIGN FOR REAL ALE (CAMRA) TO PRESERVE AND CHAMPION GOOD PUBS AND 'CASK ALES', UNPASTEURISED BEERS THAT ARE ALWAYS SERVED FROM A HAND-PUMP.

1976 JACK MCAULIFFE CREATES THE USA'S FIRST MODERN CRAFT BREWERY IN SONOMA, NORTHERN CALIFORNIA.

1992 THE BELGIAN AUTHORITIES STIPULATE EXACTLY WHAT IT TAKES TO CLASSIFY AS A TRAPPIST BEER.

2005 MAGNERS IRISH CIDER IS LAUNCHED IN THE UK – SERVED OVER ICE IT MAKES CIDER COOL AGAIN AND BREATHES LIFE INTO THE CIDER MARKET.

2014 HAVING HAD ONLY 40 BREWERIES IN THE 1970S, THE USA NOW HAS MORE THAN 2500 BREWERIES AND IS CONSIDERED THE MOST DIVERSE BREWING NATION IN THE WORLD.

2002 PROGRESSIVE BEER DUTY IS INTRODUCED IN THE UK, GIVING TAX RELIEF TO SMALL BREWERS. THIS SPARKS A MICROBREWING BOOM AND BY 2012 THERE ARE MORE BREWERIES (1000+) THAN BEFORE WORLD WAR II.

1990-2006 DURING THIS TIME A MILLION NEW CIDER APPLE TREES ARE PLANTED.

Jesus Christ

One of the best bits in the whole of the hotel room story book,
The Bible, is when Jesus Christ, the lead character, manages to turn
water into wine at a wedding.

I t's his finest trick yet it fails to withstand even the most rudimentary form of scrutiny. Jesus would never have done that. We're not saying it couldn't be done, but if Jesus was going to turn water into any alcoholic beverage at a wedding, then it would definitely have been beer.

You don't have to delve deep into dusty tomes dating back centuries, as we have done, to know that Jesus was a beer guy. Just look at his clothes. As anyone who's ever been to a Real Ale festival will testify, Jesus bore all the hallmarks of a beer boffin – a beard and sandals. And he hung around with other men who had beards and sandals.

Let's hit you with some historical fact here: Ancient Israel, where Jesus lived, was flanked by Egypt and Mesopotamia – both big beer nations. Mesopotamia was where the Sumerians first scribbled down the formula for brewing and in Ancient Egypt, beer was used as both an enema and currency (not the *same* beer). The chaps that built the Pyramids were paid with 10 pints of ale (5–6% ABV) every day – which is why they forgot to put any windows in.

Geographical evidence? In Ancient Israel, barley was grown and consumed in big quantities and not used only for bread-making. The soil was better suited to growing grain than grapes and, regardless of gender or class, every Ancient Israelite would have drunk beer in Jesus's day.

The Bible is rife with references to beer (s*hekhar*). Yahweh, God of Israel and the Judah kingdoms, drinks around 2 litres (4.2 pints) of beer every day (and even more on the Sabbath day), beer is eulogised as a medicine for melancholy (Proverbs 31:6), and moderate beer drinking is recommended – (Isaiah 5:11, 28:7 Proverbs 20:1, 31:4) with over-indulgence discouraged.

Despite numerous mentions in the original scriptures, beer often goes missing in modern translations. Why? Well, the etymological bone of contention centres on the Hebrew world *shekhar*, meaning 'strong drink'. Many attribute it to wine, but there's every indication to suggest that 'beer' is the more faithful translation.

Of the 20 times *shekhar* is mentioned, only once does it appear without the accompanying word for wine. What's more, the word *shekhar* derives from *Sikaru*, an ancient Semitic term meaning 'barley beer'.

But we reckon the real reason beer vanished from subsequent versions of the Bible is sheer scholarly snobbery. When the Bible was first translated into English in the early 17th century, beer was considered a pauper's drink, while wine was popular among posh folk.

In an astonishing display of academic arrogance, translators transformed Jesus Christ from a charitable beer-drinking friend of the people into a nouveau-riche playboy with designer sunglasses and leather loafers.

But that's not how Jesus rolled. He was a blue-collar Messiah with no wish to drink wine. After all, the Romans drank wine and, as we all know, Jesus didn't get on with the Romans.

Jesus

BEER LEGENDS

DON'T DRINK AND PILE DRIVE

WHEN ANDRE RENE RUSIMOFF WAS 12 YEARS OLD, HE WAS 1.9M (6FT 3IN) TALL, WEIGHED OVER 108KG (240LBS) AND HAD TO BE TAKEN TO SCHOOL IN A TRUCK DRIVEN BY SAMUEL BECKETT. THEY TALKED ABOUT CRICKET.

It sounds absurd, even by Beckettian standards, but these are the kind of big, bizarre things that happened in André's life. Born near the French Alps in 1946, he was diagnosed early on with acromegaly, a rare glandular syndrome that accelerates growth – particularly in the head, hands and feet.

André knew sufferers rarely reached their forties but instead of sitting on the end of his long bed, staring mournfully at his oversized shoes, André opted to attack life in an extremely large Lycra leotard.

'André the Giant' is *the* greatest professional wrestler that ever lived. Around 2.26m (7ft 5in) tall and weighing 226kg (500lbs)as an adult, the 'Eighth Wonder of the World' dominated global wrestling for twenty years. However, his canvas-based capers were nothing compared to the bravery brandished in the bar. André drank beer like mere mortals drank water during a period when American beer actually tasted like water. He consumed American beer with the throwaway contempt it deserved at the time – drinking approximately 53 bottles a day. That's around 7000 calories of alcohol. Every. Single. Day.

It didn't touch the sides, though. Bottles were mere thimbles to André and he seldom showed signs of inebriation. He drank to deaden the

discomfort caused by his dilapidating condition and to have fun. He didn't drink by himself and he would always pick up the bar tab.

Perhaps André's most infamous display of drinking derring-do saw him consume a record-breaking 119 beers in a single six-hour sitting. The 'sitting' segued into a falling over, and André passed out in the hallway of his Pennsylvanian hotel. Unable to move him, friends draped a piano cover over him. The next morning, he woke up as a dubious world record holder – one that still stands to this day.

Sadly, in his forties, despite several operations to ease his pain, André found it difficult to walk, let alone wrestle. Days after the death of his adored father, André passed away in his sleep from a heart attack, aged just 47.

NORM PETERSON FROM CHEERS

NORM PETERSON'S ICONIC ENTRANCE, HIS DAILY SLIDE ONTO THE BAR STOOL AND HIS BEER-SOAKED RETORTS WERE A CORNERSTONE OF *CHEERS*, A COMEDY THAT RAN FOR 275 EPISODES AND II SERIES FROM 1982 TO 1993.

Norm was a hardly working accountant, fully committed barfly and an elbow-bending antidote to the rampant excess of 1980s America. Less get-up-and-go and more sit-down-and-stay, Norm was a complete no-mark whom no-one noticed in the outside world.

But as soon as he was stationed on his bar stool, within reach of the beer tap and peering at life through the prism of a pint glass, he took on superhuman powers of deadpan delivery as 'Norm' – and everybody knew his name.

In the original pilot episode of *Cheers*, Norm (then called George) was the first customer and he only said one word. And that word was 'beer'. Norm's relationship with beer was a devoted, if not discerning, one. Ice cold and wet were the criteria, he wasn't too fussed for flavour* and drank steadily at a rate of 87 sips every two hours.

Even though Samuel Adams Boston Lager was emerging as one of the first microbrews in the early 1980s, Norm was very much a 'macrobrew' man whose love for beer fuelled some of the finest lines in comedy sitcom history.

'I came. I drank. I stayed.'

NORM PETERSON'S MOTTO

---

* The beer served on the *Cheers* set, complete with working bar, was a 3.2% lager that would be topped up with salt to maintain the head retention under the hot studio lights.

'Can I pour you a beer, Mr. Peterson?'
'A little early, isn't it, Woody?'
'For a beer?'
'No, for stupid questions.'

'Hey, Mr. Peterson, Jack Frost nipping at your nose?'
'Yep, now let's get Joe Beer nipping at my liver, huh?'

'What would you say to a beer, Normie?'
'Daddy wuvs you.'

'What do you say, Norm?'
'Any cheap, tawdry thing that will get me a beer.'

'How's it going, Mr. Peterson?'
'Poor.'
'I'm sorry to hear that.'
'No, I mean pour.'

'Pour you a beer, Mr. Peterson?'
'Alright, but stop me at one.... make that one-thirty.'

'What's going on, Mr. Peterson?'
'The question is what's going in Mr. Peterson. A beer please, Woody.'

BASS TRIANGLE

*There was a time when Bass pale ale, with its iconic red triangle,
was the most famous beer in the world.*

Registered in 1876 as the first ever trademark in Britain, the legendary logo that adorned Bass's brown bottle achieved global recognition at a time when most brewers struggled to establish their beers beyond a radius of a few miles.

Its fame fuelled by a swaggering British Empire, the iconic India Pale Ale slaked the thirst of British forces overseas and helped establish Burton-on-Trent as the most important brewing metropolis in the world.

It had been the London brewers such as Ralph Hodgson who initially established a thriving export trade for IPA, a hugely popular beer style brewed with lots of hops to give it the sea-legs to withstand long sea voyages from London to Calcutta.

India Pale Ale acted as sturdy ballast and actually benefited from the ships being buffeted and battered. The rocking and rollling in oak rounded off the beer's bitter edge and created an ale of mature oak-aged character.

The heat helped too. Often rising gradually to more than 35°C (95°F), it would perform a kind of natural pasteurisation, zapping any residual yeast that may have fallen through the filtering process back in London.

But by the early 1800s, it was the major brewing families of Burton, of which Bass was one, that had assumed control of the lucrative trade in IPA. Burton's water was harder than that of London and ideal for IPA. Its firm alkaline character softened the harsh bitterness of the hops yet maintained its delicate aromas.

Such was the success of Bass' flagship ale, the global market was inundated with imitators who would flagrantly festoon their bottles with the famous red triangle. Bass sought to protect itself from these poorer pass-offs on New Year's Day in 1876 when, having waited outside the registrar office overnight, a Bass employee was first in line to take advantage of the Trade Mark Registration Act and 'Bass & Co's Pale Ale' became the UK's 'Trade Mark 1'.

By the 1880s, the Bass Brewery was a business sprawled over more than 145 acres, churning out more than a million barrels of Bass beer a year and employing in excess of 2,500 workers. In an era absent of TV, radio and the internet, its worldwide renown was really remarkable and anyone in any doubt of its global iconic status need only read this extract from *Fortunes Made In Business,* published in 1884.

'It is no extravagant assertion to say that throughout the world there is no name more familiar than that of Bass... There is no geometrical figure so well known as the vermilion triangle... It is as familiar to the eye as Her Majesty's visage on the postage stamps. It would, indeed, be a difficult task to say in what part of the earth that vivid triangle does not gladden the heart of man. The word "Bass" is known in places where such names to conjure with as Beaconsfield, Gladstone, Bright, Tennyson and Dickens would be unintelligible sounds. To what corner of the habitable world has not Bass penetrated? He has circumnavigated the world more completely than Captain Cook. The sign of the vermilion triangle is sure evidence of civilisation.'

The 'vermillion triangle' most famously appears in Edouard Manet's 1882 painting *A Bar at the Folies-Bergère*, a visual enigma in which a bottle of Bass features in the foreground alongside two bottles of champagne.

Bearing Manet's signature on the label, its inclusion is not only a tribute to its own celebrity but, given that it was a beer from Burton and not Bavaria, indicative of the anti-German sentiment that pervaded the cafés of Paris in the years after the Franco-Prussian War.

Pablo Picasso, a man who regularly exceeded his recommended intake of alcohol, is another artist who incorporated numerous nods to Bass beer in his work, mostly during his Cubist period, when a lot of the bottles of Bass he depicted bore little resemblance to the original.

James Joyce is another clever clogs who became transfixed by the famous trademark. In *Ulysses*, he wrote: 'During the past four minutes or thereabouts he had been staring hard at a certain amount of number one Bass bottled by Messrs Bass and Co at Burton-on-Trent which happened to be situated amongst a lot of others right opposite to where he was and which was certainly calculated to attract anyone's remark on account of its scarlet appearance.'

According to a fusion of folklore and fact, Bass Pale Ale (India was quietly dropped from its name in the 1990s) earned the admiration of Edward VII, inflamed the imagination of Edgar Allan Poe, brought pleasure to Buffalo Bill and inspired Napoleon Bonaparte to set up a similar brewery

col. W.F. Cody. "Buffalo Bill."

From its origins in Burton-on-Trent, England, Bass beer became a global phenomenon – even wheedling its way into the drinking habits of the 'Wild' West.

in Paris – an idea he apparently abandoned when told that the water in France wouldn't be able to create the inimitable sulphuric 'Burton Snatch'.

When the *Titanic* sank, there were 500 cases of Bass Pale Ale that went down with it. It was, perhaps, an omen for a beer whose fall from grace has been as remarkable as its rise to prominence.

After years of neglect, it has ended up in the corporate hands of AB-InBev, the Brazilian owner that hails the beer's heritage overseas yet doesn't make it a priority in its homeland – preferring to push its global lagers instead.

Much in the same way that Britain itself has shuffled to the back of the world stage, Bass has been usurped by other ales in England and nearly 150 years after its trademarking, the Red Triangle is rarely seen in British pubs and bars, and the beer is no longer brewed in Burton-on-Trent.

WOMEN & BEER

HISTORY'S EARLIEST BREWERS WERE ALL WOMEN, AND WITHOUT WOMEN, THERE'D BE NO BEER. ORIGINALLY, BEER-BREWING WAS AN EXCLUSIVELY FEMALE OCCUPATION – RIGHT UP UNTIL IT WAS SEIZED UPON AS A LARGE-SCALE COMMERCIAL VENTURE.

'Brewsters' and 'ale wives' are frequently mentioned in medieval history and, according to ancient Finnish folklore, ale was first created by three women: Osmotor, Kapo, and Kalevatar. It consisted of saliva from a bear and wild honey. Not a great combination.

Ninkasi, the Sumerian goddess of beer, was the first person to write about the brewing process, scribbling a recipe on a clay tablet back in Ancient Mesopotamia. Ninkasi oversaw brewing as an exclusively female job, blessing their beer vessels and, it was believed, giving them a special spiritual connection that magically transformed grain into grog.

Ancient Egyptian paintings and pots are rife with brewing depictions and these images often show brewers as women not men. Meanwhile, in primitive society, it was women who oversaw the collective consumption of beer, fulfilling the triple roles of brewer, barmaid and bouncer.

From Queen Elizabeth I, who consumed beer for breakfast, to pop star Madonna, who has been known to tip a few pints of Timothy Taylor Landlord down her laughing gear, brewing has boasted hundreds of famous female role models from ancient times onwards.

HILDEGARD VON BINGEN

HILDEGARD OF BINGEN WASN'T MERELY A NUN. SHE WAS THE ULTIMATE MEDIEVAL MULTI-TASKER WHO FOUGHT THE FEMINIST FIGHT ON A NUMBER OF DIFFERENT FRONTS – AT A TIME WHEN WOMEN REALLY DIDN'T DO THAT KIND OF THING.

While her peers passed the time praying and pottering about the convent, Bingen became a seriously big deal in 12th-century Europe, and a sister with several strings to her bow. Popes, kings and bishops sought her counsel and she was also the advisor and physician to the German Emperor.

A prophet, a poet and a marvellous medieval musician and composer, she penned highly influential theological treatises on everything from rocks and religion to trees, tinctures and, unusually for a nun, the fictional female orgasm. 'When a woman is making love with a man, a sense of heat in her brain, which brings with it sensual delight, communicates the taste of that delight during the act and summons forth the emission of the man's seed.'

She is also the first person to write about hops in brewing. In *Physica*, the second vast volume of her famous medical work *Liber Subtilitatum Diversarum Naturarum Creaturarum*, she dedicated Chapter 61, 'Concerning the hop', to its preservative powers.

An accomplished brewer who enjoyed a daily

ration of heartily-hopped beer until she died aged 81 in 1179, Bingen added: 'As a result of its own bitterness it keeps some putrefactions from drinks, to which it may be added, so that they may last so much longer.

'If you also wish to make beer from oats without hops, but just with grusz, you should boil it after adding a very large number of ash leaves. That type of beer purges the stomach of the drinker, and renders his heart light and joyous.' Amen to that.

CATHERINE THE GREAT

LET'S GET ONE THING STRAIGHT, RIGHT FROM THE BEGINNING, CONTRARY TO RUMOUR CATHERINE THE GREAT DID NOT DIE HAVING SEX WITH A HORSE. NOR DID SHE PASS AWAY WHILE ON THE TOILET. NEITHER OF THOSE THINGS ACTUALLY HAPPENED; A SCALLYWAG MADE IT UP.

Catherine the Great wasn't called Catherine the Great either. Her real name was Sophie Friederike Auguste von Anhalt-Zerbst. The name change came about when, aged 16, she married Grand Duke Peter, heir to the Russian throne.

The marriage was miserable. Peter could barely raise a smile in the bedroom and preferred to play with his toy soldiers while Catherine's voracious sexual appetite was openly satiated by a string of lovers – none of whom were equine.

The marriage really hit the rocks in 1762 when Catherine fronted a bloodless coup and replaced Peter on the Russian throne, followed by Peter's murder six months later. Catherine denied involvement but, you know what, we're not so sure about that.

During her 35-year reign, Catherine ruthlessly crushed internal uprisings and extended Russia's imperial reach into Poland, the lands to the north of the Black Sea and, crucially, the Crimea.

An enlightened Empress, she was a close friend of Voltaire and Diderot a writer and composer of operas and a champion of the arts, who amassed prestigious art collections.

But the main reason Catherine the Great was great was because she drank stout. Lots of it – and not the flimsy 'extra cold' stuff you get these days either. Catherine the Great drank strong, strapping Imperial Stouts that would blow the faux foam 'Oirish' hats off the heads of Guinness drinkers everywhere.

These were the ports of the beer world: complex, cockle-warming bruiser beers that were smoky and silky with touches of tar and tobacco; velvety vortexes of rich coffee, chocolate and chicory that suited the Baltic and its brass-monkey, inhospitable climate.

Under Peter the Great, strong English ales had been consumed in Russia's Royal Court but Catherine became enamoured of dark British beers in the late 1700s during a trip to London, where porters and stouts were the beers of the people.

Thrale's Entire, an Imperial Stout brewed in Southwark, South London, was Catherine's favourite tipple and she ordered lots of it.

UK brewers are still brewing the kind of imperial stouts that would have satisfied Catherine almost 250 years later. Life has been breathed back into Courage's classic Thrale's recipe, while Harvey's, based near Brighton in East Sussex, matures its oily, unctuous, ink-black imperial stout for more than nine months to create a beer that is far more authentic and palatable than the completely unproven and rather tawdry, vulgar tales of horses and toilets.

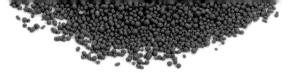

YEAST

You're about to read six, maybe seven, hundred words on yeast.
You may not expect that to be very interesting but you're wrong. It is extremely interesting. It's very, very interesting indeed.

If you're not interested in yeast, then you really should be, because yeast is easily the most fascinating ingredient in beer, and the very fact that most people don't know that it is extremely interesting is rather interesting in itself. Hey, come back here, we're not finished interesting you…

Yeast is the most interesting member of the fungus family, not including magic mushrooms. Yes, it looks funny, yes, it smells strange and no, you wouldn't want to kiss it – not even wearing beer goggles – but brewers love it. For them, no other unicellular organism comes close.

There are thousands of different yeasts, but brewers are only interested in those that call themselves *Saccharomyces cerevisiae*. Of all the yeasts out there, 'Sac c' is the sexiest. It is the single most important ingredient in brewing. Without it, beer would be as interesting, and indeed as intoxicating, as tea. It munches on sugars like a hungry Pac-Man, excretes alcohol, belches out effervescence and furnishes beer with lovely flavours and aromas.

But yeast is also a fickle and feral fellow, capable of wrecking the work of a brewer. If the wrong yeast wheedles its way into the brewing process, funny things will happen in the fermentation tank. And not in an amusing way.

A lot of breweries stick to a single signature yeast for just this reason, but if a brewer wants to showboat with a number of different styles, they'll need more than one. This is fine as long as the brewer is fastidious in keeping the different strains separate. It's like being married and taking a lover – you may be OK, but the other two mustn't meet under any circumstances.

Yeast strains in brewing can be loosely divided into two categories: ale yeast and lager yeast. In general, the former adds far more 'character' to the beer than the latter.

- Lager yeast performs better at low temperatures (1–12.75°C/34–55°F) and prefers to eat in smaller, lighter groups that drop down to the bottom of the fermentation vessel.

- Ale yeast likes warmth (12.75–24°C/55–75°F) and remains buoyant in the fermentation vessel.

Lager yeast is a clipped and rather cold dinner companion that will politely and quietly polish off everything on its plate but won't contribute a great deal to the conversation. So much so, most won't notice or remember it even being there.

Ale yeast, on the other hand, is a warmer, more gregarious guest. Rudely pushing away its unwanted plate of residual sugars (which add sweetness and texture to the beer), it spices up conversation, fires things up with the odd fruity opinion or two and happily mingles with the other ingredients at the table – getting on with some and clashing with others.

God is Good

Yeast is all around us, it's in the air, it's in your hair, it's over there and it's also over there. It's even on the inside of your leg. It's everywhere.

But back in the Dark Ages, when microscopes didn't exist and mere talk of such a thing would have you thrown down a well for being a witch, no-one knew that yeast existed. As they couldn't see, or possibly know about, the spectacular shape-shifting substance that is yeast, they assumed it was the work of a higher being.

So it, whatever it was, was christened 'God is good' – a mysterious manna from heaven that, somewhere in the froth and dregs of the beer, was somehow transforming sugars into a liquid that made folk happy and healthy.

Brewing vessels were placed in front of shrines, people would pray to pots of fermenting grain and summon the spirit of 'spontaneous' fermentation. When the 'brew' went well, brewsters would skim off the froth and use it for the next batch. This is why *doerst*, a derivative of *dros,* meaning dregs, is the Anglo-Saxon word for yeast. One of the Norwegian words for yeast was *kveik,* meaning kindling, to 'relight the fire' in the brewing process.

> ## 'Yeast is also a fickle and feral fellow, capable of wrecking the work of a brewer.'

A creamy yeast head in action at its sugar-munching best in a fermentation tank at the Skinner's Brewery in Cornwall, England. Without yeast, there is no beer.

Even by the 16th century, fermentation was still based on hunch rather than hard fact. The 1516 Bavarian Purity Law (Reinheitsgebot), which proclaimed that all beer must be made with hops and water and barley, made no mention of yeast and simply chose to ignore it.

In the 1600s, a Dutch fellow called Antonie van Leeuwenhoek was the first to identify microorganisms through a microscope. He called them animalcules (little animals) but he didn't know what they were or what they did. Theodore Schwann, a German scientist, was the first chap to correctly call yeast a 'sugar fungus' in 1837; while, a year later, Julius Meyen christened it with the Latin name *Saccharomyces.*

Biology boffin Louis Pasteur, the father of pasteurisation, looking for yeast in a bottle.

Yet it wasn't until 1857 that Louis Pasteur eventually declared that, far from being a divine gift, fermentation was a natural chemical reaction in which yeast ate, expelled and multiplied. But in terms of brewing significance, the big break-through came some years later in Copenhagen.

Great Dane

Every single day, millions of drinkers around the world inadvertently raise a glass to the memory of Emil Christian Hansen.

An itinerant odd-job man turned celebrated chemist-cum-yeast-whisperer, Emil Christian Hansen is perhaps the most important of all the white-coated boffins to have shaped brewing history, his petri-dish prowess eclipsing even that of Louis Pasteur. While Pasteur may have

first found out about the fundamentals of fermentation, it was Hansen who, working at the Carlsberg Laboratory in Copenhagen in the 1880s, managed successfully to identify, isolate and propagate individual pure yeast strains. He also worked out that different yeasts behave and feed more effectively at different temperatures. His discoveries allowed brewers to finally make yeast do what they wanted it to do and in 1833 he published a paper pronouncing the first pure lager yeast strain – *Saccharomyces carlsbergensis* – which was donated to brewers of bottom-fermenting beers all over Europe.

History has been hard on Hansen and he doesn't get the credit he deserves. Few know his name and even fewer really know what he did, but every time you lift a pint of lager to your lips, remember that you're drinking in his remarkable and historic discovery.

Beard Beer

In 2012, the Rogue Brewery in Oregon brewed a beer using wild yeast discovered within the whiskers of their hirsute head brewer.

Having initially failed to find brewing yeast residing in the brewery's hop fields, their quest to create a beer that could boast genuine 'terroir' led them in turn to the chin of John Maier, who has been Rogue's brewmaster since 1988.

Nine hairs were plucked from his face, placed in a petri-dish and sent off to a laboratory where scientist types discovered that the yeast was suitable for brewing beer. Strangely, however, it wasn't the same yeast used by Maier's in Rogue's other beers. 'Yeast is everywhere so it kind of makes sense,' said Maier, whose famed facial fuzz has been growing

since 1978. 'I can't believe it's been in front of my face for all this time' , he added. After further cultivating the yeast, and experimenting with it in different types of beer, Rogue released a 5.6% golden ale fermented with Maier's fruity Belgian-style beard yeast.

They called it, rather cleverly, 'Beard Beer'.

Lambic Beer

Lambic is what beer would have been before Louis Pasteur had his light bulb moment. It's the oldest beer style in the western world and also one of the weirdest.

For those familiar with modern beer, first impressions of this medieval liquid can daunt and dumbfound. It's closer in character to cider or fino sherry, and with its dry, sour and acidic character, it tastes a bit like a goat smells, making you draw in your cheeks as if you've seen something saucy and forbidden happening in the pantry.

Lambic beer is brewed mostly in and around the Belgian capital of Brussels between April and October, with fermentation fuelled by naturally-occurring, airborne yeast which, along with oak-ageing, gives the beer its distinctive character.

Lambic Styles

Lambic: Lambic is both the generic term for spontaneous beers from this particular part of Belgium and the name given to the base beer.
Gueuze: Normally corked and caged in champagne bottles, gueuze (pronounced *goo-zah*) is a bottle-conditioned blend of young lambic (aged for between 6 and 12 months) and old (*oude*) lambic (aged in oak for up to three years) in a ratio of one to two.

A greater proportion of older lambic brings more complexity, while gueuze blended with more young lambic will be softer in character. Just like in whisky distilling and cognac houses, blenders strive for a signature style and a certain

consistency of flavour from year to year, but every vintage tends to be different and the quest for perfection is never-ending.

Kriek

Kriek (cherry) is made traditionally by steeping sour Schaerbeek cherries, native to the Brussels area, in lambic for six months. Cherries are added whole and, during secondary fermentation, the stones dissolve to add an almond edge to the tart character.

Faro

Popular in the 19th century, Faro is lambic beer sweetened with sugar to make it more palatable to the everyday drinker but not to poet Charles Baudelaire. In 1864, he declared his distaste for it: 'Faro comes from that great big latrine, the Senne – a beverage extracted from the city's carefully sorted excrement. Thus it is that, for centuries, the city has drunk its own urine'.

Lambic beers are aged in oak barrels in much the same way as cognac or whisky. Once fermented, the beers are corked and caged in the same way as champagne.

ARE YOU A BEER GEEK?

QUESTIONS & ANSWERS

From Munich to Melbourne and Portland to Prague, the global craft brewing revolution has brought flavoursome fulfilment to millions of drinkers all over the imbibing world.

There is, however, a downside: The Beer Geek/Snob. When all beer tasted the same, beer was blissfully bereft of the kind of characters that have darkened the wine world for centuries. But with the advent of 'artisan' ale and 'boutique' lagers, and increased diversity and choice of beer, it was only a matter of time before that very same glass-swirling superciliousness swapped a Pinot for a Pale Ale and thrust its big nose of condescension into the world of 'craft' microbrewed beer.

Be warned. Beer snobbery is a sneaky fellow that is capable of creeping into your conscience without you knowing, converting a strong, natural passion for tasty brews into a serious social problem that could lose you friends.

Below is a test to see whether we've got to you too late…

You go to the pub down the road with a gang of your mates and spot a beer from a little-known local brewery that you've tried once before. Your best friend asks what you're drinking. Do you:

A. Let them have a sip and offer to buy them one if they like it.
B. Tell them a few things about the brewery and why you like the beer.
C. Pat your unsophisticated yet sweet, well-meaning companions on the head before embarking on a condescending monologue detailing the acidity levels of certain hop varieties, some mash tun circumferences and decoction techniques… until they start crying.

A well-intentioned big brewer buys your favourite yet struggling local microbrewery. Do you:

A. Lament the fact that you should have drunk more of their beer but keep things in perspective – in some parts of the world, people don't even have access to clean water.
B. Decide you'll wait and see whether the new owners dumb down the recipe before passing judgement.
C. Boycott the company's beers and their pubs and go on a one-man hunger strike atop the roof of the brewery. More importantly, you get all your pals to join you.

You return to the pub, blistered and parched, from a treacherous trek across the Sahara only to discover that the only beer available is an extra-cold lager from a big brewery. Do you:

A. Gleefully press your cracked lips against the chilled glass and dispatch the ice-cold liquid down your rasping throat.
B. Ask for a lime and soda instead.
C. Wring the moisture from your own damp under-wear to keep you going until an obscure barrel-aged beer brewed in a Belgian barn is delivered.

How would you describe a London porter?

A. 'About 5ft 10in in a uniform, a smart hat and carry-ing loads of bags to the door of your London taxi.'
B. 'Is that the one that tastes a bit like stout?'
C. 'A glowering sheen of bitter pomposity enveloped within a shroud of roasted nuttiness and a con-genial phenolic finish of Dickensian viscosity. It flummoxes the senses with equal amounts of awe and Fugglesome arrogance.'

You're out with mates and one of them orders a pitcher of macro, mainstream lager served at a very low temperature. What do you do?

A. Drink it and get on with your evening.
B. Drink it but buy something more 'flavoursome' when it's your round.
C. Attack your mate with a claw hammer.

Have you ever said the word 'diacetyl' while in the pub?
A. Dyassa… what?
B. No.
C. Yes. It's a common flavour compound imparting butter-like aroma characteristics when not fully reabsorbed by yeast.

What does IBU stand for?

A. No idea. Don't care.
B. Something to do with hops?
C. International Bittering Units; the globally–agreed standard for measuring bitterness in beer.

You have a dream about a night spent with a beautiful blond. It stars…

A. Scarlet Johansson.
B. Ryan Gosling.
C. A full-bodied, golden pale ale.

Your favourite thing about the Oktoberfest in Munich is…

A. The shapely Bavarian dirndl costumes.
B. The oompah bands, steins and big sausages.
C. The juxtaposition between the noble Hallertäu hop, pale malt and soft Bavarian water.

You're at a far-flung beer festival when a complete stranger wearing a beer T-shirt and too many badges begins talking to you about a beer you've never heard of. Do you…

A. Run away.
B. Intimidate him by comparing the beer he describes with a fictional one – until he explodes.
C. You cut off your drinking arm and hit yourself with it as punishment for not having tasted it before.

....

If you answered:
Mostly A: You've a long way to go before becoming a beer snob. Nothing to worry about.
Mostly B: You've a healthy attitude to beer drinking.
Mostly C: It's too late.

....

10 THINGS YOU NEED TO KNOW ABOUT BEER & CIDER

01 Brewing Monks
Trappist beers are rather special. They can only be brewed by the Cistercian Order of the Strict Observance.

Renowned for their rigorous religious obedience, sustained silence and strict adherence to self-sufficiency, the **Trappists have six abbey breweries in Belgium** (*Orval, Westvleteren, Rochefort, Westmalle, Chimay* and *Achel*), two in the Netherlands (*La Trappe* and *Abdij Maria Toevlucht*) and newer ones in Austria (*Stift Engelszell*) and America (*St Joseph's Abbey* in Massachusetts). At the time of writing there are 10 official Trappist breweries globally.

02 What Hops are Made of
Hops are a member of the same botanical family as cannabis. An aphrodisiac for men yet an inducer of sleep for women, they are not an altogether ideal accessory for heterosexual lovemaking. Hops are not the so-called 'grapes of beer', as they don't provide any fermentable sugars – these all come from the malt.

Hops are the spice and seasoning in beer – added early in the brewing process for bitterness, and later, for aroma.

03 Water Wisdom
Water matters in brewing. Soft water, with barely any mineral salts, is ideal for brewing lager-style beers while mineral-rich water, harder than Chuck Norris in granite underpants, is generally used to brew top-fermenting ales, porters and stouts. But modern techniques allow brewers to manipulate their water and use it to brew any style they wish.

04 Cellaring Beer
Keeping beer in a cellar can enhance its complexity and flavour. **Stand bottles upright and leave to improve over time.**

Beers that age the best are malty strong ones with an ABV of 7 or 8%. Bottle-conditioned beers carry on fermenting in the bottle, and as the yeast proceeds to eat up residual sugars, the beer becomes leaner and often finer in flavour.

05 The Bitterness in a Beer
International Bittering Units is the currency in which bitterness in beer is measured. **An IBU rating is a complex calculation** that takes the weight of hops, alpha acids, wort and alcohol into account.

Malty beers tend to have an IBU of around 15–30 while highly hopped American IPAs like Harpoon Leviathan register an IBU of 130.

06 The English Champagne?
Percy Bulmer, a Herefordshire cidermaker, began producing 'champagne cider' in 1906 using the *méthode champenoise* synonymous with the French sparkling wine.

Originally named Cider De Luxe, yet changed to 'Pomagne' in 1916, it was granted a Royal Warrant in 1911. Bollinger sued Bulmer over the use of the word 'champagne' but in 1979, an EEC ruling designated the Champagne region an area of origin rather than a process.

07 Johnny Appleseed
Core to the history of American cider is Johnny Appleseed, a man who slaked the thirst of frontiersmen by planting apple trees for settlers as they moved west.

Appleseed was born John Chapman in Leominster, Mass., in 1774. He sold saplings to the settlers to enable them to gain land grants, and the apples that were grown were used to produce **'fermented' hard cider**.

08 Scrumpy
Many believe the most traditional style of cider to be farmhouse cider, known as **scrumpy**. Unfairly associated with ruddy-faced farmer types, scrumpy is still, unfiltered cider that roams around the 6-8% ABV mark. Also known as farmhouse, it tends to boast tannin-like flavours and a feint 'farmyard' character, with each barrel differing from the next.

09 How Do You Like Them Apples?
The apple is to cider what the grape is to wine. **Cider apples** differ from their culinary namesakes because their flesh is more fibrous and therefore easier to extract juice from. High in tannin (giving body and colour) and sugar but low in acidity, they're not really recommended for eating.

10 Wassail Each January, many English cidermakers perform a 'wassail', a pagan ritual whereby revellers serenade orchards with song, banish evil spirits by pouring mulled cider on tree roots and hang soggy cider-soaked toast in its branches. A lot of cider drinking takes place too.

31

BEER RECOMMENDATIONS

There's no space to include all the great beers, so try these 10 terrific trailblazers, spanning a number of different styles, from both Europe and America.

SCHNEIDER WEISSE
5.4% ABV (GERMANY)

Georg Schneider is widely regarded as the man who saved Bavarian wheat beer in the 19th century, and his liquid legacy remains the archetypal example of the style – with all the banana, clove and bubblegum flavours becoming of a German Weissbier.

CANTILLON LAMBIC
5% ABV (BELGIUM)

An exquisite example of the art of brewing lambic, an ancient beer that is still brewed in and around the city of Brussels after more than 500 years.

Fermented once using naturally occurring 'wild' yeast and then again in oak barrels, lambic can be dry, sour and tart, making it more like wine or cider than beer. But many beer drinkers still consider it to be the purest kind of brewing.

ALASKAN SMOKED PORTER
6.5% ABV (USA)

Porter was the most lucrative liquid for London brewers in the 18th century. They then began making a stronger version which they called 'Stout Porters', stout being a generic term used to describe anything that was bigger and stronger – but it wasn't until the mid-1800s that stout became a distinct style.

Today, it is almost impossible to distinguish between stout and porter but examples don't come more distinguished than this Alaskan effort. It is brewed with smoky malt but the Alaskans do it differently from traditional London brewers, by smoking it over indigenous alder wood.

WORTHINGTON'S WHITE SHIELD IPA
5.6% ABV (UK)

Born in Burton-on-Trent and the brainchild of William Worthington, a big name in 18th-century British brewing, White Shield's tale is one of boom, wanderlust, decline, neglect, rebirth and deification.

As IPA has emerged as the style synonymous with the American brewing revolution, White Shield has enjoyed a remarkable renaissance in recent years. Yet, unlike some of the more aggressively hopped IPAs originating from America, it is beautifully balanced.

Brewed with iconic Burton well water and English hops (Challenger, Goldings and Fuggles), it's a marvellous medley of marmalade, treacle, toffee and peppery spice layered over a lovely fresh, bready base.

A classic India Pale Ale and one of the oldest existing bottle-conditioned (unpasteurised) beers still available today.

SAISON DUPONT
6.5% ABV (BELGIUM)

Historically, saisons were rustic, farmhouse ales, brewed in the winter and stored until the warmer months when they would slake the thirst of Belgian farm workers after a long, hot day in the fields. One of the best benchmarks in terms of style, Brasserie Dupont's Saison is a classic, hailing from a Walloon farmhouse brewery famed for its soft water. Zesty, citrussy and deliciously dry.

PILSNER URQUELL
4.4% ABV (CZECH REPUBLIC)

The world's first truly golden lager, the 'original pilsner' was first brewed in the Czech town of Pilsen back in 1842, by a bad tempered Bavarian called Josef Groll, using local Saaz hops and moist Moravian malt. Still brewed on the same site and matured deep beneath the brewery in cold cellars for more than a month, it is the golden giant on whose broad shoulders other, often less impressive, pilsners stand.

RUSSIAN RIVER'S PLINY THE ELDER 8% ABV (USA)

The beer that slipped a little blue pill into American craft brewing's love affair with hoppy India Pale Ales. It's a sensational and spicy Double IPA, brewed with a quartet of American hops – Amarillo, Centennial, Columbus and Simcoe – from one of the USA's most awesome and adventurous ale-makers.

ORVAL
6.2% ABV (BELGIUM)

One of six Belgian Trappist breweries, Orval is unique in that it only makes one beer that is available outside the monastery walls – a pale ale ranked by many as the world's best. Vivacious and acutely aromatic in youth, Orval's funky yeast character comes through best after six months in the bottle.

FULLER'S CHISWICK BITTER
3.5% ABV (UK)

British brewers are the best in the world at brewing beers like this. Quintessential and quenchable, and best drunk on cask, they won't buckle your knees but may well make your elbow ache.

SIERRA NEVADA PALE ALE 5.6% ABV (USA)

Back in 1980, when Californian Ken Grossman first brewed this citrussy pale ale in Chico, America was a dystopian place for beer-drinkers.

This pioneering pale ale brewed with Cascade hops, is regarded as the beer that kick-started the craft brewing revolution in California, alongside Anchor Steam from San Francisco.

CIDER RECOMMENDATIONS

Sales of artisan cider are soaring the world over. Here are a range of types, from Frankfurt and France to Somerset and Spain, to keep any cider drinker happy.

CYRIL ZANGS
THIS SIDE UP (FRANCE)

A New World-looking Normandy cider cultivated by Cyril Zangs in the Calvados region of Lower Normandy using apples grown on the coast. This cider is bottle-conditioned using 25 different apple varieties; it is tart and dry with a full-on fresh and foamy mineral finish and comes in at an ABV of 6%.

CIDRERIE DU CHATEAU DE LEZERGUE
LES 3 FRERES DEMI SEC (FRANCE)

Softly sweet, this 4.5% ABV award-winning typical Breton cider has full-bodied fruit on the nose, balanced by a bittersweet backbone. Check it out as an aperitif.

FRANKFURTER ÄPFELWEIN, POSSMANN
5.5% ABV (GERMANY)

The Frankfurt Apfelwein tradition is as strong as that of Herefordshire or Somerset in the UK or Normandy and Brittany in France. In fact, ask any Frankfurter about the origins of cider and they will swear blind that they invented it way back when.

Frankfurt is even known in Germany as the 'Big Ebbel' – the Big Apple. Its cider is typically tart and slightly sour and traditionally sipped from stone jars called Bembels, which are shared between drinkers. Possmann is the largest of the Äpfelwein brands in the city.

CASTANON 5.5% ABV
SIDRA NATURAL (SPAIN)

Based mainly around the north of the nation, Spanish cider is synonymous with a 2000-year-old tradition whereby the server, the bottle in one hand, pours the cider from as high a position as possible into a glass held in the other. It aerates the cider and creates a light effervescence, a small foamy head and a nicer-tasting cider. This rustic Asturian cider style delivers fresh fruit, and a sherbety sendoff.

LONGUEVILLE HOUSE CIDER 5% ABV (IRELAND)

An awesome Irish easy-drinker from County Cork that deftly dovetails Dabinett apples with the Michelin variety to produce a subtly sweet and effervescent affair with a flint-dry finish. Packaged, thankfully, with a crown cap. You can take the cider out of Cork but you can't take the cork out of a ….. baboomsh!

E.Z ORCHARDS
CIDRE 5.7% ABV (US)

Having been at the centre of the American craft brewing scene, Oregon is emerging as a super cidermaking region and this classy calling card suggests there may be a few sleepless nights in Europe. This cider is made with a blend of vintage French cidre apple varieties. Vivacious with verdant fruit and a ripe rusticity to it, it finishes with a lovely acidic edge.

DUNKERTONS BLACK FOX
CIDER 7% ABV (UK)

With effervescence to lift the textures off the palate, acidity to cut through the spice, and some durable tannins too, some English ciders are awesome accompaniments to fiery food. Hailing from Herefordshire, this medium-dry cider from one of the most famous and respected farmhouse producers is definitely one of them.

HENNEY'S VINTAGE
6.5% ABV (UK)

There may not be any bubbles in the bottle but this is still (quite literally) one of the best ciders to burst onto the broader British cider scene in recent times. Only using cider apples picked in a certain year, it is clean, classy and clipped with a chalky mineral mouthfeel not dissimilar to chablis.

ASPALL PREMIER CRU
7% ABV (US)

Aspall has been displaying some awesome apple skills on the English East Anglian coast for at least eight generations, using 100% fresh-pressed apple juice. For this superb Suffolk cyder, the Chevallier-Guild family combine cider apples with cooking and normal eating apples. It's crisp, it's sparkling and it's simply superb – a multi-award-winning cider.

WORLEY'S
PREMIUM VINTAGE
6.3% ABV (US)

It's fresh, it's faintly funky and it's a little bit farmyard but this satiating and rather sumptuous lightly carbonated cider made in the Mendip Hills says it all about the Somerset style. It is full of flavour with a spicy finish.

HENRY WESTONS
VINTAGE
8.2% ABV (UK)

Enormous oak vats have been maturing the ciders at Westons for centuries. The wood certainly works wonders with this classic rich and robust full-bodied cider from a large traditional producer that proves the fact that principles and profit can be paired together.

WINE
Planet of the Grapes

According to Robert Louis Stevenson, Louis Pasteur and Pliny the Elder, you will find poetry, philosophy and truth in wine. But you don't necessarily need any of these things to make wine. It's really quite simple. All you need are some ripe grapes and some yeast. The action of the latter munching on the sugars contained in the former is a naturally occurring phenomenon – you don't even have to be present at the process if you don't want to be.

HISTORY & CULTURE

Put some grapes in a big pot, leave it for a bit, come back and – just like that – you've got a bottle of wine. That's pretty much how it was in northwest Iran back in 6000 BC when wine was but a basic beverage.

Yet since then, somehow, somewhere along the way, this meek and modest grape juice has gone and got itself some serious gravitas. Today, wine is a bit of a big deal. Wine wears cravats, it totally looks good in a turtleneck and it even has those spectacles that perch so perfectly on the end of its imperious nose.

Wine pats other alcoholic drinks – grinning, smudge-faced simpletons that they are – condescendingly on the head. Right from the earliest examples of winemaking, wine has always been considered 'better' than other types of alcoholic drink. It has really revelled in its role as the most learned of libations. For the first 2000 years, wine majored in medicine as an antiseptic and was used by the Ancient Egyptians, who mixed it with pine tree resin and rosemary, to cure all manner of ailments, from herpes to a dicky tummy.

But when the Ancient Greeks and Romans turned up, wine swapped its stethoscope for some serious chin-scratching and emerged as society's most erudite of life-enhancing liquids. While beer was very much considered the preferred drink of the chest-beating barbarian type, wine was the Greek philosophers' closest companion and it was even given its very own god in the androgynous man-woman shape of Dionysus – famously worshipped by the Maenads, crazy drinking females, and satyrs sporting big beards and even bigger erections.

At Greek symposiums (See Plato and the Symposium on page 53), discerning drinking and thinking sessions, wine was used to oil the wheels of intellectual rigour, raising the wrists of those classical clever clogs that helped shape the first civilised societies.

In fact, some have argued that the Platonic Greek symposiums were the forerunners to the Passover ceder, the Jewish feast where wine is gently circulated, life is pondered and children are encouraged to ask questions of the elders. 'There is truth,' wrote Plato, 'in wine and children.'

Wine has also had its feet firmly under Christianity's pews for centuries. Holy Communion is wine served up at the altar as the blood of Jesus Christ. According to the famous hotel room story book, he also turned water into the good stuff at the Wedding of Cana (although this Biblical tale comes under some serious scholarly scrutiny on page 16 of this book).

The Messiah's most famous magic trick, however, simply can't compare with the cerebral smoke and mirrors, or the cheeky chicanery employed by wily wine-makers. Wine has been magnificent in making mystery its mightiest weapon and its popularity is partly due to it being so purposely and preposterously complicated.

That few people other than expert oenophiles

Not only an amazing vineyard packed with succulent St Emilion grapes, this is a UNESCO World Heritage site in the Gironde regon of France.

can truly fathom what on earth is going on in wine has merely fanned the flames of fascination. Incomprehensible appellations, arcane rituals, quixotic talk of terroir, varying vintages, the changing fortunes of this château or that domaine, the senselessly complex classifications, the undecipherable labels, the fickle hands of Father Time – they all come together to undermine uniformity and rejoice in the romance of unreliability.

Without this knotty network of nuance, without these endless vines of indistinct variety, wine couldn't cultivate a culture of connoisseurship in which enlightened imbibers – from Homer to Hemingway, Pliny to Plato – can legitimately indulge in displays of discernment, buying bottle after bottle, and justifying a never-ending journey to the ultimate utopian glass that remains elusive.

No two bottles of wine taste the same. In a world of homogeneous hooch, wine celebrates a lack of certitude. Is there a genuine art in the artifice? There is if you believe it. Fermented grape juice. Easy to make but almost possible to understand.

'When men drink, then they are rich and successful and win lawsuits and are happy and help their friends. Quickly, bring me a beaker of wine, so that I may wet my mind and say something clever.'

ARISTOPHANES,
GREEK PLAYWRIGHT

CIRCA 6000 BC THE FIRST RECOGNISABLE WINE MADE FROM GRAPES IS PRODUCED IN BRONZE AGE GEORGIA AND IRAN.

4500 BC WINE APPEARS IN GREECE, CRETE AND THE FAR EAST.

1323 BC EGYPTIAN PHARAOH AND ARGUABLY THE WORLD'S FIRST RECORDED WINE BUFF, TUTANKHAMUN, IS BURIED WITH WINE JARS LABELLED WITH THE YEAR, THE WINEMAKER'S NAME AND JUDGEMENTS ON WHETHER THE WINE IS ANY GOOD.

200 BC THE AVERAGE ROMAN PERSON IS DRINKING 250 LITRES OF WINE PER ANNUM.

140 BC THE ROMANS IMPROVE UPON GREEK WINES AND WINE-MAKING TECHNIQUES BY INTRODUCING CLASSIFICATION OF GRAPE VARIETIES, SOIL TYPES, RIPENING QUALITIES AND DISEASES.

600 BC CLASSICAL GREECE BECOMES THE FIRST CIVILISATION TO EMBRACE WINE. IT ALSO PRODUCES THE FIRST WINEMAKERS, WHO PLANT VITIS VINIFERA, THE FATHER OF ALL EUROPEAN WINE VARIETIES.

0 JESUS TURNS WATER INTO WINE AT A WEDDING.

71 AD THE ROMAN HISTORIAN PLINY THE ELDER RECORDS THE EARLIEST KNOWN REFERENCE TO VINEYARDS, IN WHAT IS NOW KNOWN AS BORDEAUX.

79 AD MOUNT VESUVIUS ERUPTS AND MUCH OF THE ROMAN EMPIRE'S WINE STOCKS ARE DESTROYED.

1500-1600 SPANISH CONQUISTADORS PLANT VITIS VINIFERA VARIETIES THROUGHOUT SOUTH AMERICA (MEXICO 1519, CHILE 1555 AND ARGENTINA

1336 A MONASTIC WINERY IS BUILT BY CISTERCIAN MONKS WITHIN THE WALLS OF CLOS DE VOUGEOT IN BURGUNDY.

1100S BORDEAUX WINE BEGINS TO BE EXPORTED TO ENGLAND.

500 VINEYARDS ARE BEING PLANTED THROUGHOUT FRANCE, FROM THE LOIRE AND BRITTANY TO CHAMPAGNE.

1622 ITALIAN DOCTOR FRANCESCO SCACCHI PROVIDES THE FIRST WRITTEN ACCOUNT OF SPARKLING WINE.

1633 SIR KENELM DIGBY (1603-1665) A DIPLOMAT AND SERIOUS 17TH-CENTURY SAGE, INVENTS THE GREEN GLASS BOTTLE. PREVIOUSLY, WINE HAD BEEN STORED IN BAGS MADE FROM GOAT SKIN AND IN CERAMIC POTS.

1650 CABERNET SAUVIGNON ANNOUNCES ITS ARRIVAL TO THE WORLD OF WINE.

1690s The first ship is christened with a bottle of Champagne. Hitherto, metal cups filled with blood were used.

1769 Wine-making is introduced to the state of California from Mexico.

1815 New Zealand builds its first winery.

1818 Madame 'Veuve' (meaning 'Widow') Cliquot invents the technique of degorgement.

1862 Phylloxera vastatrix, a deadly aphid, is inadvertently introduced to French vineyards when a producer plants American vines in his Rhone vineyard. The 'dry leaf devastator' destroys millions of hectares of vineyards throughout Europe.

1859 Napa Valley in California opens its first winery.

1855 Napoleon III commissions the wine-makers of Bordeaux to create a ranking of its wine estates – the classification is still considered the world's most prestigious.

1910-11 The Champagne Riots, not as fun as they sound, erupt among grape growers enraged by the appellation boundaries – a few metres making a huge difference to how much the sparkling wine could be sold for.

1939 The wing corkscrew is invented.

1982 Declared one of the best ever years for Bordeaux.

1978 Robert Parker begins publishing his Wine Advocate magazine and establishes a 100-point wine rating system that will define prices and shape consumer trends for many years after.

1963 Marlborough in New Zealand produces its first wine.

1989 A waiter at the Four Seasons hotel knocks over a bottle of 1787 Chateau Margaux. Insurers pay out $225,000.

1990s Californian wine-makers plant a lot of Merlot grapes.

2008 Robert Parker insures his nose for $1 million.

2013 Rain and hailstorms contribute to the worst Bordeaux vintage in years.

THOMAS JEFFERSON

★ ★

The history of the United States of America is drenched in drink. When peered at through a slightly woozy prism, America's past – right back to the creation of the nation itself – is soaked in the good stuff.

Alcohol induced the earliest settlers onto American soil when the ship *The Mayflower*, discovering itself bereft of beer, skidded to a halt hundreds of miles north of its intended destination.

And, seldom mentioned by scholars and school teachers, it wasn't tea that triggered the American Revolution, it was the demon drink. Long before the Boston Tea Party in 1775, the British government sowed the seeds of colonial discontent by issuing crippling taxes on domestic beer, the import of wines and molasses – and therefore rum.

The Sons of Liberty were well aware of the difference between protest and profligacy and, rather than hurling perfectly decent hooch into the sea, they tossed tea crates overboard instead and kept the booze for battle.

During the War of Independence, George Washington issued each soldier with a daily bottle of rum and a quart of spruce beer and, to secure a steady supply of revolutionary spirit, advocated 'erecting Public Distilleries in different States'. As he explained to Congress in 1777, the 'benefits arising from the moderate use of strong liquor have been experienced in all Armies and are not to be disputed'.

Alcohol coursed through the veins of all the Founding Fathers (see page 45). George Washington illegally imported rum to get his inauguration party going and during his time in office, a staggering seven per cent of his income was spent on drink. On retiring, he built a brewery and a distillery and, at one point, he was one of the nation's most prolific whiskey makers. He even grew his own barley and used ice from his ponds to keep his brews cold.

Benjamin Franklin, another founding father, took it upon himself to write a paper on wine-induced flatulence, promoting 'Musk or Lilly, Rose or Bergamot' as fragrant foils to farts caused by 'Claret or Burgundy, Champagne or Madeira'.

While few could rival Franklin's cutting-edge contributions to 18th-century science, his contemporary Thomas Jefferson displayed a more discerning approach to drinking than some of the other Founding Fathers.

An elite, enlightened elbow-bender, famous for drafting the Declaration of Independence over a glass or four of Madeira, Jefferson was a politician whose hinterland was as huge as the nation over which he presided.

He was a proper clever clogs; a polygot fluent in five languages, a scientist, an architect, a musician, an archaeologist, an astronomer and a highly skilled statesman who studied mathematics, metaphysics and philosophy. He was a rapacious writer, a voracious collector of books and historical artefacts, and even found time to rewrite the entire New Testament the way Jesus would have intended. He also kept a pet mockingbird which he called Dick.

But, above all, Thomas Jefferson was the original wine nerd. He was arguably 18th-century America's most accomplished amateur oenophile.

Thomas Jefferson

Considering he was carried around on a pillow by servants as a child, his wine tastes were refreshingly down to earth. His fondness for Bordeaux, Burgundy and Champagne (but not the fizzy wines, which he dismissed as a fad), was balanced out by a love of frugal wines from southwest France and lesser-known Italian drops, Montepulciano being his favourite. He was also partial to Port, had a soft spot for Sherry and made a habit of drinking Madeira with a touch of brandy.

He fell in love with grape-based giggle juice while at university in Williamsburg. Most students make do with the cheapest hooch they can get their hands on, but Jefferson drank some of the finest wines in all of Virginia while living with George Whythe, his law tutor, and playing violin at fine drinking parties thrown by Francis Fauquier, the French Governor of Virginia.

Both men boasted capacious wine cellars filled with the best bottles Europe had to offer and their influence increased Jefferson's thirst for Claret and Madeira in particular. They also helped hone his notoriously meticulous approach to curating wines, while he painstakingly recorded their price, provenance and age.

But it wasn't until after the War of Independence, when Jefferson moved to France in 1784, that his devotion to wine was allowed to breathe. Sent by Congress to develop commercial links with the Old World, Jefferson arrived in Paris, dressed himself like a Parisian dandy and bought himself several cases of first-class Bordeaux.

He revelled in France's laissez-faire approach to drinking: 'In the pleasures of the table they are far before us, because with good taste they unite temperance,' he wrote. 'They do not terminate the most sociable meals by transforming themselves into brutes. I have never seen a man drunk in France, even among the lowest of people.'

In 1787, Jefferson embarked on an epiphanic three-month tour of Europe's most prestigious wine regions, 'combining public service with private gratification'. He deftly disguised it as a diplomatic mission undertaken in the interests of America and told friends that he was heading to Aix-en-Provence to cure his wrist, which he'd injured while jumping over a kettle in his garden.

But it was wine that oiled Jefferson's wheels of discovery and he trundled through the vineyards of Burgundy and the Rhône Valley before dropping down into the Piedmont of Italy and back through Bordeaux. Later jaunts took in Germany's grape-growing regions, Champagne and beyond.

The trips perfected Jefferson's palate and he became quite the connoisseur of both Burgundy and Bordeaux. His wine-soaked writings, which have matured gracefully, have since proved prophetic in their praise of the regions' finest châteaux and vintages. His letters on the subject make him one of the earliest wine writers.

Everywhere he went, Jefferson took notes on the terroir; the soil, the elevation, the winemaking techniques and, crucially, any similarities between the local landscapes and those back home in America.

Jefferson had a personal vision of an American viniculture to rival that of Europe. 'We could, in the United States, make as great a variety of wines as are made in Europe,' he wrote. 'Not exactly the same kinds, but doubtless as good.'

On his return to Virginia, and using cuttings that he'd sent back from Europe, he repeatedly tried to plant grape varieties at Monticello (his mountaintop residence where he also built a brewery and a distillery). While his vines failed to take root, his vision of the USA as a wine-making nation did indeed come to fruition – albeit 150 years after his first visit to the vineyards of Europe.

A passionate plonk proponent throughout his

political and personal life, Jefferson campaigned furiously, and with great vision, to lower taxes on the import of table wines: 'I think it is a great error to consider a heavy tax on wines as a tax on luxury. On the contrary, it is a tax on the health of our citizens.'

Wine consumption, he argued, encouraged sobriety and stemmed the sinister creep of spirits on society. 'No nation is drunken where wine is cheap; and none sober, where the dearness of wine substitutes ardent spirits as the common beverage,' he wrote. 'It is, in truth, the only anti-dote to the bane of whisky.'

While Jefferson wasn't a wine snob, he was most likely a bit of a wine bore. In 1807, after dining with Jefferson at the White House, John Quincy Adams wrote: 'There was, as usual, a dissertation upon wines. Not very edifying.'

But Jefferson was generous with his wines and he had a morbid fear of a guest's glass running dry. Inspired by his time in Europe, and par-ticularly in France, his Presidential parties were, by modern standards, notoriously immoderate affairs paid for out of his own pocket and where he would order his friends to 'drink as you please and converse at your ease'.

During his eight years as President, Jefferson actually bankrupted himself with a personal wine bill of US$10, 835.90, which, accounting for inflation, would amount to a modern-day equivalent of US$146,524.40 – an average of US$18,316 for each year in office.

In 1985, Jefferson's bottle of 1787 Château Lafite Bordeaux was sold at auction for US$156,000 – which would have been just enough money to pay Jefferson's debt. What would no doubt be of greater value to Jefferson, however, is America's subsequent establishment as an esteemed wine-making nation, its vines rooted firmly in Jefferson's pioneering and won-derful wine-driven wanderlust.

THE
FOUNDING
FATHERS

Some quite epic levels of inebriation oiled the wheels of the American Revolution. The Declaration of Independence, like all good ideas, was drawn up in a pub – a tavern in Philadelphia – and signed by cider makers, wine merchants, a maltster and a cooper. John Hancock, the biggest signatory of all, was an infamous rum and Madeira smuggler.

Benjamin Franklin, the least conservative drinker among the revolutionary heroes, curated more than two hundred terms for drunkenness, including 'Getting the Indian vapours'; Con-tending with Pharaoh' and 'Sir Richard has taken off his Considering Cap'.

Contrary to millions of beer geek t-shirts, Franklin never said, 'Beer is proof that God loves us and wants us to be happy', but he did say that the location of one's elbow is proof that God wanted us to drink.

'If the elbow had been planted nearer the hand, the part in advance would have been too short to bring the glass up to the mouth; and if it had been nearer the shoulder, that part would have been so long that when it attempted to carry the wine to the mouth it would have...gone be-yond the head...but from the actual situation of the elbow, we are enabled to drink at our ease.'

WINE B(L)UFF

To really become a genuine authority on wine takes a lot of time, a lot of money and a lot of reading books and stuff. An easier way to appear an expert is to acquaint oneself with these short one-liner guides to the world's leading grape-growing regions.

ALSACE

Independent, hugely under-valued and more likely to wear lederhosen than a beret, Alsace wine runs the gamut between flint-dry and sweeter than a puppy in a dress.

ARGENTINA

Stretched out summers, rare rainfall and vineyards that are higher than a hawk on heroin give Argentinian Reds, Malbec in particular, a depth and an exuberance unrivalled in South America.

AUSTRALIA

Where once its wines had all the subtlety of a dingo steal-ing a baby (big rowdy reds and whites with loads of zing and zest), Australia's new wave of independent wine-makers, blessed with a truly eclectic range of varieties and styles, are swapping force for finesse.

BEAUJOLAIS

Forget those nightmarish Nouveau nights in November and stick to one of the region's crus, such as Fleurie, Brouilly, Moulin-à-Vent or Morgon – fruity reds best served chilled (30 minutes in the fridge).

BURGUNDY

Tastes of terroir, earthy and erotic, Burgundy appeals to one's emotions. The best ones really do taste of manure – in a good way.

CAHORS

Cahors is Malbec in old French money and, in the pricier clas-sification, it's a leaner, more learned grape that tends to box a bit cleverer than some of the haymaker-swinging pugnacious reds of Argentina.

CALIFORNIA

Mainstream California wines can be a bit Mickey Mouse, all style, science and no soul, but boutique wineries, especially away from Napa's nosebleed prices, offer good value—yet you don't tend to see the best stuff outside of the US itself.

CHABLIS

Brought up on a bed of ancient oysters, the Serein river sliding through it, Chablis at its best is sensational – subtle and stylish, clipped and classy, with a sharp and sexy tongue.

CHILE

Rather aptly for a nation whose map looks strikingly like a chilli pepper, Chile is famous for its hot and spicy reds, yet is capa-ble of cultivating some classy wines in "chillier" climates while remaining ridiculously good value. Really worth seek-ing out.

ENGLAND

Get busy with the fizzy, it's what the English do best, having planted Pinot Meunier, Chardonnay and Pinot Noir into the same Kimmeridge soil seen in Chablis – but do not expect a bargain.

GERMANY

Forget Germany's former wine faux-pas (Liebfraumilch and the ill-fated experiment that was Müller-Thurgau) and just remember one thing: Riesling – one of the world's most wonderful white grapes, grown best in Mosel-Saar-Ruwer, Rheingau, Rheinhessen and Pfalz Rheingau.'

HUNGARY

Very basic Bull's Blood aside, Hungary is hailed for its sultry Tokaji wines, a slippery sweet sip that, when poured into a glass, laces more than a shoe shop-assistant on speed. Some classics here.

LANGUEDOC

Covered with ancient, gnarled vines cultivated by copious co-operatives, there's some great value reds in them thar hills.

LEBANON

Beyond the characterful classic Château Musar, there are some beautifully balanced Bordeaux-

TEAU · MARG.
GRAND VIN

esque wines now being made in the Bekka Valley.

LOIRE

Styles, grapes and hues change with every meandering curl and coil of the river, ranging from Pouilly Fumé (greengage and gooseberry) and minerally Muscadets near Nantes to the sparkling *sec* appeal of Vouvray, the classy reds of Chinon and, of course, Sancerre – the lithe yet lively legend of the Loire.

NEW ZEALAND

Known for its New World nous, New Zealand has deftly diversified with different grapes, including the sylph-like Pinot Noirs, highly-rated Rieslings, some damn sexy Syrah and, of course, its signature grassy, gregarious Sauvignon Blanc.

PACIFIC NORTHWEST

It's all about the Pinot Noir in Oregon. While Washington State wine-makers may not be big they're awfully clever–using excellent irrigation techniques to create wines with phenomenal freshness.

PIEDMONT

Italy's great wine region. Barbaresco and Barolo wines are big, blue-blooded reds that improve in the bottle while Barbera is more blue-collar, juicy everyday drinking material.

PORTUGAL

Pass on the Port (to the left, obviously) and take a punt on Portugal's terrific table wines of the Douro valley made from blends of native grapes otherwise found in the nation's famous fortified wine - Touriga Nacional (dark and deep), Touriga Franca (plummy and perfumed), Tinta Roriz (enduring and elegant), Tinta Barroca (solid 'n' sweet) and Tinto Cao (spicy and snug).

RHONE

Beneath Burgundy and home to Châteauneuf-du-Pape, the Rhône region can be divided between the noble, steep-living Syrahs up north and some quality, quotidian quaffing wines in the South where the better bottles are adorned with Côtes du Rhône Villages – better still the name of an individual village.

SICILY

Magnificent things are happening on the slopes of Mount Etna where the indigenous Nerello Mascalese creates some cracking, complex reds.

SLOVENIA

A credible, post-Communist up-and-comer whose white wines, Riesling in particular, are worrying its more established wine-making neighbours.

SOUTH AFRICA

Old World winemaking techniques, which had been frozen in aspic during the isolation of Apartheid, have now been deftly blended, quite literally, with the best of the New World —the refined rich reds of the Stellenbosch, pricey Pinotage and Bordeaux blends are the ones to look out for.

SPAIN

Treat your tastebuds to the oaky Tempranillos of the Ribera del Duero region, embrace the aromatic Albariños Galicia or reach for Rioja – either the New World whites (fresh and citrusy) or the renowned Reserva reds – firmed up with autumnal fruit, vanilla and tobacco.

TUSCANY

Steer clear of the straw-covered bottles and seek out the Super Tuscans or the reassuring 'Riserva' Chianti. Cellar the majestic Vino Nobile Montepulciano but, if impatient, opt for the rich and raring-to-go Rosso di Montepulciano.

VENETO

Head for the hills where 'Classico' Soave and charming cherry-packed 'Classico' Valpolicella tend to wipe the floor with the lacklustre stuff lower down in the valley.

BORDEAUX

LEFT BANK

Médoc, on the left bank, is divided into eight appelations where Cabernet Sauvignon is king. In the northernmost appellations of Médoc, smaller chateaux boast some 'bargain' Bordeaux with notes of blackcurrant and a signature tobacco-like dryness. More unctuous wines await in **Saint Estephe** that, after time has tamed their tannin, become slicker than a penguin in a tuxedo, while **Pauillac** (home to Château Latour, Château Lafite-Rothschild and Château Mouton Rothschild), produces well-mannered wines uptight in their early years.

Its vines grounded in gravel and circumnavigated by streams, **Margaux's** wines are haughty yet (very) nice, posh and perfumed, with a floral, feminine touch while **Saint Julien** makes fine, fusty claret that couldn't be more archetypically English if it were a Morris Dancer, holding a cucumber sandwich in one hand and a cricket ball in the other. **Moulis**, the minutest Médoc appellation, does young, velvety wines well, while tannic exuberance is associated with the wines of **Listrac**, the most land-locked region in Médoc.

As well as some excellent earthy claret, **Graves** gives drinkers some sensational if sparse Sauvignon Blanc and Sémillon and, lest we forget, superb sweet Sauternes.

RIGHT BANK

Merlot is the main man on the eastern side of the Garonne. Made up of myriad, smaller producers, the right bank's roots dig deep into clay and limestone rather than gravel.

The oldest Bordeaux wine region is **Saint Emilion**, home to two appellations (Saint Emilion and Saint Emilion Grand Cru). Ample, approachable and of a rich and deeply coloured hue, they hit their prime before most Bordeaux. The best grapes are grown either on the steep slopes or the more gravel-y terrain towards the river.

Meanwhile, **Pomerol** wines are moneyed Merlots with youth on their side; swaggering, bejewelled prettyboys with designer watches, leaning insouciantly on the bonnet of offensively expensive sports cars. The wine of **Lalande-de-Pomerol** doesn't worry the wallet as much, while **Fronsac**, and its fraternal **Canon-Fronsac**, are unpretentious yet downright decent blue-collar Bordeaux.

And last (and for many least), wedged between two winding rivers, we have **Entre-Deux-Mers**, an improving area famed for deftly made dry whites (**Haut-Benauge** and **Graves de Vayres**), sweet whites (**Loupiac**, **Cadillac** and **Sainte-Croix**) and, increasingly, some reliable reds (**Sainte-Foy**).

WINE LEGENDS

ALEXANDER THE GREAT

HE WAS BORN INTO THE BARBARIC BACCHANALIA OF FOURTH-CENTURY MACEDONIA, TO A DIPSO-MANIAC DAD AND A MOTHER MASTERED IN THE ART OF REVELRY – IT'S EASY TO SEE WHERE ALEXANDER THE GREAT EARNED HIS QUITE EXTRAORDINARY APPETITE FOR WINE.

His dice were, quite literally, loaded from the start. In 356 BC, Macedonia was the hardest drinking nation in the Western World. The Maccedonians were phenomenal fighters, they were good at gambling and they could hunt too. But drinking, heavy drinking, was what Macedonians did best.

Unlike the Greeks, who considered their northern neighbours to be nothing but ne'er-do-wells and philistines, the Macedonians didn't bother to dilute their wine – they just necked it neat (complete with twigs, stalks and stones) in

quite extraordinary quantities. And then they'd drink some more.

No man epitomised this alcoholic excess more acutely than Philip II, Alexander's famous and hugely competitive father. Likened by his peers to a human sponge, who slept with a gold drinking cup under his pillow, Philip II was a legendary *philoptes* (lover of drinking sessions) whose prestigious displays of drinking and riotous parties cemented his royal authority, greased the cogs of diplomacy, and often ended with Philip leading a jolly jig called a *Dionysiac Comus* – which was the fourth-century equivalent of a 'Conga'.

The grape didn't fall far from the vine. From an early age, his son Alexander was determined to eclipse his old man's considerable achievements - be it with the sword, the 'amphorae' or his notoriously inquisitive 'trouser snake'.

Alexander was an across-the-board sexual omnivore, with a weakness for eunuchs, teenage boys, young girls and men of his own age. But his amorous appetite was a mere drop in the drinking jug when compared to his insatiable thirst for wine.

Initially disdainful as a young man of his father's drinking, Alexander' developed a gratitude for the grape that grew under the tutelage of philosopher Aristotle who, during his study of distillation, turned wine into water like a back-to-front Jesus. Aristotle extolled the virtues of moderation but, now approaching his twenties, Alexander was beginning to lose respect for his tutor, a man who force-fed animals with alcohol and licked his own hands to go to sleep.

By the time Alexander took the throne of Macedonia in 336 BC, he was well-versed in the ways of wine drinking and had proven himself an impressive imbiber at royal drinking bouts. He was a great drinker, but by all accounts he wasn't a great drunk. Plutarch, who penned Alexander's biography, said he was 'delightful company and incomparably charming at other times, (but) when he was drinking he could become offensively arrogant and descend to the level of a common soldier.'

When Alexander drank too much wine, bad things happened. After a goblet too many in 328 BC, Alexander killed his childhood friend and his closest general Cleitus The Black.

Cleitus, who had saved Alexander's life in 334 BC, took issue with Alexander's orders while at a banquet. Not one to take abuse on his wine-covered chin, Alexander tried to settle the matter by throwing an apple at Cleitus. When that didn't work, he pierced his heart with a javelin. On sobering up, Alexander was overcome by guilt and remorse and lay with Cleitus's body, weeping for three days.

Another of Alexander's ill-fated and wine-fuelled acts occurred five years later in 323 BC when, to commemorate the death of Calanus, a Hindi sage who'd accompanied Alexander's army through Persia, Alexander organised a kind of funereal Olympics.

But instead of running, jumping and throwing, Alexander decided the sole discipline was to be drinking, with huge money prizes on offer for the victors.

Thing is, the Indians were absolutely awful at drinking. Pretty much everyone who took part died immediately after the contest. The winner, who had seen off 12 pints of wine in one go, met his maker four days later. As Olympic legacies go, it hardly inspired a new generation of young athletes. Wine, of course, eventually ended it all for Alexander too. In June 323 BC, he died following several epic drinking sessions in Babylon,

Wine flowing in loud and generous ways, just as Alexander would have liked, at a victory banquet.

where he sank 33 pints of wine – one for every year of his life. Modern toxicologists believe political rivals poisoned his wine with a fermentable plant called white hellebore which, when consumed, tasted extremely bitter. But after 33 pints, reckoned the boffins, Alexander would have been oblivious to any kind of difference in taste.

Historians have accused him of being an alcoholic and they may be right. But he was definitely a functioning alcoholic. While mere mortals struggle to get out of bed or find their keys when suffering from the aftereffects of excessive wine consumption, Alexander managed to lead his armies to three epic victories in Persia and, in just 10 years, went from Prince of an uncouth enclave to the ruler of the biggest empire, spanning from Greece to India, that the world has ever known.

ANTOINE LASALLE

ALL HAIL ANTOINE-CHARLES-LOUIS COMTE DE
LASALLE, THE MOST FAMOUS GENERAL OF THE
HUSSARS, THE MOST DAPPER AND DOWNRIGHT
DASHING DIVISION IN NAPOLEON'S CAVALRY.

He was ferocious on the battlefield, a rascal in
the bedroom and one of very few men in history
who could successfully pull off a pair of bright,
baggy red trousers – and he pulled them off a lot,
often with the help of beautiful women.

Lasalle led his legion of chivalrous assassins
across Europe with swagger and charm. His reputation as a sensational swordsman in both senses
of the word was not dampened by his voracious
appetite for drink. One of the most powerful
weapons in Lasalle's armoury of seduction was
his ability to open a bottle of Champagne with

a swipe of his steel sabre. Called *sabrage*, it was
first and foremost a display of phallic prowess
(nothing impressed local ladies more than
effervescence erupting down a bottle's décolle-
tage), but it also happened to be the fastest way
to get the damn thing open.

Lasalle honed his technique while riding
through the Champagne region on the way to
or from battle – under the orders of Napoleon,
a fervent fan of the fancy fizz. 'Champagne!' he
proclaimed. 'In victory one deserves it, in defeat
one needs it'.

In fact, Lasalle may well have been the forefa-
ther of dégorgement. Instead of freezing the sediment, the Hussars simply got rid of the superflu-
ous lees by hacking off the top of the bottle and
drinking it.

The modern technique used today by Champagne houses, was developed in 1816 by Madame
'Veuve' Clicquot, who regularly hosted Hussars
at her vineyard, blushing as their blades brought
forth her bubbly. Did it inspire her invention?
Not sure. But it makes for a good story.

And Lasalle liked a good story. In 1806, when
he and his small 800-strong legion found
themselves isolated and overrun by 5000 men,
he hoodwinked the enemy into surrender by pre-
tending, in a move of moustache-twirling genius,
that a much bigger French army was imminent.

Lasalle lived fast, died young and expected
other Hussars to do the same. Aged 36 in 1809,
as he prepared himself for battle, he opened his
bag to find the glass favoured by his wife had
smashed, a broken pipe and a bottle of wine. It
was, he told his comrades, a bad omen, declaring
'I will not survive this day'.

Resplendent in his famous red trousers and
a long pipe perched between his lips, Lasalle
charged towards the enemy for the last time, in
full knowlege of his fate, not bothering to even
unsheathe his sword.

PLATO AND THE SYMPOSIUM

THE SYMPOSIUM WAS AN IMBIBING INSTITUTION THAT WAS CENTRAL TO CIVILISED SOCIETY IN CLASSICAL GREECE.

They were drinking parties, but certainly not of the vulgar variety. At symposiums, men of tremendous stock would come together to share stories, courteously air their opinions, perhaps pontificate a little about politics and, indeed, slacken the cerebral muscles with a moderate amount of wine.

Wine was drunk slowly, its flow moderated by a 'symposiarch' who would dilute the wine with water according to the seriousness of the subjects being discussed. Wine was watched to ensure that no single merrymaker reached a state of inebriation before another. Drink would be dedicated to the gods (Dionysus, mostly), speakers would take turns to talk, and slowly, as inhibition melted away and creativity came to the fore, the hidden truths, the candid thoughts of truly great men would emerge.

Nowhere is the symposium more elegantly eulogised than in Plato's eponymous work about man's sexual desire, where a group of men unveil their emotions and ideas about Eros, eternity, beauty and truth. Wine stars throughout – but always in moderation.

'Socrates took his seat and had his meal. When dinner was over, they poured a libation to the god, sang a hymn and – in short – followed the whole ritual.' Then they turned their attention to drinking. At that point, Pausanias may well have addressed the group: 'Well, gentlemen, how can we arrange to drink less tonight? After the excesses of last night let's try not to do it all over again this evening.'

The best way to get to know a man's true character, said Plato, was to share wine with him at a symposium – as long as it was done so in moderation. 'What is better adapted than the festive use of wine, in the first place to test, and in second place to train the character of a man, if care be taken in the use of it.'

Drinking wine, claimed Plato, was the ultimate test of whether a man can control his desires and anger and rein in his impulses. It was a test of character, yet not one that everyone passed. While Plato was a passionate proponent of the symposium in practice, he was less fond of them in reality. The symposiums were seldom sophisticated affairs but, more often than not, rather debauched descents into immorality where highbrow discourse regularly played second fiddle to complete intoxication.

Symposiums regularly got out of hand, attracting adolescent aristocratic alpha-males who didn't know how to drink. Exactly the kind of carry-on that Plato had warned against. 'The boys up to 18 should steer clear of wine,' he wrote, 'because there is no point adding fire to fire.' Ignoring his advice, young blue-blooded boys formed testosterone-fuelled drinking clubs with such names as the Autolekythoi (Pricks) and the Phalloi (Erections) and arranged performances by Pornikes, female flute girls who would play music and double-up as prostitutes (their explicit portrayal is where the word 'pornography' comes from). In reality, the symposiums would conclude in the early hours with *Comos*, a post-party pastime of roaming the streets, drinking, vomiting, urinating, looking in vain for hanky panky and behaving like complete and utter nitwits – our words, not Plato's.

ANNE-CLAUDE LEFLAIVE

'Biodynamic means respect for all that is living in the vineyard and not working with chemical products that kill the soil and the surroundings...'

Wine-making using biodynamic methods is a holistic affair entirely bereft of any herbicides or insecticides, where decisions are dictated by the cosmic calendar with every procedure linked to the position of the planets, the movement of the moon, and astrology. Fire signs such as Leo get the grapes growing with more gusto, water signs such as Pisces liven up the leaves while the roots are refreshed by earth signs like Taurus and Capricorn.

Biodynamic methods also encourage vineyard owners to get intimate and imaginative with local flora and fauna. Sticking dandelions into dead cows, cramming deer bladders with yarlow and burying manure-filled cow horns into the vines' soil – some of the stuff they get up to can seem a little far-fetched at first. But advocates of this über-organic approach may rightly argue it's no more outlandish than commercial wine-makers talking up 'terroir' while simultaneously employing laboratory chemicals.

Biodynamism is rooted in the scribblings of Rudolf Steiner, an Austrian activist, author and philosopher who first unveiled his unorthodox agricultural ideas in 1924. At a lecture filled with suspicious farmers, he said: 'I am well aware that to our modern way of thinking this all sounds quite insane... but just think of how many things

were originally rejected as crazy and after a few years became accepted.' Almost a century later, many are still sceptical but there's no doubting that the biodynamic approach results in some stunning wines – none more so than those produced by Anne-Claude Leflaive, the Burgundian queen of biodynamism who oversees Domaine Leflaive, arguably the world's best white wine estate.

Leflaive inherited the estate in Puligny-Montrachet in the early 1990s and, inspired by the work of ecological soil scientist Claude Bourguignon, she began to convert the fiercely traditional Burgundian estate to biodynamism.

It was a brave move that many questioned but, by the 1990s, Leflaive's loyalty to biodynamic principles breathed life back into the Domaine and since then, many of her Burgundian neighbours have begun to follow her lead. Having remained at the forefront of the biodynamic movement while also making stunning wines, she was named Winemaker of the Year in 2014 by the Institute of the Masters of Wine.

Accepting the award, she said: 'To make good wines that reflect the place where they come from, you have to be very careful about how you work with the vineyard. I want to spread more ecological systems so that we can all have different wines from all over the world. This diversity is very rich for everyone.'

GÉRARD DEPARDIEU

'I'm happy with very little on this earth, but I do like to have a lot in my glass.'

Built like a bashed-up Citroën 2CV with a phenomenally French face, sizeable *poignées d'amour* and a flabby andouillette of a middle finger forever raised in the direction of authority, Gérard Depardieu is a whole lot of Gaul.

A true *bon vivant* in every sense of the word, *L'Hexagon*'s favourite hellraiser has repeatedly dodged death with a classic Gallic shrug of the shoulders, surviving 17 motorbike accidents, a runway collision between his small plane and a Boeing 727 at Madrid airport, and a quintuple heart bypass.

After the operation, concerned doctors told him to drastically reduce his copious wine consumption and his 60 Gitanes a day. While the smoking stopped, his daily *du vin* interventions continued. 'When I'm stressed, I still drink five or six bottles of wine a day,' he revealed in an interview, five years later. 'When I'm relaxed, three or four, but I'm trying to cut down.'

Describing himself as an actor-wine-maker, Depardieu owns award-winning vineyards in Morocco, Spain, Italy, Argentina, Algeria, Ukraine and, of course, France too – having first bought a plot in Nuits-St-Georges, Burgundy, before snapping Château de Tigné, a 13th-century wine estate in Anjou back in 1989. Depardieu also makes Bordeaux in the Médoc with wine mogul Bernard Magrez.

Above: Depardieu purchased Chêteau de Tigné, a 13th-century wine estate in Anjou, in 1989. He now owns vineyards in several other countries.

'My love for wine,' he told *Decanter* magazine, 'dates back to childhood, during communion in church. When the priest raises the chalice and pronounces the sacred words, in the mind of a young boy wine takes on an aura of mysticism.'

His rounded, often oak-led, wines are well received with some reaching a Robert Parker rating of 94 out of 100. While not a hands-on wine-maker, Depardieu remains a romantic terroir-iste who dreams of swapping cinema for the soil of his vineyards.

'I'd rather spend my time with grape growers than actors,' he said, poignantly. 'My unrealized ambition is to tend my vines,' he confessed in his cookbook, 'to produce wine and work like an artisan. I dream of rediscovering the old traditions and customs of wine-growing… and work in harmony with nature.'

Withnail and I

Were *Withnail and I* a wine, it would be a Bordeaux. Initially overlooked by critics on release in 1987, appreciation improved dramatically over time and, like the finest vintages, it reveals new nuances every time you revisit it.

'There can be no true beauty', as Uncle Monty says, 'without decay'. Twenty five years on, it remains a vintage piece of British cinema, its polythene-covered feet firmly rooted in comic tragedy.

Overflowing with memorable lines and perpetually quoted by pub philosophers, the film has a cult status that is partly owed to an infamous (highly irresponsible) drinking game where viewers (mostly students) match the lead character, Withnail, drink for drink.

It's an acutely absurd undertaking as the cult comedy is laced with a liver-quivering quantities of alcohol; Withnail downs one pint of cider (with ice), shots of gin, six glasses of sherry, 13 whiskies, four pints of ale, lighter fluid, (replace with vinegar as they did on set), and nine-and-a-half glasses of red wine too.

Withnail, portrayed to perfection by the tee-total Richard E Grant, constantly 'demands booze' yet from his first scene to the last, fine wine is clearly his emotional crutch.

Each swig heightens his delusions of grandeur, deepening both his denial of impending adulthood and the end of the sixties, that most decadent of decades – 'My boys, my boys, we are at the end of an age', as Uncle Monty says.

Withnail's insouciant drinking of some of 'the finest wines known to humanity' is all the more remarkable when you know that the wines in the film *really were* some of 'the finest wines known to humanity'.

Some 20 years before writer and director Bruce Robinson filmed *Withnail and I*, he was offered some bottles of musty French 'muck' by the owner of a hotel in Manchester facing closure.

Unbeknown to him, the muck was made up of some of the world's finest blue-chip Bordeaux. Robinson, then a struggling actor, paid £200 for 200 bottles of Châteaux Margaux, Beychevelle, Pétrus with vintages including 1945 (an epic year), '47, '53, '59 and '61.

While Robinson had planned to use the wine solely as props before auctioning them at Sotheby's afterwards, he sacrificed a small fortune by selflessly serving them up on the film set. Some years later, during a Q&A at the British Film Institute, he said: 'We drank the lot in two weeks. It was saveloy and chips with…shall we have the Beychevelle or the Margaux?'

The bottle of Château Margaux 1953, sipped in the final scene in which Withnail recites Shakespeare's 'What a piece of work is a man' soliloquy to some wolves in London Zoo, is, at the time of writing, worth more than £2000.

BOTTLE SHOCK

On May 24th 1976, some Napa Valley nobodies went up against some of the finest names in French wine-making at the most notorious wine tasting in the history of the industry.

The 'Judgement of Paris' consisted of two blind tastings: a comparison of French/American Chardonnays and Californian Cabernet Sauvignons versus some fabulous French Bordeaux – featuring the top *Grands Crus*.

The French, of course, went into it filled with haughty hubris. The panel of highly esteemed judges consisted entirely of fellow countrymen who held American wine in low regard. But California opened a can of almighty whupass on their Old World opponents, topping the tables in both categories and knocking the established wine world off its axis.

Stag's Leap Wine Cellars' 72 from the Napa Valley (costing $6) took first place in the red wine category, closely followed by Mouton-Rothschild '70, while the winning white wine was Château Montelena 73, also from Napa – 'Not bad for kids from the sticks', exclaimed Jim Barrett, Montelena's general manager.

The French wine industry rejected the results but when the blind tasting was repeated two years later, and then again in 1986 and 2006, the Americans took first place every time.

America was hardly humble in victory. The story made the cover of the next issue of *Time Magazine* and its writer, George M Taber, went on to release a book about the tasting in 2005.

Bottle Shock, a film losely based on the story, starring a haughty Alan Rickman as Spurrier, was released in 2009. At the time of writing, a second film based on the controversy, backed by both Spurrier and Taber, was being filmed.

10 THINGS YOU NEED TO KNOW ABOUT WINE

01 The original Coca-Cola recipe was based on Vin Mariani, a *'medicinal'* drink made by Angelo Mariani who steeped cocoa leaves in French red wine for six months. Each fluid ounce contained 7.2 milligrams of cocaine and was drunk by, amongst others, Pope Leo XIII, Jules Verne, American president Ulysses Grant, Queen Victoria and the inventor of the light bulb, Thomas Edison – who claimed it helped him stay awake at night, which is why, one imagines, he needed a light bulb…

02 The word **plonk** is derived from World War one whispers on the Western Front. Sharing the trenches with the French, the British misheard them talking about *'Vin blanc'*– and mispronounced it *'plonk'*.

03 It's not true that **white wine** is made with white grapes and red wine is made with dark grapes. Oh no, that would be too simple. To make white wine, winemakers only use the juice of either white grapes or dark grapes. **Red** and **rosé**, meanwhile, use the skin of dark grapes only.

04 People often claim that the original **champagne glass** was moulded in the shape of Marie Antoinette's breasts. These people are wrong. For a start, no-one boasts bosoms like that – especially if you include the stem. What's more, the wide-mouthed glass was born in England in the mid-17th century, almost an entire century before Miss Antoinette was born. And, besides, you're better off using a flute instead of a coupe. It's better for the bubbles.

05 'Bottles of wine aren't like paintings. At some point you have to consume them. The object in life is to die with no bottles of wine in your cellar. To drink your last bottle of wine and go to sleep that night and not wake up.' **Jay McInerney**, **American author and wine critic**

06 **Red wine**, when consumed in moderation protects the body from damaging oxidising agents in much the same way as leaded paint prevents iron railings from getting rusty. Drinking a couple of glasses of red wine reduces the levels of low density cholesterols, making gummy platelets less sticky so that they don't get stuck within the arteries and form blood clots. Wines that are most beneficial in this respect tend to be young wines grown in a hot yet moist climate – like **Chilean wines** – as these possess the most flavonoids concentrated in their grape skins.

07 Avoid the second cheapest bottle on a **wine list** as, in most restaurants, this is the one the restaurateur pays the least for. Safe in the knowledge that customers don't want to appear tight, owners tend to put the cheapest wine at a price slightly higher than the house wine – thus making the most profit. In most cases, the house wine will be better and cheaper.

08 When it comes to champagne, it's not so much the quantity of bubble that should concern the connoisseur, it's the quality. The finer the foam, the finer the fizz. Big bubbles are bad, a most uncouth form of effervescence, referred to in derogatory fashion by the French as *oeils de crapaud* meaning Toad's Eyes, and synonymous with an inferior kind of sparkle.

White-coated boffins reckon that there are approximately 49 million bubbles in a bottle of **Champagne**.

Bubbles make Champagne look sexy and taste better. They begin life in the bottle as dissolved air, but after the cork is popped, carbon dioxide (CO_2) enters the little microscopic pouches of air created by flecks, specks and imperfections on the inside of the glass and little bubbles are born. As more CO_2 arrives, the bubbles expand and rise up.

On its journey upwards, a bubble gets faster and fatter. As it rises, it also hauls liquid with it to the top before dropping it down the sides of the glass, creating a kind of subaquatic fountain.

09 While it differs from wine to wine and grape to grape, on average it takes approximately **600 grapes, or approximately eight bunches,** to make just one even half-decent bottle of wine.

10 The most expensive vineyards in the world are the first growths in **Bordeaux, France,** peaking at around €1.2m per hectare. A Tuscan **Chianti** vineyard will set you back around €250,000.

WINE RECOMMENDATIONS

With so many wines from both the 'Old' and the 'New' worlds to choose from, it's tricky to recommend just ten. But whatever your wine knowledge, the broad range of styles listed here should make your cellar sexier and your wine rack more remarkable.

BELE CASEL

2012 PROSECCO ASOLO 'MILLESIMATO' (VENETO, ITALY)

Venture beyond the obvious Valdobbiadene region towards Colli Asolani, a distinctive undulating region recently promoted to Italy's top echelon of wine status DOCG (*Denominazione di Origine Controllata e Garantita*). Here organic techniques give a balance of sweet fruit and minerality.

DOMAINE FRANÇOIS COTAT

2006 SANCERRE, CUVEE PAUL (CHAVIGNOL, FRANCE)

Sancerre at its best is simply sensational but its popularity has spawned a plethora of pale imitations.

A most sincere advocate of Sancerre is François Cotat, whose Cotat Domaine is small, beautifully positioned on steep slopes and rigorously organic in its approach, with vines often harvested by hand.

GUSBOURNE ESTATE

2009 BRUT RESERVE, SPARKLING, (KENT, ENGLAND)

Since the mid-1990s English sparkling wine has been gaining an increasingly solid reputation for its quality, often standing proudly on the podium above French Champagne in blind tastings. And why not? The English climate is not dissimilar to that of Champagne and its clay and limestone soils are equally well suited to making beautiful sparkling wine.

The south-facing vineyards of the Gusbourne Estate are planted with Chardonnay, Pinot Noir and Pinot Meunier – the same as Champagne. While Chardonnay grapes provide the lion's share of the wine, Pinot Noir and Meunier add weight, depth and a subtle roundness. Berets suitably doffed.

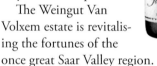

VAN VOLXEM

2012 SCHARZHOFBERGER, (SAAR, GERMANY)

Germany – and Riesling itself – make some of the very greatest white wines of the world yet, because of their relatively unfashionable status, they are very reasonable priced.

The Weingut Van Volxem estate is revitalising the fortunes of the once great Saar Valley region.

CHÂTEAU DE LANCYRE

2011 VIEILLES VIGNES PIC ST-LOUP, (LANGUEDOC, FRANCE)

Lancyre is now one of the leading lights in the enchantingly named Pic-St-Loup, a region of the Languedoc, while Vieilles Vignes is absurdly good value. It has a soft nature, making it easy to drink, and yet, still a serious wine for both enthusiasts and the cellar.

CASCINA FONTANA
2011 LANGHE NEBBIOLO, (PIEDMONT, ITALY)

One of the most enthralling Italian wines, Langhe Nebbiolo is a catch-all term for the area of Piedmont lying to the south of Alba in the province of Cuneo.

While the nose boasts the classic floral yet savoury personality (tar & roses being the common shorthand), the robust palate will have you reaching frantically for a grilled rib-eye steak as a good foil.

DESCENDIENTES DE J PALACIOS
2010 LAS LAMAS (BIERZO, SPAIN)

Alvaro Palacios is a man on a mission to recover Spain's vinous treasures. Coming from the revered wine-making dynasty of Bodegas Palacios Remondo, Alvaro successfully served his apprenticeship in Bordeaux with Pétrus and Trotanoy.

This is a region to watch, and the rapid upward direction of the prices in recent years is totally justified.

FELTON ROAD
2012 BANNOCKBURN PINOT NOIR, (OTAGO, NEW ZEALAND)

The spiritual heartland for Pinot Noir is Burgundy in France but Central Otago, home to the most southerly grapevines in the world, is the region that most closely replicates the conditions in Burgundy.

Felton Road is a relatively young enterprise, and owner Nigel Greening produces some of the very best Pinot Noir to be produced outside of Burgundy. On no account should the more junior cuvées be overlooked, but for captivating balance of power and elegance, try the 1er Cru Burgundy.

TOOLANGI VINEYARDS
CHARDONNAY (TOOLANGI, AUSTRALIA)

It's been little more than 20 years since Garry and Julie Hounsell took over the Toolangi vineyard, but in that short amount of time they have cultivated a reputation for growing some quite phenomenal fruit. Rather than producing the wine themselves, they choose an array of renowned wine-makers to work with (such as Giaconda, Yering Station, Hoddles Creek and Oakridge). As well as Pinot Noir, the 13-hectare, low-yielding vineyard is particularly cherished for its Chardonnay wine which is aged in French oak for 11 months. The low yields deliver a delightful subtlety and freshness.

CONSTANTIA GLEN THREE 2010
(CONSTANTIA, SOUTH AFRICA)

If your budget doesn't stretch to the increasingly expensive Bordeaux, try South Africa for a similar level of elegance.

In the Constantia valley, a tiny region close to Cape Town, the Austrian family-owned Constantia Glen make some marvellous wines. The key to their success, as in Europe, is the combination of marginal, maritime climate and ideal soil. The Three is the more approachable of the reds, delivering beautifully sweet fruit on the nose with a touch of sweet spice and savoury hints of tobacco and cedar. The palate is very well balanced, European yet with New-World appeal.

The authors wish to thank Berry Bros & Rudd for their advice and expertise.

WHISKY
& WHISKEY

From the troops of Henry II to the top-end style bars of Hong Kong, whisky has woven its way into centuries of history and whether it's spelt with or without an 'e', time is the all-important vital 'other' ingredient.

Whether whisky was invented by the Irish or the Scottish depends very much on whether you're drinking in a pub in Dublin or Dumbarton. Success has many fathers and both Celtic nations reckon the water of life was their idea. Theories involving St Patrick, Irish monks, Islamic Moors and Scottish clans have all been spouted but who knows?

HISTORY & CULTURE

When it comes to the origins of whisky, not even historians can agree about who first invented it, their efforts having been severely hampered by a dearth of documental evidence or concrete proof.

The Ancient Celts didn't leave many clues. Unlike the Romans and the Greeks, they weren't very good at remembering to write anything down, a problem presumably worsened by the whisky itself.

Another reason that whisky's exact origins are obscured is that everyone who was there at the time is now, rather unhelpfully, dead. So let's just mumble something about the mists of time, play the enigmatic Gaelic music and move swiftly on.

Whoever's idea it was, and whenever they had it, it's certainly been Scotland that has run with the whisky idea – not even an insistent Irishman could argue otherwise. Firstly, Scotland put a historical marker down in 1494-95, when the accountant for King James IV, an enlightened

imbiber, recorded that a huge batch of malt had been despatched under royal assent to Friar John Cor, a monk, in Fife, 'to make aqua vitae'.

Some centuries later, Scottish distillers stole a further march on their Irish counterparts when they embraced the ideas of Aeneas Coffey, the Irish inventor, who patented the continuous still in 1830. Enabling distillers to make more whisky for less money, Coffey's still served as a springboard for global domination and sent sales of Scotch soaring, usurping those of Irish whiskey.

Coffey had only offered his idea to the Scots after being cold-shouldered by his fellow countrymen, who dismissed his new distillate as too dull. It was a daft decision at the time and, as anyone who has seen Riverdance will know, one that the Irish have been kicking themselves about ever since.

Fortune also favoured Scotland the Brave. When Phylloxera, an avaricious aphid, devoured the vineyards of France during the mid to late 1800s, the price of wine and brandy rocketed and they became nigh on impossible to get hold of. Whisky, meanwhile, was cheap in comparison. It was at this point that the copious and shrewd Scottish distillers stepped in and began to export their wares throughout the world.

Leading the charge from the 1860s onwards was Tommy Dewar,

The Jameson whiskey distillery in Dublin, Ireland, is now a much-visited museum and still boasts the original water wheel that fed fresh water direct into the distillery.

who travelled the world as a salesman, not only for his own blended whisky but also to promote the Scottish nation too. Like Robert Burns before him, Dewar dovetailed the notion of whisky-drinking with the nation of his birth and, as such, his adverts were shamelessly Scottish. Print adverts featured kilted men playing bagpipes and golf, while his cinema advert of 1897, the first ever for a drinks brand, recreated Scottish battles using soldiers made of shortbread. Probably.

No other nation is more synonymous with a spirit than Scotland is with whisky. The clue, if you look closely, is in the name: Scotch. As in Scotland. It couldn't be more quintessentially Caledonian if it were a kilo of battered haggis wrapped in a Saltire and catapulted into the face of an invading Englishman.

Whisky is not merely the spirit of Scotland, it's the Scottish spirit. While every single malt is made in the same way, using the same core ingredients, each and every one is an individual, each an idiosyncratic expression of its surroundings; each a liquid legacy of a specific place and, crucially, of the lives of the people who've made it over the centuries.

From the salty, seaweed scent that blows off the sea in Skye to the smoky leather serenity of a fireside armchair in a cosy Edinburgh pub, whisky actually smells and tastes of Scotland. The peat, the barley, the water and the weather, they all strike 'terroir' into the taste and, like the 800 islands and 30,414 square miles on which it is made, whisky is hugely deserving of some serious discovery.

Behind the bar of most pubs, whisky often dwells on the top shelf beyond reach, as if it were too dangerous and difficult to understand. While that's not the case at all, it's remoteness is part of its appeal. Like an epic novel, it will reward patient perseverance like no other spirit.

This 1953 advertisement for Dewar's whisky clearly shows the company's patriotic marketing strategy.

You have to work at whisky to uncover its complexity and, like all drinks, it is best explored in context. Just as Pastis doesn't travel beyond Provence, whisky is simply better in Scotland. Scotch only seduced the Thinking Drinkers after a genuine imbibing epiphany that occurred on the remote Hebridean Isle of Jura.

Jura's Norse name means 'Island of the Deer' and after a day touring the distillery, we sat alone at sundown on a jetty, drams in hand, watching deer trying to swim across to Islay on a mating mission, hot-hoofing it across the narrow Sound in search of some sexy time.

As Bambi & Co bravely breaststroked the strong currents on their carnal quest, it all came together in an instant: the sea, the sunset, the smells, the silence, the salty air, the sheer and utter simplicity of it all. The dram adopted an added dimension and whisky adopted two more loyal and dedicated disciples.

From disputes about where whisky originated to the global spread of scotch single malt, blends and bourbon today, the whisky story is rich with romance and tradition.

1170 Henry II's troops arrive in Ireland uninvited and find the locals drinking spirits.

1494 The first written account of whisky distilling is attributed to Friar John Cor who is given malt by the Scottish Exchequer.

1506 King James IV of Scotland grants Edinburgh's Guild of Surgeon Barbers the sole right to distil whisky in the city.

1620 Settlers in Virginia, USA, are making a distillate from corn, the forerunner to bourbon.

1608 Irish landowner Sir Thomas Phillips is given licence to distil in County Antrim and Bushmills is born.

1580 The English government imposes martial law on Ireland and bans distilling. The Irish rightly ignore these rules and make illicit whiskey, or 'poteen', instead.

1690 England bans French imports such as wine and brandy. The Scots step in and fill the void with whisky.

1725 The English introduce crippling whisky taxes into Scotland. Like the Irish before them, the Scots dodge the duty by making illicit versions under the cover of darkness – hence the term 'moonshine'.

1780 John Jameson sets up a distillery in Dublin, Ireland.

1783 The Samuels family starts distilling. Their descendants now produce Maker's Mark.

1791 US President George Washington taxes whiskey. Distillers take the news rather badly and rebel.

1786 Scottish poet Robert Burns writes 'Scotch Drink' as part of his first, and most famous, book of poems.

1786 Distilling starts at the Buffalo Trace site – the oldest continuously working still in the USA.

1797 Having caused a kerfuffle by taxing whiskey in 1791, George Washington retires as president– and sets up his own whiskey distillery.

1803 The Louisiana purchase in the US opens up trade routes for Kentucky whiskey.

1816 Laphroaig Distillery founded in Scotland.

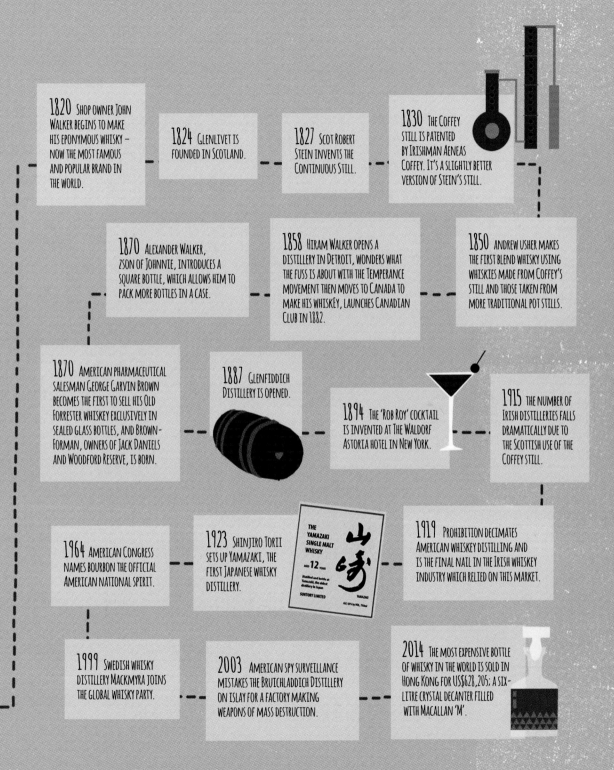

1820 Shop owner John Walker begins to make his eponymous whisky – now the most famous and popular brand in the world.

1824 Glenlivet is founded in Scotland.

1827 Scot Robert Stein invents the Continuous Still.

1830 The Coffey still is patented by Irishman Aeneas Coffey. It's a slightly better version of Stein's still.

1870 Alexander Walker, zson of Johnnie, introduces a square bottle, which allows him to pack more bottles in a case.

1858 Hiram Walker opens a distillery in Detroit, wonders what the fuss is about with the Temperance movement then moves to Canada to make his whiskey, launches Canadian Club in 1882.

1850 Andrew Usher makes the first blend whisky using whiskies made from Coffey's still and those taken from more traditional pot stills.

1870 American pharmaceutical salesman George Garvin Brown becomes the first to sell his Old Forrester whiskey exclusively in sealed glass bottles, and Brown-Forman, owners of Jack Daniels and Woodford Reserve, is born.

1887 Glenfiddich Distillery is opened.

1894 The 'Rob Roy' cocktail is invented at The Waldorf Astoria hotel in New York.

1915 The number of Irish distilleries falls dramatically due to the Scottish use of the Coffey still.

THE YAMAZAKI SINGLE MALT WHISKY
AGE 12 YEAR
山崎
Distilled and bottle at Yamazaki, the oldest distillery in Japan
SUNTORY LIMITED
ALC 43% by VOL, 70ml
YAMAZAKI

1964 American Congress names Bourbon the official American national spirit.

1923 Shinjiro Torii sets up Yamazaki, the first Japanese whisky distillery.

1919 Prohibition decimates American whiskey distilling and is the final nail in the Irish whiskey industry which relied on this market.

1999 Swedish whisky distillery Mackmyra joins the global whisky party.

2003 American spy surveillance mistakes the Bruichladdich Distillery on Islay for a factory making weapons of mass destruction.

2014 The most expensive bottle of whisky in the world is sold in Hong Kong for US$628,205; a six-litre crystal decanter filled with Macallan 'M'.

ROBERT BURNS

Robert Burns was an 18th-century blue-collar bard, more bawdy than William Shakespeare and wittier than the watered-down William Wordsworth.

A prolific philanderer with a legendary libido, Burns was monogamous in neither his love life nor in his choice of drink, but it was whisky that whetted his creative appetite, and he embraced the imaginative freedom it gave to both his pen and, indeed, his penis.

Scotch was his malted muse as he pointed his sharp-shooting wordy gun at the temples of the hypocritical Scottish church, the State, class inequality and anything or anyone that undermined the pride and the value of the common man.

Burns was the original modern poet, a libertarian lyricist whose words resonate more these days with the likes of Bob Dylan or the lewd lyrics of Bon Scott, the lead singer of AC/DC, who, like Burns, only reached his thirties. Unlike Scott who died in a Renault 5 following a quite epic drinking session, Burns was always measured in his measures, a decent drinker but, crucially, he was not a drunk and there exist very few accounts of him being overly-intoxicated in the taverns of Edinburgh. He was seldom unruly or rowdy and 'learned to look unconcernedly on a large tavern bill'.

Whisky percolated throughout Burns' prose and having spent his early years ploughing and seeding the infertile soil on his father's farm in Ayrshire, he cherished the transubstantiation of fermented grain into the fiery water of life – as depicted in *John Barleycorn*, his earliest ode to Scotland's iconic national drink:

John Barleycorn was a hero bold,
Of noble enterprise;
For if you do but taste his blood,
'Twill make your courage rise:

'Twill make a man forget his woe;
'Twill heighten all his joy;
'Twill make the widow's heart to sing,
Tho' the tear were in her eye.

Then let us toast John Barleycorn,
Each man a glass in hand;
And may his great posterity
Ne'er fail in old Scotland!

The joys of the grain, compared with those of the grape, are celebrated a few years later in his poem *Scotch Drink*, a 21-verse celebration of Scotch whisky, which deftly blends bacchanalian poetry with a cursing condemnation of Calvinism, and an attack on the evils of excise.

This proved awkward when, some years later, Burns was employed as a tax-collecting excise man in Dumfries. While he collected money on everything from tobacco to candles, he turned a blind eye to the widespread dealings of illicit alcohol among his associates and aged just 37, and leaving at least 12 children behind, he proudly went to his grave having never demanded a single penny in duty from a distiller.

Rabbie
BURNS

SCOTCH
WHISKY

THE SCOTTISH WHISKY REGIONS

Islands

Speyside

Highlands

Lowlands

Campbeltown

Scottish whisky can be divided into five key geographical regions: Highlands, Lowlands, Speyside, Campbeltown and Islands. It would be helpful if each region were prescriptive of flavour, but that's not the case. Geography provides general guidelines to the palate but history, politics, economics and science tend to confuse matters, with many caveats and exceptions.

LOWLANDS

In the Lowlands, the column still is king, and triple-distillation delivers a more delicate dram, smooth and malty in character. Famously favoured by female drinkers, the Lowland 'ladies' whiskies are light, softly spoken styles that are neither peaty nor coastal in character, more floral and less challenging on the palate. The spread of distilleries is small and sparse, with *Glenkinchie* in the east, *Auchentoshan* in the west and, to the south, *Bladnoch* and *Ailsa Bay,* which is the whisky distillery closest to England.

CAMPBELTOWN

Once a thriving hub of whisky production, with more than two dozen distilleries at its peak, the smallest of the geographical whisky-making regions, to the west of Glasgow, is far less prolific these days. It boasts only three regional distilleries, positioned on a peninsula protruding out into the sea, that tend to produce whiskies that are salty, dry and smoky. The entrepreneurial *Springbank* is the most renowned, with the other two currently being *Glengyle* and *Glen Scotia*.

HIGHLANDS

United only in their dissimilarity, Highland whiskies are vast and varied, encapsulating whisky's enigmatic, contradictory character. To the south, explore the underrated richness of *Glengoyne*; discover the dulcet tones of *Dalwhinnie* at the Highland's heart and adventure to Oban's western outpost for some fruit and spice. *Glen Garioch* is a bit of a beast in the east, ploughing a fairly lonesome furrow with some firm, full-bodied whiskies, while to the region's far north, *Old Pulteney*, in Wick, is more straight-jacket than smoking jacket; idiosyncratic expressions offer nutty notes and touches of fruit cake.

SPEYSIDE

Wedged between Aberdeen in the east and Inverness to the west, *Speyside* is to whisky what Bordeaux is to red wine.

Unrivalled in the sheer density of distilleries, *Speyside* boasts nearly half of all the stills in Scotland and, at one point, there were as many as 200 in the Livet valley alone. It's a stylistic smorgasbord but, if it helps, you can draw a fluid dividing line between distilleries that lean towards lighter styles (*Glenlivet, Glenfiddich*) and those who pay homage to the past with more robust expressions (*Balvenie, The Macallan, Glenfarclas*).

ISLANDS

An arching, remote archipelago stretching from Arran right round to the isle of Islay via the Hebrides, the 'Islands' offer whiskies that, like the islands themselves, can be inaccessible yet hugely rewarding to those who are willing to discover them.

The whiskies on the isle of Arran are laced with a lovely lightness and plenty of lemon and lime; Jura's eponymous distillery produces laid-back whiskies, while Tobermory on the isle of Mull is similarly, suitably left-field. On the Isle of Skye, *Talisker* provides plenty of peat and pepper, while up in the Orkneys, *Highland Park* oscillates successfully between smoke and sweetness.

But what of Islay (pronounced eye-la)? Peaty and smoky. The trio of distilleries to the south, *Ardbeg, Lagavulin* and *Laphroaig*, epitomise the Islay character: imagine Lapsang Souchong-sipping, pipe-puffing, smoked kippers wrapped in bacon doing laps in a loch of iodine. On the east side of the island, the understated *Caol Ila* slides the smoke dial down a notch or two before *Bowmore*, on Islay's inner west coast, slides it back up again with a touch of tropical fruit too. Further west is *Bruichladdich*, reborn in 2001 and making up for lost time with a prolific output of innovative and popular expressions that are less peaty.

WHISKY LEGENDS

AENEAS COFFEY: PLUCK OF THE IRISH

BOTH THE IRISH AND THE SCOTS WERE INSTRUMENTAL IN THE DEVELOPMENT OF DISTILLATION. IT WAS A SCOT, THE APTLY NAMED MICHAEL SCOT, WHO HELPED TRANSLATE THE SCIENTIFIC 'GIBBERISH' OF JABIR IBN HAYYAN, ALSO KNOWN AS GEBER, INTO LATIN (SEE PAGE 155 IF YOU WANT TO KNOW MORE ABOUT OUR FAVOURITE ARABIC ALCHEMIST).

Scot was one of the finest intellectuals of 13th-century Europe. Fluent in both Arabic and Hebrew, the Fife-born philosopher acted as a middle man between the East and Christendom.

Scot could also see into the future. He even predicted that he would die from being hit on the head by a little pebble, which is why he always wore a metal cap on his head. On one of the rare occasions he took it off, while attending Mass, a stone worked itself loose from the church ceiling, dropped down and hit him on his uncommonly exposed crown. Sure enough, he died soon after.

Scot's translations and further explorations into the science behind spirits laid the foundations for widespread distillation in Europe –

initially for medicinal purposes. Up until the early 19th century, all spirits were being made in small batches using the classic pot still. While iconic, it was an expensive and inefficient way of producing a distillate.

Step forward Aeneas Coffey, one of the few tax men in history who you'd happily buy a drink for. An Irishman born in Calais back in 1780, Coffey's contribution to the world of whisky transformed it from a cottage industry into a global business.

In 1824, having chased illicit distillers for more than a dozen years, Coffey was well aware of the parameters of the pot still, so he sought to develop a still that would improve both the yield and the consistency of the spirit.

In some ways, he was beaten to it by Robert Stein, a Scotsman whose 'patent still' had created a still that forced 'wash' through a column of

The Coffey still, patented by Irishman Aeneas Coffey in 1830, transformed whisky production and was adopted not just in Scotland but all around the world.

dividing panels. Stein, though, failed to generate enough funds to get his new design distilling. Coffey took Stein's still and added a twist, two in fact. A couple of pipes were inserted into the column still, which aided re-circulation of the vapours rather than allowing them to flow into the receiver. Not only did this create continuous distillation, it also produced a spirit that was stronger, smoother, lighter and, crucially, cheaper.

After gaining a patent for his new invention in 1830, Coffey took it to his fellow Irish distillers who dismissed the whiskies it produced as insipid. The Scottish, however, weren't so daft. The opportunity to make more whisky for less was wholeheartedly embraced and soon nearly every distillery in Scotland, and indeed the world, had ordered a still from Aeneas Coffey & Sons.

ANDREW USHER (JNR)

NOT LONG AFTER THE COFFEY STILL BECAME COMMONPLACE IN SCOTLAND, BLENDED WHISKIES BEGAN TO EMERGE.

Andrew Usher, a wine and spirit merchant in Edinburgh, began experimenting with blended malts in the 1840s. Yet it was his son, also called Andrew, who perfected and commercialised the blending of whisky – transforming it from a domestic Gaelic spirit to a truly cosmopolitan global one.

Born in 1826, Usher the younger joined his father's business and thrived as the entrepreneurial agent for Glenlivet in Edinburgh. In 1853, when a change in law allowed whisky of different ages to be blended 'in bond' at the same distillery, he created Usher's OVG (Old Vatted Glenlivet), the first commercial blended whisky using varying ages of Glenlivet.

Several years later, when the Spirits Act of 1860 started to allow a blend of whiskies from different distilleries, Usher added grain whisky to his blend of pot still malts; this smoothed out the flavour, made it more accessible and enabled Old Vatted Glenlivet to go toe-to-toe with the lighter, established Irish pot-still whiskies.

With this, Andrew Usher in effect rolled out the red carpet for other grocers and shop-owners to follow suit, and many of them went on to become the biggest names in blended whisky – such as James Buchanan (Black & White), Thomas Sandeman (Vat 69), Arthur Bell (Bell's), Alexander Walker (Johnnie Walker), and John and Tommy Dewar (Dewar's).

By the 1880s, within 20 years of Usher's breakthrough, blended whisky was giving the entire globe the glad-eye and, rather fortuitously, no other spirit was at that time better placed to take advantage of the phylloxera plague that annihilated Cognac's French vineyards, and therefore the cognac supply, in France.

Soon after, Scotch whisky usurped its French counterpart as the biggest selling spirit in the world. One amazing example of its supremacy is that, even today, the French buy more Scotch whisky in one month than they do Cognac in a whole year.

Scotch whisky remains Scotland's biggest export – earning the nation more than £135 per second (which would buy you approximately 40 packets of shortbread) – and of the 40 bottles that are shipped overseas every second, more than three quarters are blended whisky.

ERNEST SHACKLETON

Lieutenant E. H. Shackleton, who established the "Furthest South" record. He will contribute the story of his travels and discoveries to "Pearson's Magazine."

Ernest Shackleton, the ultimate English heroic failure – a man who never accomplished what he set out to do yet still inspired adoration.

He would have been a wonderful chap to have a whisky with. He was a charmer and a chancer, loved by the ladies but less by their husbands, a raffish raconteur whom other men would follow, even if they didn't particularly like where he happened to be heading.

Shackleton yearned not for icy adventures but for fame and fortune – and if he had to go somewhere absolutely freezing, stick a British flag in it and come back to get them then, well, that's what he was going to do.

Ever the optimist, Shackleton was led by impulse and an iron will – qualities that, many thought, made him a good leader of men. In reality, though, they just got him into more trouble. For example, while others spent years of meticulous planning before setting off for the South Pole, Shackleton gave himself just seven months to cobble together everything – money, men, equipment, boat, the whole shebang.

Scared of what Shackleton was getting himself into, Fridtjof Nansen, a Norwegian exploring oracle, offered him some advice: 'Wear the latest in cold-weather clothing, Eskimo-style parkas complete with furs and a hood.' But Shackleton wasn't feeling the whole fur thing and, instead, went with a string vest, several hats that he stuck on top of one another, and an old jacket that had no hood but did have holes to let cold air in.

Nansen also insisted that dogs were the only means of travel, but Shackleton hated dogs and dogs hated him. So, instead, he decided to take some Manchurian ponies.

Shackleton also took an actual car. When both rolled off the *Nimrod*, his car sank into the snow and wouldn't start, while the ponies kept falling down crevices. Over time, they either died or were eaten. Yet still, Shackleton somehow led his men to within a hundred miles of the South Pole – further than anyone had ever gone before – nabbing himself a knighthood in the process.

One thing Shackleton did get right was the drink. As a teenager, growing up in a quasi-Quaker Irish household in South London, he was a flag-waving member of the Band of Hope, a teenage Temperance movement that sang about the evils of alcohol outside pubs.

But 20 years later, aged 33, on May 16th 1907, Shackleton wrote a letter to the distiller Charles Mackinlay & Co of Edinburgh, ordering 25 cases (300 bottles) of 10-year-old Mackinlay's Rare Old Highland Malt from Glen Mohr Distillery, each costing 28 shillings (£1.40).

Alcohol, he'd accepted, was essential for explorers – both as a liquid layer against the crippling cold, and as a crucial bonhomie catalyst to help 15 men get along while spending nine months in a small and very cold hut.

Shackleton left New Zealand with a tonne of liquor on board the *Nimrod*. Not just whisky, brandy and port but crème de menthe, two barrels of beer from the J Speight brewery (in Dunedin, New Zealand), champagne, cider and wine too. He also packed some Forced March, pills largely composed of cocaine, designed to energize and ward off snow blindness – one white powder to protect him from another.

Each case of whisky was labelled 'British Antarctic Expedition 1907' on one side; on the other, in big black letters, were the unwittingly prescient descriptors 'rare' and 'old'. Little did Shackleton or the distillery know that, in 2006, after a century entombed in ice, three cases were to be unearthed from beneath his Antarctic hut in arguably history's most dramatic dram discovery.

With the whisky encased in a hundred years' worth of solid ice and some of the crates cracked by the cold, fears that the whisky had frozen were allayed by the soft sound of sloshing Scotch from within. Preserved partly by an ABV of 47.3% (at 40% it would have frozen), the whisky had survived the Antarctic's inhospitality yet, still, it took four years to prize a single case from Cape Royds' frosty fingers and a further eight months to fully thaw it out at a museum in Canterbury.

While a replica of Mackinlay's Rare Old Highland Malt Whisky has been released, very few people have tasted the real thing. If it's anything like Shackleton himself, then expect a balanced blend, with some seriously strong legs, some Irish malt in there, a touch of tobacco smoke, some light floral notes for the ladies and, obviously, a finish that isn't quite as good as you'd hoped.

Best served over ice. Naturally.

A replica of Mackinlay's Rare Old Highland Malt Whisky was released after the 2006 discovery of Shackleton's original stash beneath a wooden hut in Antarctica.

WHISKY & WATER

'There are two things a Highlander likes naked,
and one of them is malt whisky.'

SCOTTISH PROVERB

Whether or not to add water to one's whisky divides opinion like the letter 'n'. Some deem dilution of the dram as desecration of the distiller's art, while others wholeheartedly welcome a dash of water.

A couple of drops of water can, it is claimed, coax out complexity, unleashing aromas, agitating molecules and opening up the nose like rain hitting a pavement on a balmy summer evening.

It's a romantic notion yet one that stands up to scientific rigour. Recently, Morrison Bowmore Distillers grasped the thorny topic and discovered that a little drop of water changed the look, the taste and the smell of the whisky.

Look

When water meets whisky, the legs are not as 'leggy' as when a neat whisky is swirled around the glass. 'Viscimetric whorls develop,' explained Rachel Barrie, Master Distiller at Bowmore. 'They're the eddies and threads created when fluids of different viscosities mix.'

Smell

The most noticeable difference is very much on the nose. As the alcohol and water combine, energy is released and the liquid temperature initially increases by about 2°C/3½°F (an exothermic reaction), allowing the liquid to 'open up' and release more of the volatile aromas. 'By reducing the higher alcohol strength, it enables

our sense of smell to work better,' said Barrie, 'and the aroma paradoxically seems to increase in intensity when first adding water.'

Taste

The addition of water and the dropping of the alcohol strength creates a cooling effect on the tongue and makes us more receptive to salty and fruity tastes, rather than sweet and spicy.

But how much water should you add? Much depends on your taste, but if you're looking to analyse what's in the glass as well as enjoy it, a couple of drops will do. But be careful what kind of water you use, as different water types deliver different flavours.

When Barrie tasted Bowmore 12-year-old with three different water varieties (soft, hard and mineral rich), each delivered new sensory experiences. Mineral-rich water unlocked additional layers of floral, herbal and peaty notes on the nose, and provided a more intense and intriguing textural experience (chalky minerality) on the tongue.

Soft water, meanwhile, brought out more of the sweet honeyed and citrus fruit notes and delivered a smooth rounded taste, while acidic water brought out more peppery peat, iodine and brine with unripe fruits and cereal notes.

Ice?

Unlike water, ice locks in aroma and suppresses flavour as it brings the temperature down considerably. It does, however, reduce the burn and, let's be honest, the clinking of the ice cubes does sound quite cool.

Glassware

Whisky-making is an imprecise art. There's the style of barley, there's the method of maturation, there's the influence of the oak, there's a bit of geography in there too and there is, of course, the distinctive distillery character. To fully appreciate all this, you really need the right receptacle.

While wine had the tulip glass and champagne the coupette, whisky somehow went without its own specific glass for years – instead taking up uneasy residence in a variety of vessels ranging from rocks glasses and tumblers to balloons and snifters. But that changed in 2001 when Raymond Davidson, managing director of the Scottish-based company Glencairn Crystal, unveiled a bespoke Glencairn Whisky Glass.

Devised in consultation with whisky distillers and based on the copita glass used for sherry, the unique patented design welcomes both single malts and aged blends. Accommodating a 35ml measure with room for some water, the bulbous bowl enables appreciation of both the body and the colour of the whisky, while keeping the liquid in contact with the air to coax out the aromas. A staple at specialist whisky bars all over the world, the Glencairn Glass is a classy container in which to enjoy your whisky.

WHISKY GALORE!

In the early hours of 4th February, 1941, Captain Beaconsfield Worthington steered eight thousand tonnes of ship and 250,000 bottles of Scotch onto the rocks off the island of Eriskay.

No-one really knows how it happened, but it did. Was there a German gunship on the starboard side? Was Worthington worse for wear because of whisky? Or was it magnetite's fault? The most magnetic element on earth, it drives compasses crazy and plays havoc with a ship's navigation; and, crucially, it lives within the island's stony outcrops.

Or was the real reason, and a far more romantic one, that *SS Politician* was pulled into Eriskay's arms by the sheer, whisky-deprived will of the islanders? Back in 1941, life on the isles was pretty bleak, the Outer Hebrides were the first line of defence during World War II, movement was restricted, whisky consumption was rationed and there was a bristling antipathy towards the English who, having ratcheted up duty on whisky, were placing it beyond the reach of the common crofter.

Everyone was in dire need of a dram. So when word spread that 'Polly' was packed with terrific, tax-free whisky (worth £7,836,447.50 in modern money), and with official salvage attempts abandoned, the islanders quickly got in their boats in search of the boozy booty.

Let's get one thing straight here. It wasn't stealing. The islanders were 'rescuing' the whisky, selflessly 'saving' the bottles from being swallowed up by the sea. Customs and Excise, it turns out, didn't distinguish between 'rescue' and 'robbery', so it was under the cover of darkness that the hordes of thirsty Hebrideans descended on poor *Polly*.

Clambering out of their bobbing fishing boats, they climbed 15m (49ft) rope ladders that swayed in the wind well away from the hull of the heavily listed ship. Once on the slippery deck, tottering around with Tilley lights in one hand and home-made hooked spears in the other, they fished out the whisky from the dark oily, salty depths of 'Hold No 5' – like a high-stakes game of hook-a-duck at a fairground.

The task was rendered more difficult by the swirling sea and more surreal by hundreds of black-faced Hebrideans shouting at each other, knocking back free whisky and wearing women's clothes.

'Most men brought some old clothes with them to save their own,' recalls one local. 'But even these became so clogged with oil that, after a few visits, some of them had to raid their wives' wardrobes, carrying off dresses, overalls and even skirts to pull over them.'

Back on land, the Eriksay islanders employed increasingly elaborate ways to hoodwink the Excise men. Bottles were buried in the grassland (*machair*), planted in peat bogs, poured into chamber pots and hot-water bottles and even kept in coffins and old ladies' tights. The islands, almost overnight, became a better place to be. It wasn't just the whisky that created the carnival atmosphere. People were riding oversized bikes, wearing ill-fitting clothes and trading with rolls of South American currency – all of which had 'washed up' on the shores. Someone even 'discovered' a grand piano but no-one had a home big enough to house it.

Customs and Excise, inevitably, came after the islanders. While some smugglers were taken to court, they were mostly given laughably light sentences or fines. Eventually, the authorities ordered *Polly* to be blown up. 'Dynamiting whisky,' exclaimed Angus John Campbell, senior crew member on the *Polly*. 'You wouldn't think there'd be men in the world so crazy as that.'

After the war, cases would mysteriously emerge on the machair while some of the whisky is reputed to still be buried beneath the runway of Benbecula Airport. Locals are forever stumbling across bottles in the most unexpected of places.

Consisting of hundreds of different labels, and mostly distilled in 1938, the stash contained some highly distinguished drams from some very decent distilleries, and in 2013, two bottles from the wreck fetched £12,050 in an online auction.

Even today, whenever the islanders of Eriskay go to whet their whistle with whisky, they raise a toast to the 'Captain of the *Polly*', Beaconsfield Worthington (below). The tale was told in a 1947 novel by Sir Compton Mackenzie and was soon followed by *Whisky Galore*, a 1949 Ealing Comedy that warmed up an austere post-war Britain.

'Don't ask me why I'm feeling sad,
My thoughts are melancholy.
The truth is that I've had a dram
of whisky from the Polly.
For that's the ship that came ashore,
And you never saw her like before –
She'd whisky in the hold galore.
And it's led me into folly'

TOAST TO BEACONSFIELD WORTHINGTON, CAPTAIN OF THE SS POLITICIAN

WHISKY APPRECIATION
FROM SPLENDID BLENDS TO SINGLE MALTS

BLENDED IS SPLENDID

The vast majority (93%) of Scotch whisky is blended. Blends are more fluid in their pursuit of flavour and without blends, single malts probably wouldn't survive.

Each blender (Johnnie Walker, Chivas Regal, Cutty Sark, J&B) boasts its own character and strives for consistency in flavour while reacting to different drinking trends and new occasions that may emerge.

The blender's art is an incredibly complex one. They must choose whiskies from a consistently inconsistent collection of casks and deftly dovetail them into a signature house style which may change over time to meet different tastes.

GO WITH THE GRAIN

Blends are a collection of single malts combined with grain whisky – a mix of malted barley (less than 10%) and other grains (corn, wheat) and distilled in a column still. Often unfairly dismissed as a subordinate distillate, grain whisky is more than just a plain canvas to make malts look better. Grain whisky must, by law, reflect the character of the grain and its role in blends is a crucial rather than a cameo one.

LESS MAY BE MORE

What makes a quality blended whisky is not the quantity of malts nor is it the proportion of malt in the whisky. It's all about the harmony – regardless of how many malts it's made from.

While all malt whisky in a blend must be at least three years old, blends don't have an age statement and most will contain between 15 and 40 per cent malt. So-called deluxe whiskies, however, tend to contain whiskies that are at least 12 years old and consist of at least 45% malt.

SINGLE NOT READY TO MINGLE

Single malts are key to the unlocking of what Scottish whisky is all about. These malts provide the spirit's DNA and form the basis of our understanding and appreciation of Scotch whisky in all its forms. Single malt whisky must:

a) Come from one distillery.
b) Be aged for a minimum of three years in oak casks.
c) Be bottled at a minimum of 40% ABV.

MALT OF THE EARTH

Malt whisky is made from cereal that is then mashed, mixed with water, fermented, distilled and aged. In the case of malt whisky, the cereal must be barley only. Malt whiskies vary dramatically; this is all down to the distillery approach to production, the shape and size of its copper pot stills and the way that wood-ageing techniques impact on the character.

COPPER CONVERSATION

This has nothing to do with helping the police with their enquiries. All stills are made with copper as it's malleable, conducts heat and – crucially – reacts (converses) with unwelcome sulphur notes and reduces/removes them from the whisky. Generally, the more the spirit interacts with the copper in the still, the lighter the spirit.

STILL LIFE

The size and the shape of the still is a massive influence on the final whisky. Taller stills create greater reflux (the condensing of alcoholic vapour). Steam turns back into liquid, drops down to be redistilled and a lighter whisky is produced. A further factor is the angle of the swan neck/lyne arm at the top of the pot still. An upward angle will produce greater reflux while a neck that is level or quickly drops down will create spirits heavier in character. Any kinks or dents are crucial too and will be deliberately added when certain parts are replaced by distillers.

OAKY DOKEY

Whisky off the still is called 'new make' and is reduced in strength before it cosies up in oak casks. The casks previously contained other spirits or wines, usually sherry or bourbon. Bourbon barrels are made with white American oak and give whisky notes of pine, cherry, vanilla and spice while sherry ones are European oak and impart dried fruit, orange and clove.

Other finishes are used such as port, rum, wine and even beer. The wood allows oxygen in, which rounds off harsh notes in the whisky. At the same time the whisky takes on the characters of the wood such as valuable vanillins. Barrels can be filled more than once. The first fill whisky takes on more wood character; the second fill less; and eventually the wood can simply give no more and is re-charred for new use. No two barrels will ever react with the whisky in the exact same way but working with the wood, and managing its influence within different warehouses, is all part of the distiller's art.

AGE-OLD DEBATE

Age is just a number, right? Yeah, man. Except that number is a crucial identifier in determining how old something is. So, really, the number is rather important. It'd certainly be daft to dismiss it in the world of whisky because it reveals how long a whisky has spent in a barrel, which has a huge impact on flavour and, often, price. That said, approach an age statement with caution. Don't splash out on the old kit for the sake of it; sometimes age brings neither wisdom not maturity. Besides, anything from around 10 to 15 years for single malts gives you great complexity and a fine understanding of the distillery that produces it. Explore older age statements as you learn to appreciate a distillery style. An emerging trend in whisky is 'no age statement' expressions such as Glenlivet Alpha or Talisker Storm.

WHISKY GLOSSARY

Angels' share: the whisky lost in evaporation during ageing – around 3% a year.
Cask strength: when the whisky has finished maturing it will be around 50/60% abv and is then reduced with water.
Dram: a measure of whisky, size varies according to your host.
Finish: how long the flavour sticks around in your chops. A long finish is only useful if you enjoy the flavours. Most of us simply want a happy finish.
Hogs Head: The 250-litre/ 63-gallon cask most commonly used in maturing whisky.
Nose: a physical protuberance converted into a verb: *to nose.* Simply means to smell.
Peat: carbonised soil. It's an ancient mix of decayed vegetation set down over centuries on wet, boggy ground. Peat is cut, dried and burned in a kiln to adorn malt with its smoky character.
Single cask: Unlike single malt which comes from one run-off per still, single cask simply means it come from one barrel.
Stills: where the whisky is distilled. Each distillery has its own and it gives the new make its distinctive character.

SCOTCH WHISKY
RECOMMENDATIONS

From soft and aromatic Glenkinchie to strong and smooth Laphroaig.

GLENKINCHIE
12-YEAR-OLD, 40% ABV

Light but by no means a lightweight, this lovely Lowland whisky is crisp and fresh, serving up some subtle citrus notes and a fine floral, faintly fruity finish. This is the whisky to offer those who say they don't like whisky. **DRINK WITH:** Ceviche.

THE GLENROTHES SELECT RESERVE
NON-VINTAGE, 43% ABV

A non-age statement whisky that deftly straddles different styles, starting soft before suggesting a step-up to something sturdier. Firm in its autumnal fruity notes, it slowly opens up to reveal almonds, vanilla and cashew nuts. **DRINK WITH:** A plate piled with pulled pork.

THE GLENLIVET
12-YEAR-OLD, 40% ABV

In the 19th century, there were more than 200 distilleries huddled around the town of Glen Livet. Most of them were illegal and most made oily, heavy whiskies. When, in 1824, distiller George Smith went legitimate and began making lighter whiskies, he distinguished his distillery, both literally and legally, as The Glenlivet. This is a most delicate and aromatic dram that will have you saying fruity stuff like 'pears', 'apples', 'melons' and 'I'm going to help myself to some more'. An excellent aperitif. **DRINK WITH:** Strong cheddar cheese.

OBAN
14-YEAR-OLD, 43% ABV

Oban is a perfect spot from which to set off on your journey to the Islands and smokier, stronger single malts. There's a soft spine of salt, seaweed and smoke here but it plays second fiddle to fruitcake, marmalade and a trace of treacle on the front of the tongue. **DRINK WITH:** Smoked salmon on sourdough bread.

DALWHINNIE
15-YEAR-OLD, 43% ABV

A classic whisky from as high up in the Highlands as you can get. Well known for its honeyed tones. Age adds an oaky edge to proceedings, and there's a touch of toffee-apple too, with a smooth, gentle finish. **DRINK WITH:** Goat's cheese and walnuts.

GLENFARCLAS
15-YEAR-OLD, 46% ABV

The huge stills of Glenfarclas are the biggest in Speyside, and are traditionally heated with direct fire rather than steam, to give the whisky some weight and not inconsiderable gravitas. Nutty, with a smouldering, strapping sweetness, it embraces the oak yet isn't overly familiar and delights drinkers with a forceful, but warm finish.

DRINK WITH: fresh lobster.

LAGAVULIN
16-YEAR-OLD, 43% ABV

When compared to its Islay counterparts Ardbeg and Laphroaig, there's less choke to the smoke lacing the whiskies of Lagavulin. Spice and Lapsang Souchong on the nose with an exquisite unctuous texture on the tongue; the palate picks up oak. iodine and a crème brûlée sweetness. A sweet yet smouldering smoky send off.

DRINK WITH: Rocquefort cheese or fresh lobster.

TALISKER
10-YEAR-OLD, 45.8% ABV

Set on the shoreline amid the uplifting isolation of the stunning isle of Skye, Talisker's malts talk clearly of smoke, and mirror its spectacularly beautiful surroundings. The 10 year-old is a tender introduction, softly spoken seaweed and smoke with a bit of brine and bacon, rounded off by a flint-dry, peppery finish. This is the 'King of Drinks' according to Robert Louis Stevenson.

DRINK WITH: A fresh oyster with a dash of Tabasco.

HIGHLAND PARK
12-YEAR-OLD, 43% ABV

The output from this Orkney distiller ranges from sizeable smoke bombs to mild, delicate malts, yet the 12-year-old encapsulates its signature style. Using barley that's floor-malted on the distillery site, it perfectly pairs the peat with soft nutty sweetness and fires off fruity notes when water is added. Michael Jackson's favourite 12-year-old (the whisky writer that is, not the singer). **DRINK WITH:** Bacon-wrapped scallops.

LAPHROAIG
18-YEAR-OLD, 48% ABV

A phenomenal, phenolic distiller whose own floor maltings furnish it with a distinct peaty flavour profile. The muscular medicinal notes of the new make are mellowed by 18 years in American bourbon barrels that slide in a signature sweetness, balancing out the smoke and oak.

DRINK WITH: Dark chocolate.

WORLD WHISKEY

Today you can find wonderful whiskey in all corners of the world.
Although, it's worth pointing out, the world is actually round.

Bigoted xenophobes look away now, because aside from Scotch there's a wide world of whisky out there. You've got your Irish, your American, your Japanese; you've got your Indian, your Australian, your Swedish, your Taiwanese; then you've got your Dutch, your Belgian, your French, your German, your Welsh; you've even got your English. The English! Making whisky! And all of these countries, coming over here with their whisky, speaking a different whisky language into our mouths and taking jobs off hardworking Scottish single malt workers. Disgusting. Still, it all makes for a diverse drinks cabinet, and while it's true that the Scots have mastered the marketing, today we can enjoy a genuinely tasty global gurgle of the good stuff in many other countries.

The Irish stake the biggest claim on inventing the spirit. Granted, the geek clique consider this is a bone of contention big enough to choke an Irish wolfhound, but Emerald eyes were certainly smiling in the 13th century when Irish monks made a habit of rustling up grain-based distillate. They said it was whiskey, so who are we to argue?

Needless to say this epic whiskey history inspires an illustrious list of Gaelic guzzlers, with the likes of literary legend James Joyce referencing it through the pages of his novels,

and Oscar-winning Peter O'Toole sharing a drop with Omar Sharif under the stars while filming *Lawrence of Arabia*. A dramatic decline during the 20th century left it a poor commercial cousin compared to Scotch, but it's on the up, remaining as Irish as blarney and bicycles on the ceiling while Guinness is a painfully clichéd Celtic quaff (stout is English, you know), whiskey is the original native nip.

But the most significant world whiskey outside Scotland, from a volume perspective at least, is bourbon. America's self-proclaimed national potable is integrally linked to the taming of the Wild West, and while we cannot condone the cruel obliteration of a native people, we can at least give a nod to the sidebar story of grain spirit.

America's fascination with liquor came over on 'the boat' as parched puritanical passengers on the *Mayflower* mixed seasick with spirits and burned wine to make a distillate. They offered this crude concoction to the first natives they met, who drank so much they subsequently renamed their home Manahachtanienk (Manhattan), 'the island for crazy people'. Irish and Scottish immigrants embraced the natural resources they discovered in the New World and converted grain to whiskey, the abundant rye around them was adopted first, with spicy rye

whiskeys appearing on menus towards the end of the 19th century.

As the settlers moved south and west, corn was utilised to create what we recognise today as a sweeter style and it tickled the tongues of the great Americans who built the country. George Washington would distil at his Mount Vernon plantation, Andrew Jackson overindulged in Tennessee whiskey during his 1829 inauguration party and while Abraham Lincoln abstained, he still sold plenty of the liquor at his Illinois grocery store. His assassin John Wilkes might have been a useful customer. On the night of the dastardly deed, he reputedly necked enough to put down a loyal elephant before he decided he'd rather put down the President. Tourists too enjoyed a nip, Oscar Wilde amongst them. In 1882 the over-dressed dandy writer lectured the Leadville miners on interior design at a saloon and while the miners ignored the presentation, they were impressed when Wilde later drank them under the table.

Up until the 20th century, this was rough-and-ready, gunshot whiskey, the sort of sauce that induced high-noon-style flare-ups in the mouth.

Above: Passengers on the *Mayflower* distilled on board. *Right:* The Japanese enjoy award-winning whisky. *Opposite:* Classic bourbon.

But this is a million miles from today's whiskey experience. The Wild West bourbon fighting juice image is the smashed-in, boarded-up front-window façade of American whiskey – the arrière-boutique of the modern spirit however, is distinctly deluxe with protective, scientific distillers using proprietary yeast and matching carefully crafted spirit with marvellous wood management to create big and beautiful vanilla, toffee and spice notes.

America and Ireland are the historic harbingers of this lovely liquid, but there are many countries outside Scotland where wonderful whiskey can be discovered. Whether they spell it with an 'e' like the Americans and the Irish, or drop an 'e' like the Japanese, Canadian and social drug-users of northwest England, quality whiskey can these days be discovered all over the planet.

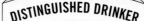

HUNTER S THOMPSON

The author of Fear and Loathing in Las Vegas, *and one of the most important writers of his generation, Hunter S Thompson often kept a bottle of bourbon within touching distance of his typewriter.*

Legendary journalist Hunter S Thompson will likely be lionized for weapon worship and drug abuse. But his mind-stabbing prose, which made him one of the most important writers of his generation, owes much to his love of grain spirit.

To cherry pick one alcoholic beverage for Thompson is as contentious as his copy, with rum, tequila and even fernet branca inspiring his literary exploits. But his affection for whiskey was consistent throughout.

The author of *Fear and Loathing in Las Vegas* usually kept a bottle of bourbon within touching distance of a typewriter. Photographs often capture him brandishing Wild Turkey, while tales of his bourbon 'trapped' in a Secret Service car boot and fuelling his Superbowl coverage can be found across old pages of *Rolling Stone* magazine.

Public appearances also fortified his fondness. Angered by the hospitality at a Duke University engagement in 1974, Thompson called the audience 'beer hippies' and 'pig farmers' before throwing bourbon about the place and reminding staff he would 'insist on drinking my own beverage while speaking and that it would be either Wild Turkey or something stronger". His demands hadn't been met on that occasion, nor was his request that organisers knock $100 off his fee and supply a gram of coke. Hence his ire.

In amongst his best journalism, though, is a feature for maverick magazine *Scanlan's Monthly* (a title later investigated by the FBI) about the-

Kentucky Derby called 'The Kentucky Derby is Decadent and Depraved'. Thompson attended the race in 1970 and the night before overindulged with Wild Turkey while he fingered a mace gun over dinner. He started the following day with Bloody Marys, before reporting on the 'thousands of raving, tumbling drunks, getting angrier and angrier as they lose more and more money. By mid-afternoon they'll be guzzling mint juleps with both hands and vomiting on each other between races... The aisles will be slick with vomit; people falling down and grabbing at your legs to keep from being stomped. Drunks pissing on themselves in betting lines.'

Beautiful bourbon-soaked words, but this was a style that carved an angry niche in the line-up of literature's most enduring legends. Thompson would eventually follow in the fatal footsteps of another iconic American writer, Ernest Hemingway, by killing himself in 2005, using a gun to transport him to the other side. Welsh artist and long-time collaborator Ralph Steadman wrote that Thompson had told him: 'I would feel trapped in my life if I didn't know I could commit suicide at any time.' In a final flourish his ashes were fired from a cannon on a150ft (46m) tower, overseen by friend Johnny Depp.

Thompson's writing was visceral enough to earn him a place with a whiskey by Satan's fire, but the afterlife wasn't his concern. He lived large and let us know about it with words, and that was his legacy.

Hunter S Thompson

THINKING DRINKING COWBOYS

WHISKEY WOULD WHET THE WHISTLE OF MOST COWBOYS CROSSING INTO THE WILD WEST, BUT SOME HOMBRES HOGGED THE HOOCH WITH SUCH VERVE THEY STRUGGLED TO GET THE GUN UP WHEN IT MATTERED. IF THEY WERE LUCKY THEY WOULD END UP IN THE CALABOOSE, OTHERWISE IT WAS THE COFFIN. HERE, THEN, ARE SOME OF THE INFAMOUS NAMES TO MIX WHISKEY WITH WILD RIDING. IN EACH CASE WE'VE AWARDED POINTS FOR GUN-FIGHTING SKILLS, BASIC SURVIVAL AND, OBVIOUSLY, WHISKEY DRINKING.

WILD BILL HICKOK

A heroic whiskey fan, Hickok drank so intently he earned the name 'Wild Bill Hiccup'. Some claimed his whiskey ways didn't impair the ol' six shooter and the 'King of the Pistoleers' could reputedly hit an ace of spades at 50 paces. Others claimed he was too often found face down in the mud and simply shot foe down when they weren't looking. Not really cowboy cricket. Certainly this wasn't the case with friend Mike Williams, whom he accidentally shot in the stomach as he defended him during a gun battle at Abilene's Alamo Saloon. Apparently both men were gutted. Jack McCall, meanwhile, thought a bullet in the back was as much as Hickok deserved when he shot him dead in 1876 as he played cards in Deadwood, South Dakota. Hickok was 39, but his hand was a winning one. A pair of aces and a pair of eights. He was inducted into the Poker Hall of Fame a year later.

BIG ON THE BOOZE, BUNGLING IN THE OTHER COWBOY BUSINESS: 6/10

BEN THOMPSON

A notorious killer who womanised and drank whiskey hard. So enamoured was Thompson with the saloon, he used his gambling take to open his Bulls Head Saloon in Abilene, Texas, with Phil Coe, who was later shot dead by Wild Bill Hickok over an argument regarding the bar's image of the bull, which showed off the animal's testicles. Feared by most, Thompson once went crazy with a gun and filled a local newspaper building with lead; he did the same at the keno hall, the police headquarters, the variety saloon, three cat houses and, randomly, an Italian hand organ. Despite this, he was made a Marshal. Big cowboy points here. He didn't quit gunslinging though and was killed at the tender age of 40 during a rather bloody showdown in a vaudeville theatre. He was hit 13 times and the man who finally blew Thompson's brains out was so excited afterwards he accidently shot himself in the leg and died.

THOMPSON HAD HIS OWN BAR AND DESTROYED AN ITALIAN HAND ORGAN: 7/10.

CLAY ALLISON

Clay Allison might have enjoyed his whiskey more had saloon owners not occasionally shut up shop when hearing he was in town. He got into a knife fight with a neighbour over a fence dispute and grimly battled the adversary in an open grave to save the others from having to haul a body into a hole. He also joined a rival for a genial dinner and plenty of whiskey in a saloon before killing him in a gun duel – when observers asked why he ate with a man who was going to start a gunfight, he said: 'Because I didn't want to send a man to hell on an empty stomach.' He also invented streaking. Unfortunately he died in 1887 after falling off a wagon at age 46. Not so cool.

HE DIED OF NATURAL CAUSES: 6/10

MIKE FINK

It wasn't all about the dusty plains of the mid west, some of the loons of liquor were water based. Fink was a flatboat man from the 1820s, known as 'King of the River Missouri' and described by Davy Crockett as 'half horse, half alligator', which leaves little room for 'half man'. In his spare time he rode dangerous bulls, shot a man's heel off and drank so much Monongahela rye, he seared the inside of his belly. To compensate, he ate a buffalo rug, believing the hair would line his stomach. He also played a game of shooting whiskey glasses off a friend's head. He shot the friend in the head.

YOU CAN'T GO AROUND SHOOTING YOUR BUDDIES IN THE HEAD: 6/10

WILLIAM 'BAT' MASTERSON

Part-owner of the Long Branch Saloon with a stake in a gambling joint with Wyatt Earp, Masterson was actually referred to by some as the 'Deadliest Gun in the West'. In his first gunfight duelling over a girl, he took a bullet in the pelvis. Sexy stuff. Much of his reputation was based on hearsay, it transpires he wasn't one for shooting without good reason and in later accounts he insisted he killed only eight of the 30 men he was reported to have killed. A gambler, buffalo hunter, resident of Dodge City and US Marshal, this was a real man of the Wild West, but perhaps most impressive of all, he lived out his days as a sportswriter at the *New York Morning Telegraph*, dying of a heart attack at his desk, aged 67, as he wrote his last column.

DRANK WHISKEY, SOLD WHISKEY, HAS A CANADIAN RYE WHISKEY NAMED AFTER HIM, SAMPLED AND SURVIVED THE WILD WEST: 10/10

LIVELY LADIES

★ ★ ★ ★ ★ ★ ★ ★ ★ ★ ★ ★ ★ ★ ★ ★ ★ ★ ★

The absence of a female form on our list is largely due to the fact that women weren't welcome in Wild West saloons. There were exceptions, strippers and prostitutes, for example – the first bottomless strippers appearing in a San Francisco Saloon in 1869, which you might view as progress. Amazingly, McSorley's, a saloon in New York, didn't permit girls to drink their giggle juice until 1970. Some wicked women did make a nuisance with a gun, prostitutes would wisely carry pistols for deserving customers, but there were other more notorious gunfighters to rival the men. Calamity Jane was one of the various legends. She earned her name by inflicting venereal diseases on men. Have that. Regardless, Jane loved her whiskey, it killed her in 1903, in fact.When she was once refused a drink she fired four shots into a wall in disgust. She got the whiskey.

THE WILD WEST BAR

Yee-haa to all the rootin'-tootin', whiskey-drinkin', chaps-chaffin', six-shootin', hoss-drinkin'-from-a-trough-ridin', wild-west-wanderin', bar-stool-sittin' cowboys. Yee-haa indeed, because the very best cowboys drank whiskey and supped most of the spirit in the Wild West saloon, an iconic remnant of a liquor lovin' past that deserves a proper bullets-in-the-air salute.

When early 19th-century frontier pioneers headed west to trap beavers or poke cows, their exploits were being fuelled by whiskey, and for a brief spell, the best and worst of the spirit was served in the Wild West saloon. Cinema occasionally sketches a somewhat suspect illusion of this establishment, gaudy and glittering with fancy Dans and tuneful music to complement the flutter of a little lady's flouncy dress. True, later incarnations came close to a romantic silver-screen imagining, but early saloons were desperate holes of horror, where women weren't welcome, music was unheard of and whiskey was rancid.

By 1812, some of the westerly wandering American wagons had ceased due to a touch of local conflict, and settlements started to pop up. Essential services quickly evolved, the bar being the most important, and by 1822 the first officially recorded saloon swung open its doors on the borders of Wyoming, Colorado and Utah.

As more bars followed, men stampeded to these joints, coining a host of unusual names, from jug houses to bughouses and whoop-ups to water holes. There was the 'barrelhouse' where whiskey flowed direct from barrel to glass; the 'deadfall' where those who fell had invariably been shot dead; the 'pretty waiter saloons' with girls in short skirts; even 'hells on wheels' – saloons that could be transported on trains.

And so the saloon became the hub of the settlement. Here was an establishment that could mix drinking with a bath, and be a place to stay for a cowboy and his steed. Saloon owners added casinos, courtrooms and churches, billiards, barbershops and bordellos, attracting everyone from beaver trappers and brothel keepers to buffalo hunters, prospectors, even Native Americans.

With all these cultural clashes, the infamous high-noon showdowns were inevitable and the saloon became as notorious for gunslinging as the shooting of whiskey. But this simply drew increasingly curious cowboys to the bar, so that by the 1880s, saloons had sprouted up everywhere. The 1879 census of Leadville, Colorado, listed four banks, four churches, 10 dry goods stores and 120 saloons. Even the names of towns in the state reflected the influence of imbibing: Boozeville, Drunkenman, Delirium Tremens, Whiskey Park, Whiskey Hole and Whiskey Springs.

It had taken 60 years for the phenomenon to arrive but soon it was dying off just as quickly. By the1880s, half of America was going dry due to the pesky Temperance movement, and by 1920 Prohibition had stamped out many bawdy booze houses. Despite its historic resonance, the saloon's life was over as quickly as Billy the Kid's draw.

Grand Designs

Saloons started life as tents, shacks, and if patrons were lucky, mud bricks. The Gold Rush inspired the interior decorating most commonly associated with the Hollywood-style saloon: the mahogany fixtures and fittings, grand back-bar mirrors and

even pianos were only in place after the 1850s. The mirrors served a dual purpose, enabling punters to see a gunslinger approaching while they drank at the bar, and giving the bartender eyes on the punter when he turned to the till. But even with the glitz and glamour of a mirror, many of the saloons operated with a false front. A two-storey wooden façade implied grandeur, while behind it languished a lurid single storey. It didn't help that toilet facilities came to towns long after bars – and sewers for that matter – so conditions were often squalid. The saloons had baths at least, so the dirt stayed outside; towels hung from rails to mop up the spillage of beer, while sawdust lined the floor to absorb what the towel missed.

Like the prostitutes they offered, these saloons came in all shapes and sizes: Walker's Saloon in Denver was big enough for six at the bar, while the Brown Palace had glorious marble columns. Bar length was a matter of competitive pride: Breen's Saloon in San Francisco was 22m (73ft), but was shamed into shrinking from the spotlight by Erickson's in Portland, Oregon where the bar's breadth reached 208m (682ft). Erickson's also attracted the first all-female saloon orchestra.

Finally the swing doors: a notorious design. So synonymous did they become with the violence in saloons that they were actually made illegal in some states. As was the actual word 'saloon'.

On the menu

Whiskey was the Wild West drink of choice and most had a slug problem, neat shots being what all cowboys wanted. Strange labels told the punters all they needed to know, assuming they could read, with names like Skull Bender, Panther Piss or Snakehead Whiskey, complete with a snake head in the barrel.

Among the most celebrated sips was Toas Lightening, made in San Fernandez de Taos in

New Mexico in the 1820s. It was a corn-based beverage, a forerunner to bourbon, distilled by Peg Leg Smith, who cut off his own leg after being shot by a Native American. But on the whole, this gear was as dangerous as a rattlesnake bite, deliberately bulked out with strychnine, sulphuric acid, varnish, turpentine and fuel oil.

Things improved as the saloon entered the 1860s and bartenders made a name for themselves. Jeremiah 'Jerry' Thomas became the first bartender to earn star status and write a recipe book; specials boards listed 'Fancy Drinks' with whiskey fixes and Thomas's special, the Blue Blazer, where he set the whiskey on fire and poured it between tin cups – undoubtedly killing some of the nasties as well as his eyebrows. As famous as this era has become for its cocktails though, macho saloon patrons turned their nose up at such concoctions, and even ice was seen as a feminine *faux pas*. Many classic cocktails were conceived at the end of the 19th century, but this was also the era of the boilermaker and few fancied more than a beer and whiskey chaser.

When it came to food, the cowboys kept it equally simple. Early settlers had to rob honey from bees and make gruel from corn, and the bar snack was also seasoned with gunpowder. By 1822 at Brown's Hole the food seemed to have progressed but still reflected the sign on the door, being flame-grilled buffalo intestine.

THE ANATOMY OF A WHISKEY BARREL

A bit of liquid learning for you, but don't worry, this piece is a barrel of, er, information. If only it were a barrel of monkeys, eh? We like monkeys. If you're sipping a sophisticated whiskey while you're reading then, first of all, well done you, we owe you a medal. If you're not, go and fetch a discerning drop and take a gander at the glass. Consider what you see. As you will discover the liquid is brown. I know, education, education, education, no wonder you paid so much for the book. It's perhaps more interesting to note (perhaps) that the whiskey wasn't always this colour, and that when the distiller runs spirit off a still it is always 'water white' or transparent. It is the process of maturing spirit in wood that engenders all the leathery, tanned tint.

When ageing a spirit most producers will use oak barrels of varying sizes, and many of the brown spirits you'll be familiar with, rum and Scotch for example, will rest in American oak ex-bourbon barrels or else in European oak, such as former sherry butts. American oak grows faster and imparts softer flavours, while European oaks take longer to grow and develop a greater wealth of tannin in the wood.

Bourbon barrels are particularly prevalent in aged spirits because, according to the regulations of bourbon, the whiskey must be matured in new, charred

American oak barrels. This legislation was implemented to protect the coopers, the craftsmen who make the barrels. This not only ensures that each bourbon run gets a spanking new vessel, but also supplies the rest of the world with plenty of barrel stock. It ensures that the American whiskey industry is important worldwide both for the distinguished distillate it delivers and the barrels it crafts in the process.

Why do they use oak then? Because it can be fashioned into a shape that provides perfect ratios of liquid to surface area, it's waterproof, yet also breathable, and, what's more, it brings that oaky colour to the party, along with some generous flavour gifts.

When spirit is rested in an oak barrel it permeates the wood, dipping into and out of the pores for the duration of its stay. The oak holds congeners, or flavour compounds, so as the spirit makes itself comfortable, it extracts new flavours. Vanilla is a regular bedfellow of American whiskey; this comes courtesy of vanillin in the wood. Elsewhere the eugenol keeps things spicy under the sheets and lactones deliver a lovely bunch of coconuts.

The charring process of the barrels was originally employed to kill off other flavours and aromas, with wines being stored in barrels that might previously have been used for fish. But producers soon learned that this layer of carbon ended up subtracting harsh congeners from young spirit.

Levels of char vary. In America a 1000°F flame is burst into the empty barrel for 45 seconds or more, depending on how heavy a char is required, and this in turn develops rich, creamy, vanilla and caramel flavours.

Meanwhile, it helps that the oak itself is not hermetic as it ensures the whiskey has air, which is vital in the process of oxidisation. While some of the spirit evaporates, taking out some of the harsh congeners with it, within the barrel oxygen, wood and spirit come together to enhance or soften flavours. Depending on the climate, this occurs quickly or slowly. In warm conditions water evaporates first, so the alcohol content of the spirit rises, resulting in more spirit penetration with the wood. In the case of stone buildings in Kentucky, natural weather conditions fluctuate between cold winters and warm summers, all impacting on wood interaction.

The balance of extracting the elements of the oak without damaging the drink is the tricky part, so maturation is carefully managed from beginning to end, with some distillers even hand-picking the trees for the wood. If the spirit gives you too much wood, it will be a confusingly, unsexy experience: the drink can be overpowering and dry and kill the essence of what the distiller was originally aiming for.

Tannins, the phenolic substances that wood imparts, are astringent and bitter. Too much of them and the overall taste will become too tart. Blending is a final part of the ageing process, where wood doesn't get a say, as producers work with a selection of barrels to marry the spirits and find consistency in flavour – key to creating a successful flagship brand.

The craft of the cooper is worth bearing witness to, and a few distilleries still keep their own cooperage. Amongst the most impressive facilities we have witnessed is the Bluegrass Cooperage in Louisville, one of the world's largest producers of white oak whiskey barrels. The epic factory is a din of machinery but the barrel-building, or 'raising', is still done by hand, with wooden staves hammered into the metal brackets by burly men.

We had a go, we were rubbish, as hard labour hurts our delicate hands, but they turn around thousands of barrels a week, with each one being sold for approximately £72. By doing it this way, coopers retain a historic tradition in the whiskey world, which makes the price of a bottle of bourbon even more justifiable for a thinking drinker.

LITERARY DRINKING GAMES

Celebrated scribe Graham Green liked whiskey. He also liked opium. And prostitutes. And Jesus. But it was the regular mention of alcohol through his most righteous reads we've chosen to focus on, because folks, this a book about drinking, not Jesus or opium.

Greene's appreciation of whiskey is well documented, both his love of Scotch and adoration of American bourbon. He's not unique of course, peers such as Tennessee Williams, Ernest Hem ingway and William Faulkner, all famously sipped as they scribbled, Faulkner saying: 'I usually write at night. I always keep my whiskey within reach.' (We always keep the TV remote control close Bill – procrastination across the nation).

However Greene was more than capable of putting his affection for alcohol on hold when tinkling his typewriter. It seemed to work for him and along with penning countless global bestsellers, his most enduring works, *Brighton Rock* and *The Third Man*, were also served up on the silver screen to great acclaim. Added to this, Greene made it to a ripe old age of 86 having mixed drinking and writing for 60 years, surviving a stint in Sierra Leone for MI6, a battle with a bipolar condition and riding his luck through 'games' of Russian Roulette with his brother on Berkhamsted common. That is to say, actual Russian roulette. With a real gun. 'I was beginning to pull the trigger about as casually as I might take an aspirin tablet,' he reputedly said. With all this in mind, we'd argue the liquor can't have done him a great disservice.

The sipping scribe's most infamous ode to alcohol is the draughts game he describes in *Our Man in Havana*. The satirical spy story is soaked in great spirits, from hefty daiquiris at the Havana Club, to pilots paid with whisky. But it's the drinking game played out by protagonist Jim Wormwold and Cuban copper Captain Segura that seems particularly germane for our thinking drinker journey.

Among the quirks of Wormwold, a feckless vacuum salesman, is a collection of 100 whisky miniatures, and early in the novel the ill-fated Dr Hasslebacher suggests he should adopt them as pieces on a draughts board. 'When you take a piece you drink it,' suggests the doctor, the idea being that as the better player drinks more, the strategic senses are dulled and a natural handicap comes into play. The rule is used to great effect later in the novel as Wormwold outwits Segura.

It's a great idea for a game isn't it? Not only does it provide frequent tasty treats it also delivers a valuable lesson on drinking boundaries, determining the fine line between drink-inspired confidence and overindulgence leading into arrogance and ineptitude.

In his book, Greene pitches Scotch against bourbon, this being long before the whiskey globe expanded. We, however, have decided to update the game and our version pitches American whiskey v The Rest of the World. We've also called our game 'Daft Draughts, Havana Style'. It's much safer than Russian roulette.

GRAHAM GREENE

DAFT DRAUGHTS, HAVANA STYLE

Draughts is a funny name for a game isn't it? Spelled in an entirely different way, it implies a current of cool air, or spelled the same way, a method of beer dispense. But it's a game as well.

In the version described by Graham Greene in *Our Man in Havana*, two people play on opposite sides of a chess board, one using white pieces, the other dark—in this case, one using Scotch, the other using world whisky. (See pages 82-83 for some of our top recommendations for Scotch whisky you could use in the game, and pages 96-99 for world whiskeys.)

Say you use world whisky; line the pieces up on the dark squares only, working forward from your end. You can get up to 20 pieces on there.

The aim is to take the opponent's pieces and you do so by jumping over their piece as you move to an empty square. You will each move one piece at a time, taking alternate turns.

Scotch goes first, moving forward only. You move diagonally only. As you jump over your opponent's pieces

you take them and—this is the important bit—you drink them.

If you manage to move a piece all the way to your opponent's end of the board, it then becomes a king and can be moved both forward and backward. The winner is the last man standing.

In *Our Man in Havana* Wormwold replaces all the pieces with whisky, but crucially he uses miniatures—so steer clear of 70cl bottles. Remember our mantra: Drink less, drink better.

Our game is more fun than actor Alec Guiness's face implies in the film of Graham Greene's *Our Man in Havana*, 1959.

AMERICAN WHISKEY

MAKER'S MARK
45% ABV

With whiskey traditions dating back to 1780 there's heritage in them thar hills and the Maker's mashbill of corn, with higher levels of wheat than many others, delivers a soft and super sweet, laid-back bourbon.

E.H. TAYLOR SMALL BATCH
50% ABV

Wormwold played with Old Taylor in *Our Man in Havana* and this is a more recent incarnation, paying homage to Col. Edmund Haynes Taylor Jr, a pioneering 19th-century distiller. The bourbon is aged in warehouses Taylor built and boasts a lovely lick of butterscotch and pepper with a tobacco finish.

WOODFORD RESERVE DISTILLER'S SELECT
43.2% ABV

A distillery where boffin distiller James Crow made his name and one that sports its own cooperage (see page 93). The flagship Kentucky Straight Bourbon ramps up the rye in the mash bill for a beautiful balance of spice and sweet. One of our go-to bourbons.

RITTENHOUSE RYE
40% ABV

To make the first Stateside spirits, wannabe distillers farmed the abundant American rye. Corn wouldn't become popular until settlers moved south and west. This straight rye is a fine exponent of the original historic style. Big, bolshy and bitter with the poke of pepper and a long rye spicy finish.

KNOB CREEK 9-YEAR-OLD
50% ABV

This luscious liquor, full of rich, sweet qualities is from the Jim Beam distillery set up in 1795 by Jacob Boehm (becoming Beam).

WILD TURKEY 101
50.5% ABV

Hunter S Thompson's favourite (see page 86), this rich but rustic bourbon is old school, free from new-fangled fripperies. Rocking its chair to a rhythm of rye, it takes a walking stick whack at the tongue with spicy clove before making up for its loud behaviour with soft maple syrups and treacled toffee.

FOUR ROSES YELLOW LABEL
40% ABV

Yeast matters in American whiskey and there are five strains here to complement two mash bills. It's a modern mellow yellow marvel of a whiskey and excellent value for money, a smooth and creamy sip. Worth a try for sure.

JACK DANIEL'S SINGLE BARREL
45% ABV

The rock 'n' roll rascal of the back bar steps down an octave with this bassier, rich and sweeter variant. Careful selection of the barrels results in big banana notes on the nose converting to a sweet then spicy treat on the tongue.

EAGLE RARE 10-YEAR-OLD SINGLE BARREL
45% ABV

From the award-winning National Historic Landmark Buffalo Trace Distillery, home to the oldest continuously working still in America, more than 200 years old, this whiskey swoops across the tongue with warm cherry notes, flights of orange peel and droppings of thick rich burnt sugar before it claws at the finish with a dry and lingering crisp, dry oak.

GEORGE DICKEL OLD NO.12
45% ABV

A lesser-spotted Tennessee whiskey that employs differing chill filtering method from its neighbour Jack Daniels and which presents a smoother proposition, with light herbal notes and warm cooked spicy fruits. With hints of vanilla upfront, this is a gold standard Tennessee whiskey.

OLD FORESTER KENTUCKY STRAIGHT BOURBON
43% ABV

Also featured in Graham Greene's *Our Man in Havana* and conceived by the bourbon brainbox George Garvin Brown in the 1870s, this historic hero finds some pepper and allspice from the high rye, blending with warm orange and soft vanillas. Ticks all the tastebud boxes.

OLD FITZGERALD 12-YEAR-OLD
45% ABV

A big belt and braces city boy of a bourbon, bounding out of the glass with fat-cat smoky cigar and leather-bound scents that launch an aggressive management buyout on the more apprentice-like proboscis. A beautiful balance of honey, chocolate and vanilla plus oak.

WORLD WHISKEY

LARK SINGLE MALT SINGLE CASK
43% ABV (AUSTRALIA)

A Tasmanian devil of a drink that smacks itself hysterically around your cheeks with some hot pepper before running out of steam and slow-pacing with rich toffee and fruit-cake flavours.

CANADIAN CLUB RESERVE 10-YEAR-OLD
40% ABV (CANADA)

Hiram Walker's role in whisky-making is honoured here with a typically spicy Canadian style Plenty of rye offset by some toffee and a touch of fresh mint.

PENDERYN SHERRYWOOD
46% ABV (WALES)

By picking a pronounceable name, complete with valuable vowels, the Welsh Whisky Company ensures this is a safe order at the bar and since the dry oloroso sherry barrels didn't leek, they've unearthed a lighter, floral style of whisky with plenty of sultana sweetness on the finish.

ENGLISH WHISKY CO. CHAPTER 6
46% ABV (ENGLAND)

While English whisky is a relic of the 19th century, this is one of the few existing today. The bourbon casks twist a fresh whisky into something softer, with a hint of oak. A tasty dram and early evidence that Scottish independence might not be so difficult for the English to deal with.

BUSHMILLS 16-YEAR-OLD
40% ABV (IRELAND)

Distilling began here in 1608, when they got their licence, but 1784 was the year they opened. The only dates that matter will be found on the warm palate – alongside sweet fruit, spice and raising notes courtesy of maturation in bourbon, port and sherry casks.

REDBREAST 15-YEAR-OLD
46% ABV (IRELAND)

From the Middleton distillery in Cork, home to Jameson, this is a massive mouthful of a whiskey. With a leviathan length that will keep anyone with a leather fetish happy, it delivers a deliriously happy finish of spice, fruit and a not inconsiderable dose of wood.

KAVALAN SOLIST PORT CASK FINISH
57.8% ABV (TAIWAN)

Made in Taiwan from high-quality ingredients. An unusual port to call at for your whisky but we've cast our nets wide and the tropical conditions aid the ageing here and help them create a super-sweet whisky with rich oak and berry nice fruit.

MACKMYRA BRUKSWHISKY
41.4% ABV (SWEDEN)

A sexy Swede of a spirit, Mackmyra is tops. Its use of bourbon barrels, sherry and Swedish oak casks as well as some smoked malt makes for an interesting addition to your daft draughts board drinking game (see page 95).

AMRUT FUSION
50% ABV (INDIA)

Indian whisky? Thank you please. India has long been a whisky heartland, so it's no surprise they make their own. Amrut has enjoyed international acclaim with this slightly smoky offering that has a touch of orange marmalade.

MILLSTONE 8-YEAR-OLD
43% ABV (NETHERLANDS)

From the experienced crew at Zuidam, the Dutch once again prove they can take an apparently alien concept, twist it with some Netherlands know-how and raise an eyebrow. Mixing innovative wood experimenting and ancient windmill techniques allows this Dutch master distiller to deliver winter fruits, a touch of warm citrus and cinnamon spice.

BAIN'S CAPE MOUNTAIN WHISKY
43% ABV (SOUTH AFRICA)

Introduced in 2010, this is the first single grain whisky to come out of South Africa. It is sweet, it is sultry and it has really grasped the vibe of single grain whiskey. Spirits fans worldwide are clamouring to sample it.

HIBIKI 17-YEAR-OLD
43% ABV (JAPAN)

Explore Japanese whisky and you'll find plenty to enjoy. This blend is a fine example of their fantastic efforts – sending honey, sherry chocolate and woody notes up the nose and taking them right through to the tongue.

TEQUILA
Agave to margarita

If your last tequila induced illness, chances are it's due to your shooting it after an irresponsible amount of lousy lager or value bucket vino.

The generalisation that the spirit is rough and ready is unfair. Many 100% agave tequilas are now balanced, subtle, fruity, sweet and even rich enough to rival a decent scotch or brandy. It's probably time you sorted out your life and tried it again.

HISTORY & CULTURE

Tequila was once described to the Thinking Drinkers as a schizophrenic, a Jekyll and Hyde of a drink. Now, we're not doctors, we're drinks writers. Even so, we're confident the comparison is insensitive. Schizophrenia is a nuanced condition with a host of symptoms beyond a split personality. But, after smugly wagging a finger at the lazy stereotypists spouting slightly wonky medical analysis, we realised the analogy is not entirely distorted. Tequila is packed with myriad, complex characters, inspires muddled thoughts and if abused, can even spark hallucinations.

A dusty, gun-slinging, donkey-riding spirit for the shot glass, tequila, while complex, can conversely be sultry and sleek in a delicate flute; stern and serious for the old boy's snifter, or mixed and metrosexual for more-ish Margaritas. In short, what we're saying here is, tequila's personalities are split...

This should, logically, ensure that tequila is all things to all people. The prom king and queen of the round. The problem is, most of us tend to think of it as a less popular personality: the college Goth. Tequila has an unhinged, brooding, dark side to it, something you're afraid of because you don't really understand it. You know it's brighter than you, but it's easier to criticise it behind its back; and while you'll approach it after carousing with the popular beer or wine, you'll never consider it a first choice when picking drinks teams. You don't much like its get-up, not as transparent as vodka or gin, nor as aesthetically pleasing as a rich, aged rum or whisky. Meanwhile it smells odd, slightly vegetal, rustic and earthy perhaps, but with an occasional hint of vanilla essence. There's also a suspicion that something very bad is about to happen with tequila, that at a moment's notice it'll flip and inflict a massacre on your mouth.

With all this in mind, it's best to leave it well alone, right? Push the dusty bottle to the back of the drinks trolley. Don't think about your drink, pour another whisky instead, right? Or alternatively you could 'man up' and have a word with yourself in the mirror, because if you're ignoring tequila, you're bypassing one of the best drinks on the backbar.

Tequila's history alone makes it worthy. The significance of its main ingredient, the agave, reaches, quite literally, into the annals of Mesoamerican history. From 900 AD Aztecs were utilising every element of this plant, for items ranging from footwear to furniture, and ritualistically gorged on the fermented juice from its heart, even consuming it through straws via their rear ends.

The 15th-century Spanish conquistadors, dashing as they looked in their dapper red shorts and big shiny helmets, arrived and did a *right* number on the Aztec culture. After taking a nap under a tree and kicking sand in the faces of unsuspecting Nahuatl nerds, they inadvertently introduced smallpox to the people. They systematically extinguished many Aztec cultural references, including the intricate drawings and

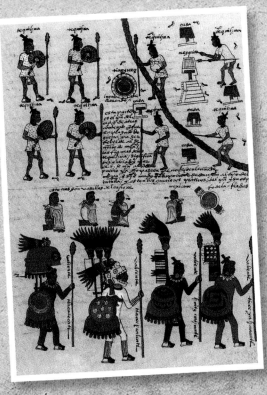

The Codex Mendoza Folio is an ancient picture of the Aztecs doing some stuff and things. Look at it, it's really good. They've got big brooms and crazy hats.

after sinking seven pints on a Saturday night. Demand was high and producers responded by mixing the agave spirit with other sugar-based distillates made with sugar cane and then these 'mixto' tequilas flooded the international market. As the quality dropped, and as we skulled shot after shoddy shot, tequila's reputation dropped lower than a rattlesnake's belly. The only time we reached for one was at the end of the night, but anyone who drank to excess and happened to finish the evening with a tequila blamed the spirit for the ensuing headache the next day, in almost all cases very unfairly.

It's been a long, dusty road back for the Mexicans, with the government so intent on reform it established the *Consejo Regulador del Tequila*, a body set up to preserve the spirit's integrity. This helped the tide turn as producers were monitored and information spread; we started learning about 100% agave tequila, mixtos were improved and the rise of other agave spirits such as mezcal widened the category. As bartenders looked for authenticity in drink they combined history with modern techniques and made us think again.

True, certain tequila can slice through the palate. Some Mexicans claim the word 'tequila' referred to 'stone that could cut', and the spirit can cut through the palate. But those in know, the thinking drinkers, were enjoying tequila years ago. Rather than a naughty, child-like daub on the newly decorated drinks cabinet then, tequila's mark is now a celebrated piece of alternative street art. So stick silly stereotypes under an oversize sombrero and muffle the mutterings of malcontent under a massive moustache, because it's time we showed tequila some respect.

carvings that must've taken those Aztec guys absolutely ages to create. They did, however, embrace the local liquor – a mark of how tasty agave really is. Taking baked agave juice they created a distillate to replenish ailing brandy stocks, and then mezcal wine became tequila.

Tequila subsequently fuelled the expansion of the country, its New World evolution. It would inspire revolution as the likes of Emilio Zapata, master marksman and heroic horseman, galloped into battle with a fiery spirit in his belly. When Mexicans recognised the global value of tequila it started to make waves north of the border, initially among West Coast Americans suffering from the absurd 1920s Prohibition and then, as the margarita flaunted with fashionistas in the 1950s, tequila hit the bar scene in California.

Somehow it lost its way with the rest of us. Perhaps it was the daft rituals that became *de rigueur* during the 1980s. Salt and shots suddenly seemed appropriate as sadsacks turned to tequila

Tequila, when drunk in moderation, has a tendency to make one relatively content. It has done so over thousands of years. Here we cherry-pick some of said years in a chronological order.

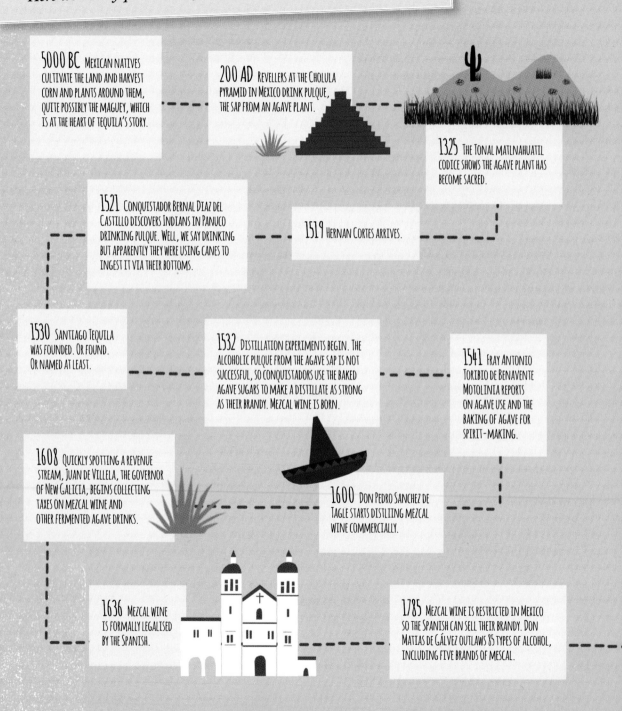

5000 BC Mexican natives cultivate the land and harvest corn and plants around them, quite possibly the maguey, which is at the heart of tequila's story.

200 AD Revellers at the Cholula pyramid in Mexico drink pulque, the sap from an agave plant.

1325 The Tonal matlnahuatil codice shows the agave plant has become sacred.

1521 Conquistador Bernal Diaz del Castillo discovers Indians in Panuco drinking pulque. Well, we say drinking but apparently they were using canes to ingest it via their bottoms.

1519 Hernan Cortes arrives.

1530 Santiago Tequila was founded. Or found. Or named at least.

1532 Distillation experiments begin. The alcoholic pulque from the agave sap is not successful, so conquistadors use the baked agave sugars to make a distillate as strong as their brandy. Mezcal wine is born.

1541 Fray Antonio Toribio de Benavente Motolinia reports on agave use and the baking of agave for spirit-making.

1608 Quickly spotting a revenue stream, Juan de Villela, the governor of New Galicia, begins collecting taxes on mezcal wine and other fermented agave drinks.

1600 Don Pedro Sanchez de Tagle starts distliing mezcal wine commercially.

1636 Mezcal wine is formally legalised by the Spanish.

1785 Mezcal wine is restricted in Mexico so the Spanish can sell their brandy. Don Matias de Gálvez outlaws 85 types of alcohol, including five brands of mescal.

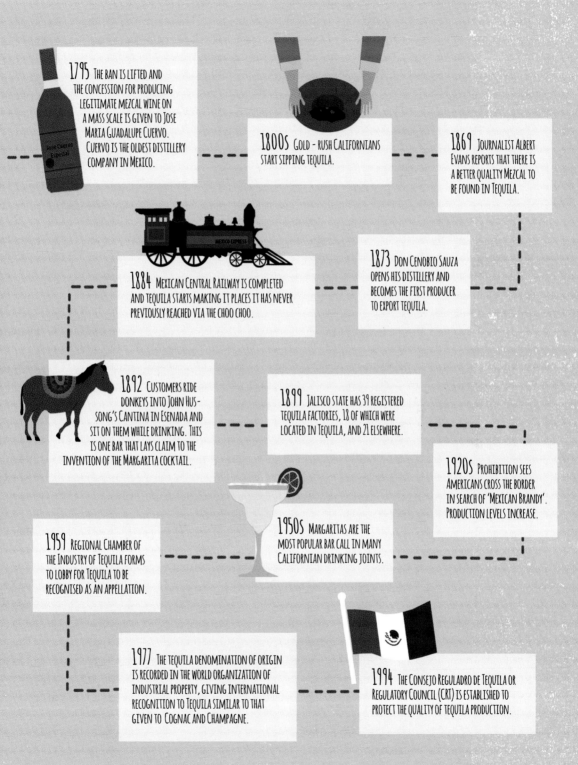

1795 The ban is lifted and the concession for producing legitimate Mezcal wine on a mass scale is given to Jose Maria Guadalupe Cuervo. Cuervo is the oldest distillery company in Mexico.

1800s Gold-rush Californians start sipping Tequila.

1869 Journalist Albert Evans reports that there is a better quality Mezcal to be found in Tequila.

1884 Mexican Central Railway is completed and Tequila starts making it places it has never previously reached via the choo choo.

1873 Don Cenobio Sauza opens his distillery and becomes the first producer to export Tequila.

1892 Customers ride donkeys into John Hussong's Cantina in Esenada and sit on them while drinking. This is one bar that lays claim to the invention of the Margarita cocktail.

1899 Jalisco state has 39 registered tequila factories, 18 of which were located in Tequila, and 21 elsewhere.

1920s Prohibition sees Americans cross the border in search of 'Mexican Brandy'. Production levels increase.

1959 Regional Chamber of the Industry of Tequila forms to lobby for Tequila to be recognised as an appellation.

1950s Margaritas are the most popular bar call in many Californian drinking joints.

1977 The Tequila denomination of origin is recorded in the World Organization of Industrial Property, giving international recognition to Tequila similar to that given to Cognac and Champagne.

1994 The Consejo Reguladro de Tequila or Regulatory Council (CRT) is established to protect the quality of Tequila production.

DISTINGUISHED DRINKER

MAYAHUEL

Mayahuel was worshipped by the 13th-century Aztecs. As a goddess, she proffered pubescence, watched over wombs, manifested herself as a maguey plant – and had 400 breasts.

Mayahuel's story is crucial to the ancient culture of the Aztecs, particularly in connection with tequila, and we'll get to that, but to stress: she had 400 breasts.

The tall tales and myths about gods and goddesses are littered with betrayals and heavy-handed persecution, habitually resulting in sacrifice or martyrdom, and generally some rather painful deaths. Mayahuel's story is no different, but having many breasts might well have been her biggest burden. It's doubtful her disciples designed a sports bra to compensate, added to which her many mammary glands were used to feed 400 children. Rather than milk, Mayahuel's greedy sucklings gorged on pulque, the fermented alcoholic sap of the agave plant, and, tasty as this sounds, it meant that Mayahuel was forever filled to feed. Now, any woman who has been through breastfeeding will be acutely aware of the discomfort Mayahuel endured – from lactating to latching, engorgement to expressing, breastfeeding is tough. But multiply it by 200 and you've got a lot on your plate.

But the breasts are only part of the story. Mayahuel's beginning, middle and her end also warrant notice, not least since further investigation reveals she was the personification of the maguey or, more pertinently, an agave. The agave (see page 113) is the plant at the heart of tequila's essence, crucial in production and, thanks to Mayahuel, spiritually vital. Mayahuel started life (well, afterlife) as the goddess of fertility and embroiled herself in an unmitigated disaster of an affair when she paired off with the god of medicine Patecatl. Having dropped some sultry Barry White tunes and cracked out the chocolate body lotion, Patecatl played pat-a-cake on Mayahuel's love bumps, riling her priggish grandmother in the process.

Nanny Mayahuel didn't believe in half measures so sent out demons to hunt the pair down. Running scared, the star-crossed lovers turned themselves into branches of a tree. Nifty as this disguise was, they were discovered by the demons and the tree was split in two, Mayahuel being destroyed and buried as branches.

But, much like Jesus, Mayahuel rose again, this time in the form of the maguey plant; even more heroically, she bore 400 offspring along the way. Visiting friends and family were forced to lie about how bonny the babies were when they discovered they were actually rabbits, but Mayahuel and her rabbits were adopted by the Aztec people as deities. The bunnies became gods of intoxication while struggling single mum Mayahuel's maguey form was used for its mind-expanding alcoholic pulque sap, and to make sewing needles, sneakers and shelters. Eventually it was baked, with fermented sugars used in the very first incarnation of tequila.

Patecatl went on to give us mescaline but we would argue that drugs are for mugs, and Mayahuel was the true champion of the tale, a woman who is at the heart of the tequila legend.

TEQUILA

MEZCAL

MAYAHUEL

TWO TEQUILA LEGENDS

DON JAVIER DELGADO CORONA

TEQUILA HAS ENJOYED A RENAISSANCE IN RECENT YEARS AND THERE ARE MANY MODERN DAY TEQUILA LEGENDS WE COULD CELEBRATE.

   Tomas Estes who runs Café Pacifico in London spreads the tequila love around Europe; Tommy Bermejo did the same for the rest of the world from his base, Tommy's, in San Francisco, a beautiful bar and home to Tommy's Margarita. In terms of production, distillers such as Jesús Hernandez, the late Don Julio or the Camerena family all warrant a nod. But the most sterling contribution comes from an octogenarian Mexican who ties all these people together. Don Javier Delgado Corona runs the La Capilla cantina in Tequila town and has been serving customers since the age of 15. As a result he's become rather good at making drinkers feel welcome and comfortable in his rustic, dusty bar. La Capilla has had its doors open for nearly 30 years; it is free from airs and graces and is revered by the local tequileros as well as the global tequila community. Indeed many of the most avid imbibers in the drinks industry will have the bar on their bucket list. A common bar call there is Don Javier's trademark Batanga (tequila and coke) and if you're not sipping quality tequila neat, you'll often find it's topped up with a mixer of fizzy pop from a huge plastic litre bottle and stirred with whatever is close to hand, be it a spoon, knife or pen. The bar and the man sum up the spirit; laid back, lacking in pretention, comfortable in its own skin. Should you visit the Mexico, then La Capilla is a must-see.

Above: Don Javier entertains the troops from behind his bar. Below: A typically rustic Mexican cantina.

JACK KEROUAC

TAKING US BACK TO OUR EARLIER MENTION
OF SCHIZOPHRENIA, WE PRESENT MR JACK
KEROUAC, DIAGNOSED WITH THE CONDITION
AND AS A CONSEQUENCE DEEMED 'UNSUITABLE'
FOR THE US NAVY.

Forced to ditch the naval career he ventured
forth as an American novelist, poet, and writer,
and, even if he might not have agreed, we're
undoubtedly better off because of it.

Kerouac is included here as an advocate of
Mexico as much as tequila having written enough
about it to please a tourist board. In his short
story collection, *Lonesome Traveller,* he delivers an
ode to Mexico, a defence of a country that was, at
the time, regarded as perilous. He loved crossing
the border from America's southwest states, comparing it to sneaking out of school, walking into
a bar and grabbing a drink while 'fellas cooked
tacos, wearing sombreros, some wearing guns on
their rancher hips... It's the feeling of entering
the Pure Land.' He added: 'Mexico is gentle and
fine even when you're travelling with dangerous
people, which I did.'

In *The Dharma Bums* he writes: 'Enjoyed the
real Mexico where there were girls at a peso a
dance and raw tequila and lots of fun.' And that
does indeed sound like a laugh, Jack. So Kerouac
drank and dug the scene in Mexico then travelled
back to Mexicali where he partied with a truck
driver and enjoyed more tequila and Mexican
whores. Beat that, people.

His first experience of Mexico came when he
visited fellow beat writer William Burroughs in
the summer of 1950. Together the two shared
tequila as they hung out in Mexico City and
probably wrote some words down in their note-
pads. Great days. This anecdote might've been
more charming were it not for Burroughs' over-
enthusiastic appreciation of booze and narcotics.
Burroughs is probably a man to associate with
gin, since this was what he was drinking when he
allegedly shot his wife in the head during an ill-
fated William Tell re-enactment.

As with Burroughs, we walk a tightrope when
celebrating Kerouac as a drinker. The man found
himself at the bottom of a bottle and we know
that there are no useful answers to be found there.
But he loved tequila, it inspired some of his work
and he wrote about it, and for that we honour
him. He even had a drink named after him at
Vesuvio in San Francisco – a shot of tequila with
some rum, and a dash of orange and cranberry.
A debate rages about whether the man actually
drank it. He apparently drank 'anything brown'.
We're not sure we like the sound of that order.

MEZCAL
DAY OF THE DEAD

Mexico's surreal Day of the Dead can be vividly intensified after one too many slugs of agave spirit. During a three-day public holiday the festival sees the deceased commemorated and celebrated with private altars (*ofrendas*) created for the dead and adorned with marigolds and gifts.

Morbid as it sounds, the Day of the Dead is supposed to be a merry event, as men in terrifying masks cavort around on stilts, people chant rhymes about the dead, kids eat skulls (candy skulls), skeletons roam the streets and folks cuddle gravestones in cemeteries. Hilarity ensues. Despite the fun, if you're high as a kite the celebrations can be a weird trip, as explained in the 1947 novel *Under the Volcano* by the Mexico-based novelist Malcolm Lowry:

'The Consul now observed on his extreme right some unusual animals resembling geese, but large as camels, and skinless men, without heads, upon stilts, whose animated entrails jerked along the ground.... his room shaking with daemonic orchestras, the snatches of fearful tumultuous sleep, interrupted by voices which were really dogs barking... The wailing, the terrible music, the dark spinets: he returned to the bar.'

It should be noted that Lowry's protagonist was an alcoholic who gunned endless bottles of mezcal during his final, violent hours alive. That his demise coincided with the Day of the Dead festival was unfortunate – if he'd drunk less but better Mezcal, he may have enjoyed his experience.

Mezcal is referenced throughout *Under the Volcano*, as well as tequila, and both are agave spirits, but they are very different beasts. Mezcal operates as an umbrella term for agave distillates, so Tequila is a mezcal in the same way that Cognac is a brandy. The 16th-century Spanish conquistadors christened all agave creations 'Mezcal Wine'. This wasn't wine, it was a potent potable, but as the Tequila valley and Jalisco regions started to perfect blue agave cultivation,

The Day of the Dead *(Dia de los Muertos)* ceremony in Patzcuaro town, Michoacan state, Mexico. The annual celebration takes place from 31 October to 2 November.

tequila gradually formed its own identity and became less associated with mezcal.

Mezcal has always been important to the Mexicans, but its popularity was dead and buried for the rest of the world as the margarita and tequila put it under. Now we are seeing the spirit enjoy a resurrection.

Today when we refer to Mezcal we more readily associate it with a set of artisan distillates becoming increasingly as revered as tequila. There are plenty of similarities, but unlike tequila, mezcal is not constrained by the use of the blue agave, and can be derived from many different agave species, and while it has an Appellation of Origin like tequila, production is geographically spread. That said, there is a definite heartland for Mezcal in Oaxaca and they do favour a particular agave, the Espadin. As with tequila, 100% agave is the official guarantee that there are no other fermentable sugars in there.

Along with Quauhnahuac, the scene of the Consul's demise, Oaxaca is also referenced in Lowry's novel as an ardent advocate of the Day of the Dead, making this region of Mexico perfect to enjoy both the dead and a reborn spirit. The Mezcal distilleries in Oaxaca are often tiny in comparison to the commercial juggernauts of tequila, but this is part of the charm, with rural settings and small producers employing traditional methods including the stone-lined pits to bake the agaves. The resulting mezcal is ragged and raw, smoky and full of rustic character, just how the Consul would like it; not a spirit to be wasted on the dead.

Del Maguey
The prodigal son of Mezcal is Ron Cooper who has helped resuscitate the category from its morgue. Del Maguey is one of the largest brands in the mezcal world. Cooper insists on preserving painstakingly artisan and small batch processes

with a 'single village' approach, visiting a number of villages (*palenqueros*) and protecting each producers techniques to retain individuality. Worth trying.

Papadiablo Mezcal
Produced in Miahuatlan, Oaxaca, and distilled using a copper still heated over an open fire for subtle notes of agave and sweet peppers. This ensures a mouthful of subtle agave and sweet pepper character. A finish of sweet smoke is impossible to exorcise, but merits a celebration.

 Festival Spirit

Pechuga mezcal is a traditional Mexican festival favourite, with spices and fruits added to the distilling process. Think pungent pineapple or bold banana, gorgeous guava, quince, or almonds, even anise and rice. Not to mention, wait for it, a raw, skinless piece of chicken breast. Yep, clucking amazing. The pechuga process sees a carcass of meat suspended in the bell of the still and, as the percolating distillation rises, steam cooks the chicken, its fat absorbing the stronger smoky Mezcal compounds. The smoke still comes through, but it is tempered by sweet fruits and a salty quality, to the point that few of the egg-samples you'll encounter actually taste meaty. It's hard to put your finger on what it tastes like, but reassuringly it's more complex than chicken, so expect more of the fruits and spice under that smoke. Chicken is merely the starter though, as other deli counter contributions to this unique spirit include turkey, rabbit and an expensive piece of ham in Del Maguey's Iberico.

RIDING THE REVOLUTION

When agriculturally adept Aztecs harvested agave, they scraped the plant's core to propagate a flow of sap, fermenting it for their tasty beverage *pulque*. Much like the Aztecs then, we too scraped the bottom of something, and so we include a horse as one of our fellow thinking drinkers.

But don't get long-faced about it, this is hardly a contribution we came up with on the hoof. Our research has revealed that the horse is actually a blessed beast who plays an instrumental role in tequila production.

A mane-stay of Mexican revolutions, noble steeds were ridden into battles by legends like Emiliano Zapata at the turn of the 20th century, and their bravery was recorded in legendary tales and songs. Perhaps the most famous on four legs was Siete Leguas, owned by the Mexican insurgent Pancho Villa.

Siete Leguas earned his name, Seven Leagues, in recognition of his exceptional equine pace and stamina, as exhibited during the brutal battle of Ojinaga in 1913. In the warm-down, Villa rewarded Leguas's nag nerve by serving him a nip of tequila, this despite the fact that Villa himself was a teetotaller. A rampant womaniser, Villa loved Siete Leguas almost as much as the ladies and enjoyed the nickname the 'Centaur of the North', half-man, half-horse, which we've assumed was due to his affection for the mount rather than his overexposed endowment – or his insistence of being the centaur of attention.

Pancho Villa, half-man, half-horse. Mostly man though.

Villa was thrilled when Marina Adeo, AKA *La Bandida*, a revolutionary and lady of the night, wrote a song, *El Siete Leguas*, in tribute to his equine buddy. A paean to the hooved hero, it was sung in tequila-fuelled catinas:

Siete leguas el caballo,
que Villa más estimaba,
cuando oía silbar los trenes,
se paraba y relinchaba,
siete leguas el caballo,
que Villa más estimaba.

Beautiful stuff, and so catchy. The legend of Siete Leguas lives on in tequila thanks to the distillery and its tasty Siete Leguas Añejo 100% tequila brand, and horses still play a role in tequila production – they are employed to pull the tahona, a huge stone that crushes cooked agave to extract the fermentable sugars. The tequila itself is aged for 24 months in American oak and consequently gallops up the nose with heroic hints of vanilla.

THE ANATOMY
OF AN AGAVE

At the centre of tequila's story is the agave. This revered plant is crucial to quality, and just as single-malt whisky lovers celebrate patient ageing in barrels, agave takes anywhere up to 12 years to reach maturity and that's before the process of making tequila can even begin.

Agave comes from the latin *agavus*, meaning admirable or illustrious or Thinking Drinkers, and is a generic name given by 18th-century Swedish botanist Carl Linnaeus to plants with big spiky leaves and pineapple-style bases. The agave is extremely hardy, a perennial that is resistant to drought and to frost. There are hundreds of agave varieties but for tequila you require the blue agave, because by law tequila uses sugars from the *Agave tequilana weber azul*, harvested in the Jalisco region. It's worth pointing out that it is not a cactus – it's actually part of the asparagales order. Eating it may or may not make your urine smell.

Blue agaves grow in rich volcanic soil, and in Jalisco the best are found south of Guadalaraja in the Highlands, or Los Altos, where they are slower maturing and higher in sugar – a great example of the style is *Tapatio*. Tequila producers also use agave from the Lowlands, which gives more earthy flavours, vegetal and lime. Herradura is an example of the type.

Agave reproduce sexually, but also asexually, which has a much less significant impact on their wallets. The downside is they have a maximum life span of around 12 years.

The large outer leaves or the '*penca*' have sharp spines and needles and are removed by highly skilled and rather hunky *jimadors* (pronounced him-a-doors. Him a man, though, not a door. Geddit?). *Jima* means to prune or cut and these men will still use a *coa de jima* (a circular blade around 20cm/8in in diameter) that's super sharp and has a long wooden handle. A jimador can harvest an agave in six minutes, averaging 100 agave a day. Since the agaves mature at any time, the *jimadors* work all year round and their aim is to strip it back to the heart of the plant, which is like a massive bulb and is called a *cabexa* (head) or *piña* (pineapple), as this contains the juice.

The agave was revered by the Aztecs, who propagated then fermented its sap to an alcohol volume of around 4 or 5% ABV to make 'pulque' (pool-kay) and it's still sold in Mexico from the side of the road in plastic jugs called *curados*. In the case of tequila though, distillers require the juices from a baked agave. When the *piña* is roasted, the high concentrations of insulin and chemical compounds in the plant convert to fermentable sugars. These are obtained when the agave is crushed or shredded; the resulting juice is then fermented and distilled to make tequila.

TEQUILA AT THE MOVIES

MEXICAN MOVING PICTURES

Tequila is the nihilistic, macho man of the movie drinks cabinet. While whisky ruled the Wild West, the hard-core cinematic cowpokes on the Mexican borders were only ever rustling for pocket change to buy rusty mugs of mezcal.

But these gutsy guzzlers are no more, tequila has latterly suffered a hijacking from the world of Hollywood and product placement pollutes our viewing. The appearance of Patrón being daintily sipped by pinkie-protruding romcomers in *No Strings Attached*, or an 'all-star-cast' clinking cutely cut glasses of 1800 in weepy *He's Just Not That Into You*, suggest that tequila is a fighter on the ropes.

So if we want to celebrate tequila at its turbulent cinematic best, we must look to the past, and Mexican maestro, director and actor Emilio 'El Indio' Fernández provides us with our star.

Enjoying his peak as a Mexican film director during the 1930s and '40s, Fernández was a winner of prestigious top prizes and, more importantly, helped promote the image of tequila. But he was as mysterious and misleading as the spirit itself, his stories

a margarita mix of fact and fiction, shaken up – largely by the man himself.

Fernández's childhood alone beggars belief. Born in Mexico in 1904, he was nine when he caught his mother with another man and killed him then fled to join the revolutionary campaigns of Venustiano Carranza. After a spell in military school he joined up with Adolfo de la Huerta (who previously overturned Carranza… hang on a sec…) in 1923 during yet another revolution.

When that failed, Fernández was arrested and sent to prison for 20 years, but escaped and fled to Chicago. Here he befriended superstar Rudolph Valentino, an admirer of Fernández's tango, but simultaneously fell out with infamous bank robber Baby Face Nelson, forcing him south to Hollywood.

These brilliant but arguably bogus beginnings are dashed with the occasional corroborated fact. We know that Fernández sipped

his tequila with silent film starlet Dolores del Rio. She was married to the art director for Metro-Goldwyn-Mayer, who convinced Fernández to pose nude for an artist, and the image was subsequently used as the basis for the first Oscar statuette in 1929. We also know that when his exile from Mexico was lifted, he returned home to enjoy his tequila on tap and became one of the key film- makers in Mexico's film history. Indeed his celebrated cinema made him the leading exponent of classical Mexican cinema between 1935–1955. And in 1946 he raised a tequila toast as his film *Maria Candelaria* won top prize at the first ever Cannes film festival.

His fortunes waned in the '50s and by the '60s he turned to acting. When he struggggled critically he managed to raise eyebrows and heart rates by shooting a reviewer. In the *cojones*. And he became more familiar to cinema fans in the 1960s when mezcal-fuelled mayhem with film director and felllow loose cannon Sam Peckinpah led him to assume the roles of mad Mexican Mapache in the

classic *The Wild Bunch* and El Jefe in *Bring Me the Head of Alfredo Garcia*. Both memorable characters. But it was at a party in 1962 that he showed the current crop of marketing executives about product placement, introducing tequila to Marilyn Monroe.

Marilyn, the most famous woman in the world at the time, was a guest at his Mexican Coyoacan home and a photo of him showing her how to drink the spirit was distributed globally, placing tequila on the map.

Look a little deeper into Fernández's life story and he becomes embroiled in the kind of hyperbolic hearsay that reads like a Walter Mitty adventure. But by mixing myth with fact, Fernández became a true embodiment of tequila. Labelled a rogue and brimming with balderdash, but still basking in sun-drenched mystery. Fernández and his cinema: classics.

Above: Marilyn Monroe. *Right:* The Mexican movie star Emilio 'El Indio' Fernández.

115

TEQUILA BAR BORE TIPS

The best way to learn about this spirit is to visit Tequila Town, but in lieu of an expensive air fare, learn a bit about the technical traditions and values of tequila and you can make the man insisting you shoot the stuff look rather ignorant.

SPEAKA THE LINGO

The *agavero* is the agave grower, the *jimador* harvests them by cutting off the leaves with a *coa de jima*, meanwhile a *tequilero* is anyone who works in the tequila industry. A *cantinero* is your bartender, ask him for a *direcho* to order your tequila neat. And *mariachi* is Mexican folk music.

HORNOS OR AUTOCLAVE?

When Hubert and Philomena start banging about their AGA over tequila, shame them into silence with your oven know-how. Traditional *hornos*, or masonary ovens, tend to be used for a slow cook, and many feel it provides the final product with a unique character that is lost in the pressure cooker or autoclave. Imagine cooking anything in a clay pot or a metal pan and you get the point. Some mezcals still use pits lined with stone – even more artisan than the *hornos*. No one really uses AGAs.

GIVING 110%

We advocate the consumption of 100% agave tequila where possible. Mixto tequilas will not have 100% agave on the label and by law must only include 51% agave sugar. The remaining 49% can comprise anything – well, not crack or puppy ears, but any other sugars, so it could be cane spirit instead. There are some palatable mixtos out there and their conception was necessary to protect a tequila industry under pressure from demand, so we're not knocking the category. Even so, 100% will give you a reassuring guarantee of agave spirit.

LABELS MATTER

Look for a NOM on the bottle, it means *Norma Official Mexicana* and protects the appellation of origin. It relates to the company producing it. You also want the stamp of the CRT and, assuming you're not after a mixto tequila, the vital words '100% Agave'.

IS THAT A GUN OR ARE YOU JUST PLEASED TO SEE ME?

Either way, don't shoot. The addition of salt and lime to the rookie drinking ritual is possibly of Mexican origin, since the Mexicans will add lime to most things. But they don't tend to shoot tequila, bite lime and lick salt off their hands. The only reason to drink it this way is if your tequila is cheap and nasty, and frankly, we're not sure why you'd be drinking stuff like that anyway. If you want to drink it in a traditional fashion try the Bandera: a shot of tequila, a shot of lime, and a shot of quality sangrita, sipped alternately.

AGE CONCERN

While ageing is revered in whisky or rum, it can have a negative impact on tequila. Too much time in wood can impact the delicate agave characteristics of the spirit, so don't base an expensive purchase on the age statement. For quality, we look at the agave, the production methods and then ageing, usually under five years.

DON'T EAT THE WORM

Why? Because it's a worm, you dummy. It appears in mezcals, not tequila, and invariably in sub-quality spirits as a touristy gimmick. And more accurately it's actually the larva form of an agave moth. Eating it will not induce hallucinations, nor will it make you look cool. In fact you'll look like mug.

REGIONAL DIFFERENCES

While Jalisco is the most famous region for tequila, you might want to head off the beaten track and sample tequila from other states sanctioned to produce it: Nayarit, Guanajuato, Michoacan and Tamaulipas are all sanctioned regions. Chinaco was the first tequila distillery to open outside Jalisco.

WORD PLAY

The word 'crud' probably comes from the Mexican language – *cruda* means hangover. I feel like *cruda*. But actually tequila won't give you a hangover any more or less than any other alcohol drunk to excess.

IT'S NOT CACTUS JUICE

Nor does it contain mescaline. These are two common misconceptions about tequila.

THERE ARE FIVE RECOGNISED EXPRESSIONS OF TEQUILA

Blanco *(silver):*
No minimum age requirements.

Joven or Oro *(gold):*
A blanco that has been softened by abocado (caramel, oak extract, glycerin and sugar syrup). Could also be a blend of blanco and reposado.

Reposado *(aged):*
A tequila that is aged for a minimum of two months in oak.

Añejo *(extra aged):*
A tequila aged for a minimum of one year in oak barrels that each have a maximum capacity of 600 litres.

Muy Añejo *(ultra aged):*
A tequila aged for a minimum of three years in oak barrels, each with a capacity not exceeding 600 litres.

TEQUILA RECOMMENDATIONS

Far from the average tequila you'll find in a dive bar, quality 100% agave spirit is immensely sippable and comes in a number of styles. Here are a few to try.

OLMECA ALTOS
BLANCO TEQUILA 38% ABV

Olmeca's legendary spiritual guide Jesús Hernandez included the input of bartending duo Henry Besant and Dre Masso when distilling this tequila, ensuring it's a terrific tipple to shake and stir into mixed drinks. Rustic in its agave aggression, with pepper and an earthy quality, it backs it up with soft sweetness and lime.

CALLE 23
BLANCO TEQUILA 40% ABV

A tequila created in Mexico by a French woman. Sophie Decobecq is a microbiologist fascinated with yeast and agaves, who converted classroom theory to prosperous practice in Mexico. Specifically selected yeast strains bestow this blanco with a character that is silky smooth, but beyond that it bounds around the 'bouche' with bananas and tropical fruits, green pepper and vegetal agave. Then a French 75 of spicy pepper booms the back of the tongue before you enjoy a fresh flourish on the finish.

DON JULIO
REPOSADO TEQUILA 38% ABV

Renowned for its agricultural care of agave, Don Julio takes a cultivated core and then fires up brick ovens and injects wild yeast into the fermentation. After distillation the reposado is aged for up to eight months in white American oak. All these components deliver a tequila with a hint of vegetal agave but complemented by sweet vanilla and almonds, as well as a touch of cinnamon-coated apple and light chocolate.

TAPATIO

ANEJO TEQUILA 38% ABV

Created by Don Felipe Camarena, an appreciator of all
things artisan who aims to do
as much as he can by hand.
Production methods are over
100 years old, with the traditional tahona wheel used to
crush agave. Agave juice and
fibres are mixed by (hopefully
clean) feet, wild yeast strains are
added and agave juice
is fermented in wood
after 18 months in
American oak without
dilution. The result-
ing spirit fills your
chops with choice
flavour, gorgeous
caramels and vanil-
las and chocolate
under a beautifully
baked agave char-
acter, with cloves
and cinnamon
working together
for a moreish pud-
ding of a tequila.

JOSE CUERVO RESERVA

EXTRA ANEJO TEQUILA 40% ABV

Every part of the process is premium here, from the 10-year-
old agaves, hand-selected and
harvested at the peak of their
growth, to the traditional ovens
they are cooked in for a pains-
taking 72 hours, right up to
the five years it spends ageing
in French Limousin and ex-
American whiskey casks. They
even blend in some tequilas
aged for as long as 30 years.
The bottles are hand-numbered
and sealed with
wax, and each
new collectible
has a hand-
painted wooden
box. Sweet, fruity
and a hint of
spice on the
finish.

OCHO AÑEJO SINGLE-BARREL CASK STRENGTH

VINTAGE TEQUILA 54.8% ABV

Ocho has taken tequila in a vintage direction, releasing tequilas
noting a specific year or harvest
and the location of the agave
plants. A collaboration between
Tomas Estes (the man who gave
us Café Pacifico) and renowned
distillers, the Camarena family,
this rare single-barrel bottling
of Ocho Añejo tequila, is cask
strength but has
successfully found
the balance between
agave and oak char-
acter. Plenty of rich
qualities, with the
nuts and chocolate,
spice from the
wood, as well as
some sweet
pepper and
agave to go with
warm, dried
fruit and spice.

119

TEQUILA RECIPES

★ ★ ★ ★ ★ ★ ★ ★ ★ ★ ★ ★ ★ ★ ★ ★ ★

MARGARITA

A cocktail with a contested etymology. Depending on who you speak to it might have been named after a 1930s dancer in a Tijuana club who later became known as Rita Hayworth (real name, Margarita Carmen Cansino); was the work of barman Danny Negret at the Garci Crispo Hotel in 1936 as he struggled to think of a wedding gift; or came to us courtesy of Carlos 'Danny' Herrera of the Rancho La Gloria Bar in the 1940s who shook it up as he dreamt of a showgirl. There are other tall tales but frankly we're more interested in making a drink.

GLASS: MARGARITA/MARTINI
50ml (1¾fl oz) tequila
25ml (1fl oz) Cointreau
25ml (1fl oz) fresh lime juice
GARNISH: LEMON OR LIME SLICE

Rim a chilled glass with salt then shake all ingredients hard over ice and strain into the glass. Garnish with a slice of lime.

PALOMA

Margarita? Do me a favour, far too much hassle. This is Mexico's answer to a gin and tonic and its simplicity is what makes it the nation's most popular tequila serve.

GLASS: HIGHBALL
60ml (2fl oz) tequila
3 tsp lime juice
ice cubes
grapefruit soda, to top
GARNISH: GRAPEFRUIT SLICE

Dip half the glass rim in salt (optional) then add the ice, tequila and lime juice in order. Stir, top with grapefruit soda and garnish.

TEQUILA SHOT

We don't generally advise drinking tequila in shots. So, why one here? Well, we're not suggesting you simply nail a shot, but we do advocate sipping quality, aged tequila neat. That is a thing of joy. So pour a nip in to any glass and then sip it slowly with food such as white meat or fish, preferably with added spice.

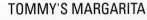 **GLASS: SHOT**
60ml (2fl oz) 100% agave
    tequila blanco

Pour the tequila into the glass, then sip slowly.

BATANGA

The La Capilla bar in Tequila is a tried and tested drinking hole for the tireless tequileros, and the octogenarian owner Don Javier is an agave-loving icon. This simple mix is his creation.

GLASS: HIGHBALL
salt to rim glass
ice cubes
60ml (2fl oz) tequila
3 tsp lime juice
cola, to top
GARNISH: LIME WHEEL

Salt the rim of the glass, then add the ice, tequila and lime juice in that order. Top with cola.

TOMMY'S MARGARITA

Created by Julio Bermejo who runs Tommy's in San Francisco, one of the best tequila bars in the world, this contemporary classic is the perfect foil for any drinker who recoils at the frosty bitter zest of a margarita.

GLASS: ROCKS
60ml (2fl oz) tequila reposado
30ml (1fl oz) lime juice
3 tsp agave syrup
ice cubes

Shake all the ingredients, pour into a glass and serve with ice.

VODKA
FROM GRAIN TO GLASS

Vodka, eh? You probably know it. It's that water-white spirit with a history embedded in Eastern Europe. Enjoyed with simple mixers, it's sometimes served as a shot with cold fish, maybe in a martini if you're James Bond. It's strong, but it's neutral. It's the standard stalwart spirit of the back bar. These days new and interesting producers are taking a more considered approach to the spirit, proving that there's much more to this noble nip than you might imagine...

HISTORY & CULTURE

Vodka is a dichotomy of a drink. Once a catalyst for cataclysmic change, fuelling revolution while delivering a rustic tang that made eyes water, today it postures around poncey bars celebrating a neutral, often insipid purity. The honest history-maker has become something of a con, an eastern prize-fighter put out to a western pasture.

If you're not a fan of the spirit, you'll agree with this sentiment. You might have once paid through the nose for a night out with vodka, selecting a stylish bottle before peeling away the façade to discover something maddeningly middle-of-the-road, leaving you feeling cheated, fed up and financially worse off. You won't be the first or the last to be hoodwinked in this way – because distilled deception is what vodka does best. Vodka may be transparent in colour, but it's not always clear what you're drinking.

With thousands of 'neutral' spirit brands fighting for attention, vodka is mired in everything from the bafflingly bland to the completely aroma-less and those undetectable in a mixer. Some vodka will chisel more than the ice in your glass. Even its name, which derives from the Russian word for water, is a dangerous half-truth.

But as with any form of art, if you understand vodka in context and take time to marvel at the spirit's highs and lows, you will not only appreciate its crucial role in alcohol's history, but also learn to love it in its finest form.

And if you do your homework, you'll even discover that, beyond the rakish frauds leading you up a garden path to flavour frustration, there are exponents of the vodka-making art who respect the past and deliver a drink worthy of your time.

Vodka captures the imagination with the stories of an emergent Eastern Europe and understably so. From the early 15th century, this is the heartland of the spirit where it has imbued and inspired Tsar and Tsarina, revolutionaries and dictators, even (less discerningly) modern presidents. Its role in history is emphatic, particularly in Russian lore. Take Ivan the Terrible, a man pushing early incarnations of vodka on his subjects as early as the 16th century. Ivan's was a simpler time and you could get away with a hell

Barley is one of the ingredients used to make vodka. Other bases for the spirit include potatoes, beets and onions.

of a lot more back then – his crimes included unleashing bears on monks, and chucking puppies from the top of buildings. This was how he rolled – but he also recognised vodka as a valuable source of national income, and his advocacy inspired the Tsars who followed, among them Peter the Great, who took his affection abroad.

But vodka's 20th-century success is arguably more laudable. Like a hyperactive apparition, it has taken the spirit world by storm at a scarily rapid pace. Largely ignored outside northern Europe until the 1930s, vodka stole a march on its spiritual peers in the decades that followed.

Pablo Picasso loved a drop and noted the best things to emerge in post-war France were 'Brigitte Bardot, modern jazz and Polish vodka'. He did not say Orangina, which was an error on his part, but that man knew how to draw, so we should take heed. And by the 1950s Americans had fallen for it, Prohibition had effectively killed the whisky industry, and vodka was well placed to satisfy conservative palates. Soaring vodka sales had almost single-handedly saved the spirit-driven cocktail culture in the western world.

Today vodka is the biggest spirit category in the USA. In the UK, home to gin and whisky no less, it now represents a third of all single spirit orders at the bar, making it impossible, and indeed foolish, to ignore.

While the success has enabled some to clamber on a bland bandwagon, there is a new wave of vodka with character. Vodka can be distilled from any fermentable agricultural product, which is a very loose stipulation and has seen everything from grapes and potatoes to beets and onions used. While these organoleptic characteristics are lost in the distillation, the aim is for more dynamic producers to now deliver a spirit with a remnant of its original ingredients. This embrace of more traditional styles makes for a wider range and more varied flavours.

Soviet propaganda poster of 1941, prior to operation Barbarossa 'The Motherland is Calling'.

But more than that, vodka gives us the base for cocktails and enhances other spirits in a mixed drink. Vodka has also been instrumental in advancing techniques in distillation and filtration which, in turn, have benefited other spirit categories. And since vodka can be manufactured from any agricultural base, it continues to drive innovation in production and marketing.

Vodka: Neutral, Transparent. Lacking in aroma. But is it really? Well, yes, in some cases. But there's a lot more to vodka. It courses through Eastern European history and has recently been embraced by more caring producers. So here's a chapter to convince you it's worth another shot.

Vodka history started in Russia and Eastern Europe, travelling onwards via a Polish pharmacist and the invention of the column still – and not forgetting James Bond and a few hapless presidents.

1405 The first written evidence of grain spirit (not actually called vodka) being made in Poland appears in the court records of Świętokrzyskie province.

1426 The Genoese bring a gift of distilled spirit from Asia to the Russian Prince Vasily III of Russia.

1450 Grain spirit is purportedly distilled in Moscow at the Chudov Monastery.

1470s Vodka is now sold to the Polish as medicine from apothecaries. It's not medicine. Never has been.

1534 Polish pharmacist Stefan Falimirz writes a guide to medical treatments and features the word vodka. It's still not medicine.

1474 Ivan the Terrible imposes a monopoly on vodka production in Russia. He liked being the boss.

1546 Polish cities Krakow, Gdansk and Poznan become distilling heartlands. Poznan still is today.

1648 Rising Russian taxes inspire peasants to go nuts and behead leading noblemen. The powers that be end the riots by hosting a huge feast complete with unending servings of vodka.

1725 Catherine the Great, whom Russian soldiers claim 'drank like a man', serves troops vodka to help her secure the throne.

1741 Elizabeth Petronova follows Catherine's lead, charming generals with a heavy dose of Russian courage and a few fluttering eyelids, before tipsy troops help her pinch the throne from baby Tsar Ivan VI.

1823 The continuous still is invented. The method of column distillation sees production of vodka improve.

1793 German chemist Johann Tobias is teaching at St Petersburg Academy of Sciences and experimenting with charcoal filtration.

1756 Sweden is playing the vodka game comprehensively, now operating 180,000 stills.

1941 Brit John Morgan pours his ginger ale with John Martin's Smirnoff vodka into a copper cup, they add some lime and the Moscow Mule is born, becoming an omnipresent bar call and making vodka a star spirit in the USA.

2010 Vladimir Putin wages war on Russian vodka consumption. Boo. To be fair, it seems by this point a lot of people do have a drinking problem.

1861 The Smirnov family is making vodka.

1961 The film 'Dr No' sees James Bond say 'yes' to a pretty girl and a vodka Martini. This was a departure from his standard bar order – in the books he drank a Vesper with gin, vodka and Kina Lillet.

SMIRNOFF

1933 Vladimir Smirnov sells rights of Smirnoff to Rudolph Kunnett who starts distilling the iconic vodka in the USA.

1879 Absolut genius Lars Olsson Smith launches Absolut Rent Brannvin, sneakily setting up shop outside the Stockholm city limits and undercutting the state monopolised vodka prices. He earned a packet.

1978 The Polish try to sue Russia over ownership of vodka. In retaliation, Russian researcher Vilyam Pokhlebkin becomes a national hero when he (bogusly) claims in his book Istoriya Vodka that vodka is Russian. This is not held up by future historians, but then Pokhlebkin also claims that if you don't drink before 3pm or after midnight, you're not a 'professional' alcoholic.

2004 Sidney Frank sells his Grey Goose vodka brand to Bacardi Martini for $2bn. He dies two years later.

1904 Tsar Nikolai II nationalises vodka.

1921 Ferdinand Petoit makes the first version of the Bloody Mary. It's really quite the hit.

1991 Yeltsin drives in a bus-load of vodka for troops in order to overturn a coup d'etat.

1917 The Russian Revolution kicks off big time.

1917 The Swedish government cottons on to Olsson's money-making scheme and nationalises vodka.

ABSOLUT.

1979 Absolut launches in the USA and creates a premium market there for vodka.

PETER THE GREAT

The Great loved his vodka and he used it to fuel his extraordinary, if sometimes slightly aggressive, reign as Russian Tsar. In his time he also designed a device that created a triple-distilled vodka.

Peter is not a name to inspire awe. You've got your Peter Rabbit, Peter Pan, Peter O'Toole and the guy who let Jesus down, but really it's a slightly average name for a king. A Russian Peter who ruled the country in the 17th century saw this coming and enhanced a potentially forgettable Christian name by adding 'the Great'. And while this self-imposed moniker was confusing during games of football in the playground, Peter the Great did well by his super surname later in life, particularly with vodka.

By the time he was 20, Peter stood 2m (6ft) tall and was already keeping things real. When he wasn't overthrowing military leaderships abroad or modernising medieval laws, he was enforcing a tax on beards, all with a cup of vodka by his side.

Create St Petersburg? Peter did it and toasted it with a vodka. Rescue iron workers in the freezing Finnish sea? For sure, and he warmed up with a vodka. Celebrate the lives of dwarves with a dwarf wedding and have them jump out of pies? Naturally, and there was vodka for afters. Have a favourite pet monkey to sit on the back of his throne? Yep, and the monkey got a nip. Train a bear to serve vodka? He actually did that. Earn a reputation as the antichrist in some circles? That also happened.

Stories of vodka parties followed the Tsar wherever he travelled and landlords were regularly put through their paces. In 1698 English author John Evelyn hosted The Great at his estate for three months and the zany Tsar wrecked the joint, using family portraits for target practice and ruining hedges by ramming his mates through them in wheelbarrows. Russia was subsequently sent the bill for these bonkers bacchanals.

Admittedly Peter had a tendency to push the boundaries of responsible behaviour. He set up the 'All-Joking, All-Drunken Synod of Fools and Jesters', aiming to 'get drunk every day and never go to bed'. But his verve for vodka didn't affect his work ethic and he was never seen struggling during a morning-after moment. He toiled throughout and, according to the peasants, worked like an actual peasant. They lauded his get-up-and-go attitude, possibly because he would often hand them bottles of free vodka from his bear-drawn sleigh.

The Great cared about vodka so much in fact, that he improved production standards and used his engineering expertise to design a device that created a triple-distilled vodka. In doing so he popularised a quest for purity in vodka that still exists today. Meanwhile, the revenues he secured from vodka ensured Russia's financial stability for future generations.

In 1725 it all caught up with him and he found himself reclining on a deathbed in his early fifties. He probably didn't drink much of anything as he approached his demise, since his urinary tract was blocked, and an autopsy post-death (which all autopsies should be) revealed that he had gangrene in the bladder. Still, what a guy, a true vodka legend.

Peter the Great

10 THINGS YOU NEED TO KNOW ABOUT VODKA

01 The word **vodka** originates from the Russian voda, meaning water. *'No dear, I'm not drinking, I'm just enjoying a pint of water.'* The Polish use a w, so woda or wodka is the Polish equivalent. **Wodka** was recorded in Poland for the first time in 1405, but in Cyrillic it dates back as far as 1533, and was used to denote a medicinal drink that was transported to Russia from Poland at that time.

02 By law vodka can be produced from a range of fermentable agricultural products. This tends to be grain or potato.

Vodka Bases:

Potato: Round mouth feel, smooth and silky.

Rye: A little spicy kick.

Wheat: Touch of citrus and often a fresh aniseed finish.

Barley: Low in oil, so a crisp vodka.

Others: Vodka's lack of restrictions opens it up to all manner of bases. Ciroq, for example, distills fermented grapes. There was one that used onions once, but we don't recommend that. The countries that most commonly produce vodka are Russia, Poland, Finland, Lithuania and Sweden.

03 Try dropping the word *'congeners'* into vodka conversations at the bar. Do remember to use it in the correct context, though; don't say, for example: 'when I go to bed I wear congeners instead of pyjamas.' You don't get any points for that. Congeners are important organic compounds that give alcohol its flavour. In vodka, many of these are regarded as *'impurities'* (conversely, in rum or whisky they might be used for adding flavour), so producers filter many of them out.

04 The Russians drink vodka neat with food. You can do this too. If you like. Or don't. It's up to you really. We've successfully paired **Chase Marmalade Vodka** with a **glazed ham**, or **Copper House Barley Adnams Vodka** with a slice of **salmon**. All very middle class.

05 Vodka must be distilled to a minimum of **96% ABV** and then diluted in column stills, which are the most common in production. They are tall and have a number of plates inside to enable the accurate extraction of preferred alcohol flavours.

06 What matters in vodka is the base ingredient. The success of the distiller relies on his ability to remove the congeners (see 03) that carry the less pleasant aromas and flavours, yet still retain the character of the base ingredient (see 02).

07 Tags like **premium**, **super premium, ultra premium** and **super dooper premium** simply mean expensive, more expensive, too expensive and unnecessarily expensive. Luksosowa's bottle is basic and worryingly affordable and yet it's an incredibly tasty beverage. Don't spend for the sake of it.

08 Don't be hoodwinked by marketing, always look a little deeper into the product to discover the true story. Or... do be hoodwinked and back one randomly as you might a horse, by picking interesting names – **Rodnik** and the lesser spotted **Koch** vodka are among our favourites. These brand names have a certain sense of Russian authority to them, potential kings or queens among the numerous vodka brands trying to grab your attention the most.

09 Vodka can be distilled anywhere in the world. There are no laws on geographical restrictions, although the **Vodka Belt** of Northern Europe is its true heartland.

10 One of the most common questions we are asked is, 'Why are you looking through my window with binoculars?' and, after that, 'What is the purest vodka I can buy?' People are obsessed with the pursuit of **purity** and while it does matter in vodka, it shouldn't come at the cost of character. Column still distillation and filtration promote purity and, in the past, vodka was rounded off using fining agents as unusual as egg, fish bladder and soil, but today charcoal is the darling of the process. Charcoal can absorb heavy compounds and increase the mellow nature of a spirit. It's used alongside quartz, sand, gold and silver, lava rock and even algae. Not all vodka requires filtration, some is marketed as unfiltered, so don't get hung up on it – it's all about finding a vodka that suits your palate. The fun is in the sampling and comparing, so get to work with your tasting hat on and enjoy.

THREE VODKA LEGENDS

ISIDORE OF KIEV AND JAILHOUSE ROT

AMONG THE LEGENDARY FIGURES OF VODKA PRODUCTION IS A GREEK MONK CALLED ISIDORE OF KIEV WHO, ALONG WITH PRAYING, PICKED UP SOME RATHER NIFTY DISTILLATION TECHNIQUES DURING AN ITALIAN FIELD TRIP IN THE 1430S.

Returning to Russia, Isidore uttered a few unforgivably crude comments about his adopted homeland and riled the authorities so much that he was subsequently locked up in the Chudov Monastery.

So far, so religious nut persecuted, but it's here that the story gets really interesting, because it was while Isidore was in this prison that the Russians claim he distilled the first vodka – apparently pre-dating the Polish in the process.

There's a rich history of prison cons creating special sauce inside, and much like cigarettes and shivs, hiding the homemade hooch from screws has always been crucial.

Keeping contraband up their keisters is no mean feat. Just ask Neil Lansing, a Florida inmate, who, in 2011, managed to fit 31 items up there, including lip balm. But lip balm is small and round, and most of the jump juice produced in 'Grandma's House' over the years has been fermented, not distilled.

So how the hell did Isidore get away with distilling vodka? Did his jailers really sanction stills to craft hard spirit during his hard times? Seems unlikely. So it would appear we've picked a hole in the story as big as the one created by that chap Andy Dufresne in *The Shawshank Redemption*.

Even so, legends are legends (by which we mean lies), and Isidore was supposedly given the kit to produce his vodka from grain – which also just happened to be in his cell...

In the autumn of 1441 Isidore cemented his legendary status when he served his jailhouse rot to unknowing guards, rendering them drunk and enabling his escape. Carrying the distilling apparatus within him was not an option (Neil Lansing take note) so it was abandoned in his cell, allowing the Russians to have a crack at making vodka on their own.

VLADIMIR THE DEATH DEFYER

IN THE LATE 19TH CENTURY, PYTOR ARSENIEVICH SMIRNOV, BORN A SERF, DEFIED THE ODDS AND BECAME THE WORLD'S MOST FAMOUS VODKA MAKER. HIS IS AN INTERESTING STORY, BUT EVEN BETTER IS THAT OF HIS SON VLADIMIR, WHO REVIVED THE BRAND AND CREATED SMIRNOFF.

After Pytor's death his vodka business broke up and by 1918 a combination of World War I, Prohibition and the Russian Revolution had destroyed the Smirnov empire. Despite financial ruin, the Bolsheviks targeted the once-privileged Smirnov family and Vladimir was arrested, receiving a lengthy spell in the clink where he suffered beatings, starvation and, perhaps more worryingly, a death sentence.

Incredibly, Vladimir faced the firing squad six times, and survived. We're no sniper squad, but we're confident we could clip a blindfolded man from a few metres away. The Russians didn't miss though, Vlad simply mixed luck with moxie.

Vladimir's first evasion came through song. While marching to the execution location, Vlad convinced the guards to sing with him. So engrossed were they that they marched beyond the shooting range, forgot to do the deed and got so peckish they took everyone back to the cells. The song must've been really catchy.

Vlad then endured five mock executions and dodged death throughout, eventually escaping to Turkey. With little to his name, except his name, he launched Smirnov vodka in Bulgaria, Poland (where he added the two Fs) and, finally, Paris. He failed almost everywhere, but still fighting in his late fifties, destitute and close to death, he found a buyer for Smirnoff in Rudolph Kunnett, who took Smirnoff to the USA and, along with American drinks distributor John Martin, created one of the biggest drinks brands in the world.

THE STOLICHNAYA CHALLENGE

WHILE WE UNDERSTAND THAT THE WATERGATE CARRY-ON DAMAGED HIS REPUTATION A BIT, RICHARD NIXON IS AN UNLIKELY VODKA HERO IN THE USA. IN 1959, IN A DEMONSTRATION OF AMERICAN INTERVENTIONIST ARROGANCE, HE ATTENDED THE FIRST US TRADE EXHIBITION IN MOSCOW. Now cramming a conference centre full of American homeware nick-nacks in a celebration of capitalism was always likely to really wind up then Soviet Union leader Nikita Khrushchev, but Nixon had a plan to cool the Premier's pique. Directing him to the Pepsi stand he invited him to take a little sit down and to sip something sugary. The Krush-meister loved the stuff and for years after, the Russians flirted with Pepsi. In 1973 (shortly after Nixon's involvement in Watergate, in fact), Pepsi's chief executive Donald Kendall signed a deal to sell the sugar-crazed Russians his fizzy pop, exchanging it for Russian vodka. And not just any vodka but Stolichnaya, the state-owned sauce. As the Russians started a love affair with fizzy pop, so the Americans lapped up the new vodka, helping the spirit's sales surpass bourbon for the first time. By the mid-1970s vodka was the number 1 spirit, all due to Nixon's tête-à-tête over a soft drink.

VODKA AT THE MOVIES

THE BIG LEBOWSKI

From James Bond's Martini to the Cosmopolitan in *Sex and the City* and John Candy's arcane but equally admirable Orange Whip in *The Blues Brothers* (a blend of vodka with rum, cream and orange juice), vodka has enjoyed plenty of silver-screen time over the years. But if we had to choose one movie to honour above them all it would be The Dude's White Russian.

The Dude, or 'his dudeness, duder or el duderino', takes these adventures on with the vacillation of a man regularly nipping on vodka. Which he invariably is. A legend of liquor, he frequently parades his love of a White Russian, mixing the cocktail at various stages during the film with reckless abandon. So habitual is his tipple it becomes part of his armour, earning the drink infinitely more gravitas than Bond's predictably shopworn shaken and stirred martini.

When there isn't a spoon, The Dude stirs his drink with a finger. If there's no cream or milk, he'll use powdered. He rarely checks the vodka label. He makes a milk moustache look cool. He calls the drink a 'Caucasian'. And when he's bellicosely bundled into a limo by a chauffeur, the drink comes first, he won't spill a drop, he simply says: 'Hey, careful, man, there's a beverage here.'

Through strikes and gutters, The Dude abides, and he drinks right though.

The Dude's favourite cocktail was originally born out of the popularity of vodka in the late 1930s and 1940s. Forerunners included the Russian – crème de cacao and gin – and a cocktail called the Barbara (seriously, there was a drink called Barbara) introducing vodka and cream to the mix. The 1961 *Diners' Club Drink Book* then added a Black Russian to the menu, and lo, there must be a white, and so it evolved. It was subsequently a star of the 1960s, but, much like The Dude, lost its way and was eventually discussed as a drink for those who don't like the taste of booze, or perhaps like it too much.

No more though, The Dude has made it cool, and was the main reason for the revival of the classic mix. We won't spill any spoilers about the film here, you should watch it, it's well worth your time, but we will add that the film also catapulted Kahlúa into multiple drinks cabinets courtesy of The Dude's immortal line:

'I'm sorry if your stepmum is a nympho, but, ah, you know, I'm not sure what this has to do with… do you have any Kahlúa?'

THE
WHITE RUSSIAN

We highly recommend a White Russian (also commonly known, thanks to The Dude, as a Caucasian). It was The Dude who was single-handedly responsible for Kahlúa becoming a mainstay in most home bars.

■ **GLASS: OLD FASHIONED**
60ml (2fl oz) vodka
30ml (1fl oz) Kahlúa
15ml (3 tsp) double cream
15ml (3 tsp) full-fat milk
ice cubes

Shake ingredients, strain into glass over ice. Or, pour into a glass with ice and stir with your finger.

★ ★ ★ ★ ★ ★ ★ ★ ★ ★ ★ ★ ★ ★ ★ ★

★ ★ ★ ★ ★ ★ ★ ★ ★ ★ ★ ★ ★ ★ ★ ★

POLITICAL DRINKING GAMES

As long as Russia has had a ruler it has relied on vodka to rule. This applied to Tsars like Ivan the Terrible who insisted on his staff drinking to the death, as much as to Stalin's squiffy Soviet Politburo, charged with so much vodka they thought he was sane. So, while some of the best ideas come to us in the pub, we struggle to defend some of the decisions delivered by these characters after they cut loose their carafes.

Of all the Russians to showcase the folly of too much hooch in the hot seat though, it was bonkers Boris Yeltsin who raised the bar.

No other prominent statesman is more synonymous with a particular spirit than Boris is with vodka. He was actually raised as a firm believer in temperance and early on in his career was openly disgusted by the drinking of his peers. But by the time he was in office, Boris was hooked and his affection for alcohol affected his image. Yet it was vodka that facilitated Yeltsin's rise to power.

In 1991, as the old Soviet Union structures crumbled under Mikhail Gorbachev's *glasnost*, Vice President Gennady Yanayev and Prime Minister Valentin Pavlov launched a *coup d'état*. On the day of reckoning, these bunglers had been in the boozer necking vodka to the point that they forgot to arrest their key opponent Yeltsin, the then President of the Russian Republic. At the time, Boris was meeting with the Kazakh president and was also drunk. Even so, the error gave Boris an opportunity to overturn the coup. Sobering up, he secured strong support and during a heroic moment, climbed on a tank and dodged sniper fire to thwart the coup, all the while refusing a drink.

Alas, this sober moment of clarity was not how he intended to go on. In the immediate aftermath, as Yeltsin's role as Russian leader was delicately discussed with the three newly separated republics, he got drunk and fell off a chair. This was how he intended to go on.

The consequences were immediate. Driving his country towards democracy, Boris was supposed to be creating a new market economy but drinking and ham-fisted flailing inspired ill-advised, quick-fix solutions followed by a hyperinflation hangover and mass unemployment. In two short years he had passed a wind of political despair and rivals forced a referendum on the issue of his leadership. He very nearly lost when he turned up at a crucial rally hammered, but this narrow escape did little to quell his quaffing.

Reinvigorated, no doubt with more vodka, he quickly launched his own coup to prevent another attempt to de-throne him. He succeeded, but he was oblivious. The win required military intervention and Boris was passed out drunk when the orders were given to save his bacon.

Opposite: Vodka legend Boris Yeltsin.
Above: Khrushchev, Stalin and Churchill.

And so it continued. When he met Kyrgyzstan president Askar Akayev, Boris drank heavily and played the spoons in a percussion style. On Akayev's bald head.

When Boris visited Germany to see the last Russian troops off German soil, he had a few and stopped to perform as an impromptu conductor with a brass band. Part of the act saw him wave his arms and dance in front of the press like a demented goose. His finale was a drunken groan he emitted 'in tune' with the music.

He also once inappropriately handled a female delegate. On camera. It looks like he'd definitely had a drink. Crazy guy. When in Stockholm he compared the face of Björn Borg to meatballs, declared massive cuts in the Russian nuclear stockpile and almost fell off the stage. Drunk. And in 1995, when the man who brought democracy to the East visited its ideological heartland, America, crowned his drinking antics when, after a few, he snuck past secret service bodyguards in his underpants and hailed a taxi in the street in search of pizza.

Political drinking games litter Russian vodka history, all the way up to the 20th century. Stalin was one of the most complicit. The surviving aids of the Soviet Politburo would often leave boozing bouts at dawn. By the 1950s Nikita Khrushchev would claim 'Stalin liteally forced us to drink!' Winston Churchill visited Stalin in 1942 and himself endured overindulgence while discussing World War II, but at least tolerated the toasting game by switching to weaker wine. But none of these displays of drinking compare to Boris, who is a reminder that drinking less but better is a wise approach.

VODKA RECOMMENDATIONS

*From a classic Polish rye grain prizefighter to a Russian supreme premium,
a Canadian craft classic to a Swedish sizzler, here are 10 unmissable vodkas.*

BELUGA

A bolshie big hitter of a vodka and flag-bearer of a more general Russian grain style. Flowers delivered and very welcome on the nose, with a touch of vanilla that carries through to the taste with a lightly fiery pepper and crisp fennel finish. They call it 'premium', but we prefer not to get bogged down in too much marketing guff. Either way it's perfect for drinking straight, the Russian way.

WYBOROWA

A Polish rye grain prizefighter that packs a punch. Take out the gum shield and enjoy its dry, savoury pepper taste, balanced with some sweet relief. Then spray some water in your mouth and spit in a bucket.

VESTAL

The Hawaiian Tropic tanning lotion of vodka, oily with subtle mango and light coconut on the nose, made by small-batch producers who obsess over potato quality. A Polish family-owned vodka, it is designed for mixing and is double-distilled to retain as much character as possible. It won't protect you from the sun if you smear it over your body, but then, in 600 years of its production, there's not really been that much sun to worry about in Poland.

KETEL ONE

The Dutch go with a wheat base here, along with plenty of character, splitting the bill between clean, fresh citrus and a moreish, smooth mouth-feel. The name is derived from the Dutch word for pot still, *distileerketel*. This is also available in flavoured versions.

CRYSTAL HEAD

Don't be tricked by marketing or celebrity endorsement, unless the vodka comes in a skull-shaped bottle and was made by Dan Aykroyd. In which case, *do* be tricked by marketing and celebrity endorsement.

FINLANDIA

Barley vodka from, wait for it, Finland. We like a brand that does something constructive on its label. In the tasting there's a crisp crack of pepper and it's fresher than a teenager on a first date. But it's clean with it, no lingering taste on the tongue when you're done.

AYLESBURY DUCK

Made in the western Rockies, this is a Canadian craft offering to go truly quackers about. Taking its name from a breed of bird reared for eating, it's a perfect wheat-based vodka that's soft and easy to drink. Good to paddle into a mixer, yet better as a neat sip, with sweet ginger flavours before Peking with a subtle rhubarb finish. Shoot it and get in a flap about it. Ducks.

KARLSSON'S GOLD

We love most things from Sweden, the cars, the crime thrillers, the cheap meat hot dogs in Ikea. And when it comes to Swedish spirits, this is one of its best. Potato-based with a natural richness, and a super-smooth, slightly sweet send-off.

CHASE ENGLISH POTATO VODKA

Achingly artisan, Chase Vodka, founded by the eponymous William Chase, goes as far as growing its own potatoes with which to make its vodka, fermenting and distilling gluten-free King Edward and Lady Claire potatoes on its Herefordshire farm site in the UK. The result is a big, creamy vodka. An award-winner.

REYKA

Not much grows on Iceland but vodka does. And by grow, we mean it's distilled here. The country's stab at the spirit includes spring water direct from the Grábrók Spring, found under a 4,000-year-old lava field. This vodka has a barley base that balances buttery notes with a crisp finish.

FLAVOURED VODKA

I n the *Financial Times* of vodka's net value, flavours are the Fortune 500 – a cigar-chomping, leather chair-swivelling bank of plenty. So financially rewarding are flavours that producers have explored every essence imaginable in a bid to tantalise tongues.

But, frankly, it's gone too far, folks. From sad savoury efforts such as salmon to sickly sweet varieties like strawberry bubblegum, faddish flavoured vodkas merely take your money and mug off your maw.

It wasn't always like this. When the Russians and Polish started centuries ago, it was an artisan affair. By the 1600s flavoured vodka was prolific in Russia and Poland but production was far from perfect so, to mask any cheesy feet tang, they added natural ingredients. Amongst the most popular were wormwood (the star of the absinthe show), tree bark, acorns and ash. More palatable were the berries, cherries and natural herbs and spices – all of which were readily available natural ingredients.

Latterly, however, lots of the flavoured vodkas lack subtlety, and sledgehammer our sense of taste

with cloying variants. Taste is subjective but here at Thinking Drinker Towers we draw the line at wedding cake vodka. Really, we do.

If you're looking for artisan authenticity, your best bet is to sample vodkas that infuse genuine ingredients. The worst-case scenario in flavouring is cold-compounding – this involves pouring concentrates directly into the spirit. It's cheap, low-grade flavour fare. So look for natural macerations or infusions where possible.

A rule of thumb when choosing flavours is to stick with citrus. Orange, lemon and grapefruit peels often deliver a fresh and discernible dimension. Belvedere Cytrus is a fine example. Carefully selected Spanish spring and winter lemons (which are sharper) and Colombian limes are macerated, the vodka is then redistilled and

lightly filtered for potent aromas and flavours.

Californian brand Hangar One is another example. With a background in creating *eaux de vies* and a passion for fresh ingredients, Jorg Rupf and former US Navy nuclear engineer, Lance Winters, furnish their vodka with plenty of vivid fruit character.

Hangar One's chipotle and chilli infusion is particularly interesting and other herbs, spices, grasses and light berries work well. Siwucha is a stylish Polish rye with sloes in the mix. English brand Sacred adds Indonesian cubeb berries, angelica, nutmeg and frankincense to the mix. And Zubrówka takes a traditional Polish route by filtering rye vodka through a local grass. Skorppio Vodka has a scorpion in the bottle. We're not above a scorpion in a bottle, who is?

VODKA COCKTAILS

★ ★ ★ ★ ★ ★ ★ ★ ★ ★ ★ ★ ★ ★

VODKA MARTINI

A serve for James Bond of the silver screen, first ordered this way in the film *Dr No* in 1962.

GLASS: MARTINI
60ml (2fl oz) vodka
15ml (3 tsp) dry vermouth
ice cubes

GARNISH: OLIVE OR LEMON ZEST TWIST

Stir the ingredients in a mixing glass with ice and strain into a glass. Garnish with an olive or lemon zest twist.

BLOODY MARY

A fêted first drink for those with a delicate disposition. Created by French bartender Fernand Petiot, and since the French know their cuisine, it must be good.

GLASS: HIGHBALL
50ml (1¾fl oz) vodka
12.5ml (2½ tsp) lemon juice
4 dashes Tabasco
8 dashes Worcestershire sauce
1 bar spoon horseradish
pinch of celery salt
200ml (7fl oz) tomato juice

GARNISH: CELERY STICK AND LEMON SLICE

Rim the edge of a glass with salt and pepper. Place the other ingredients in a shaker, tumble gently and pour into a glass over ice. Garnish with a stick of celery and a slice of lemon, if liked.

BLUE LAGOON

A blue drink. Need we say more? Created in the 1960s by Andy MacElhone, son of Harry from Harry's New York Bar, Paris.

GLASS: HIGHBALL
50ml (1¾fl oz) vodka
50ml (1¾fl oz) blue curaçao
ice cubes
lemonade, to top

GARNISH: MARASCHINO CHERRY AND ORANGE SLICE

Pour the vodka and curaçao into a glass over ice and top with lemonade. Garnish with a maraschino cherry and a slice of lemon.

PHARMACEUTICAL STIMULANT

This is a forerunner to the modern-day classic espresso martini first mixed by Dick Bradsell in 1984 at Fred's Bar in Soho, London.

GLASS: ROCKS
35ml (1¼fl oz) vodka
15ml (3 tsp) Kahlúa
5ml (1 tsp) sugar syrup
30ml (1fl oz) espresso coffee
ice cubes

GARNISH: COFFEE BEANS

Shake all the ingredients hard with ice and strain into a glass over fresh ice. Garnish with fresh coffee beans.

MOSCOW MULE

A marketing gimmick that became a classic when the American owners of the Smirnoff brand mixed the ingredients at the Cock 'n' Bull bar on Sunset Strip in Hollywood.

GLASS: MULE CUP
juice of ½ lime
60ml (2fl oz) vodka
ice cubes
ginger beer, to top

GARNISH: LIME WEDGE AND A SPRIG OF MINT

Cut the lime into quarters and squeeze the juice into a glass or cup, dropping the shells into the drink. Add the vodka and ice, stir and then fill with ginger beer. Garnish with a lime wedge and a sprig of mint.

COSMOPOLITAN

Initially made famous by Dale DeGroff at the Rainbow Rooms, and latterly by *Sex and the City*.

GLASS: MARTINI
40ml (1½fl oz) citrus vodka
15ml (3 tsp) Cointreau
10ml (2 tsp) fresh lime juice
20ml (4 tsp) cranberry juice
ice cubes

GARNISH: FLAMED ORANGE PEEL OR LEMON OR LIME SLICE

Place the ingredients in a shaker, tumble gently and pour into a glass over ice. Garnish with flamed orange peel or slice of lemon or lime.

RUM
SWEET, WHITE, DARK

Rum is a sexy swashbuckler of a spirit, tempting the tongue with a softly, softly stroke, and tasty in your tum. Sporting eye-patch, parrot and peg leg, it yo-ho-hos and hornpipes into a glass just like a pantomime pirate and is aaaaarguably the most amorous companion behind the bar. But best of all, rum is sweet, matey, so if you've avoided it until now, it's time to bounce down the plank and dive in.

HISTORY & CULTURE

Ahoy there! Swashbuckling pirates are a tired rum-drinking stereotype for us to use as a rum hook, no doubt. But if you've been reading this book up until now (have you?) then you'll understand this is hardly a barrier for its writers. Besides, there's plenty of jollying and rogering to be done when you've had a few glasses of the stuff. Are we right, you guys? Except, of course, quite a few pirates were rapists and murderers. Some of them even nailed innocent captives to the deck, others hung them from the mainsail, and modern-day pirates take over freight carriers with very unromantic AK47s. So it's worth emphasising that, while rum's bountiful estery bananas, pungent pineapples, voluptuous vanilla backdrop and sweet sugar heart might charm the chops, behind the fancy-dress façade is a pokey punch of alcohol that'll run you through like a cutlass.

Rum might well revel in this roguish status, assuming it was a person with feelings and that. Certainly it's preferable to rum's previously perceived guise of something thick and gummy that old Uncle Albert drank. If you didn't have an uncle Albert in the family, he tended to be a salty old seaman with a sun-bleached beard who, irrespective of your interest, regaled you with tall tales about taller mainsails and wars he missed, all while downing dark, treacly, navy rum. Navy styles still

exist and Albert is very welcome to use the spirit to fuel his yarns (lies), but rum doesn't need to live on past glories, as it's in the midst of a remarkable and rather refined renaissance.

Today, rum retains the wanderlust it enjoyed at conception, but more than that, it has acheived 'cool'. This is possibly fine by you, but added to its cool is the fact that it's sweet. For those taking their first trepidatious steps into dark aged spirits, then rum represents a perfect place to start exploring barrel-aged booze.

Rum's history is as up and down as high-sea ships and the dubious morals of a pirate. Integrally linked with sugar, the spirit emerged from the countries that tied up the cane trade, first the Portuguese in Brazil and then the Dutch, French, Spanish and English in the Caribbean. While the sugar was sweet, the behaviour of the Europeans was anything but, and this period of global expansion was accompanied by the unpleasant, nefarious slave trade. The triangular exchange of humans for goods lasted centuries, from the first public sale of an African slave in 1444 to the 1780s, when one slave ship left Britain every other day and half the slaves on board would die during the voyages. It's an inescapable blight on rum's otherwise righteous passage into today's glasses.

Having travelled the world, sugar cane was first consumed in fermented liquid form and Alexander the Great recalls drinking an early sweet treat in India in the 4th century BC. When it was eventually distilled in Brazil, it became cachaça and then evolved again in the Caribbean during the 17th century to become the rum we know today. It appeared in print when the likes of Richard Ligon recorded Caribbean life in his book *A True and Exact History of the Island of Barbados* in 1647, and it soon became a global spirit, traded and enjoyed by the very countries that had fought for the land in the region, the landlubbers on the shores of England and the east coast of America.

As soon as it seeped off stills, rum was remarkably popular, so much so, that some even went to war for the spirit. When the English tried to invoke a tax on the American's supply it sparked a revolt. Long before the Boston Tea Party, it was the impact on the diminished supply of rum that really rankled.

Meanwhile, rum's association with boats kept it on the move. Far from being an exclusive preserve of pirates, it also worked its way into the wages of the British Navy. Not everyone thought that giving sailors rum daily was a good idea. By 1850 insurance companies were cottoning on, reducing rates for captains who banned booze.

Wherever sugar went, rum would follow, so today we can indulge in beautiful boutique

brands from across the Caribbean, Central and South America and beyond, with no restrictions on where it is made.

And while rum is cool, it's not pretentious, it doesn't sneer at you through fake-lens, horn-rimmed glasses as it passes you on a single-speed bike. No, rum is fun. It basks in the sunshine, donning swimming trunks no other man would dare to wear. It fuels the extrovert, including the bikini-clad winged whiners from the epic carnivals in the Caribbean and Brazil. With a healthy sense of humour, it has sparked cocktails like the Pina Colada and Zombie and inspired the Polynesian tiki party that started life in the 1930s.

It's a wicked spirit, in all senses of the word, and is one of the favourites at Thinking Drinker Towers. We're confident that, once you take the time to cosy up to it, you'll be on board. Because, you know, like ships and things. On board a ship. On board. Ahoy there?

Left: Some tiki mugs do 'sad face' but you'll be happy drinking rum. *Above*: Sugar cane. It's what you make rum with.

Rum has a history and this is it. It's a history at a glance, so you can just glance. And it's presented in a timeline. So you follow rum history, over time. We, know, it's pretty good, right?

6000 BC SOME DUDES WHO DIG IN THE GROUND DISCOVERED EVIDENCE THAT SUGAR CANE WAS GROWING IN INDONESIA AND INDIA AT THIS TIME.

326 BC ALEXANDER THE GREAT'S NAVARCH NEARCHUS (NAVAL LEADER) HOLIDAYS ON THE INDUS RIVER AND SEES LOCALS KICKING BACK WITH FERMENTED SUGAR CANE DRINKS.

1493 CHRISTOPHER COLUMBUS TAKES SUGAR CANE WITH HIM ON GLOBAL ESCAPADES AND PLANTS IT WHEREVER HE CAN.

1625 BRAZIL HAS BECOME THE SUGAR CAPITAL OF THE WORLD AND IS EXPORTING THE HIGHLY DESIRED SWEET TREAT TO EUROPE.

1595 SUGAR MILLS NOW OPERATE IN CUBA, JAMAICA AND PUERTO RICO.

1563 SIR FRANCIS DRAKE SETS SAIL FOR THE CARIBBEAN, ALL THE WHILE DRINKING WHAT IS BELIEVED TO BE A SUGAR-BASED DISTILLATE.

1655 BUCCANEER HENRY 'CAPTAIN' MORGAN SWAPS SWASHBUCKLING FOR SUGAR PLANTATIONS IN JAMAICA AND PICKS UP A KNIGHTHOOD.

1635 HEALTH AND SAFETY GETS THE BETTER OF THE BRAZILIAN AUTHORITIES AS THEY BAN SUGAR DISTILLATE CACHAÇA.

1637 DUTCHMAN PIETRE BLOWER BRINGS SUGAR CANE SEEDS TO BARBADOS ON HIS TRAVELS.

1655 VICE ADMIRAL WILLIAM PENN NOTES THE ANTI-FRENCH FEELING ON BOARD HIS SHIP AND SWAPS THE CREW'S DAILY BRANDY RATION FOR RUM.

1687 A RUM RATION BECOMES A PART OF THE BRITISH SAILOR'S WAGE.

1672 THE DUKE OF YORK IS NAMED THE GOVERNOR FOR THE ROYAL AFRICAN COMPANY. IN 17 YEARS IT IS RESPONSIBLE FOR TRANSPORTING NEARLY 90,000 SLAVES.

1660 THE PORTUGUESE LEVY TAXES ON CACHAÇA IN BRAZIL, INSPIRING A REVOLUTION IN RIO DE JANEIRO.

1690 RUM IS BEING PRODUCED ON THE EAST COAST OF AMERICA.

1703 MOUNT GAY RUM COMPANY IS FOUNDED.

1733 THE BRITISH TAKE THEIR FIRST STAB AT A SUGAR & MOLASSES ACT, IN A BID TO FORCE AMERICANS TO BUY SUGAR FROM BRITISH ISLANDS. THE AMERICANS TELL THE BRITISH TO GET LOST.

1740 VICE-ADMIRAL EDWARD VERNON ORDERS THE TAMING OF THE RUM RATION BY MIXING IT WITH WATER. HE ALSO DEMANDS THE ADDITION OF LIME AND SUGAR TO MAKE IT MORE PALATABLE, CREATING AN EARLY DAIQUIRI, OR PUNCH.

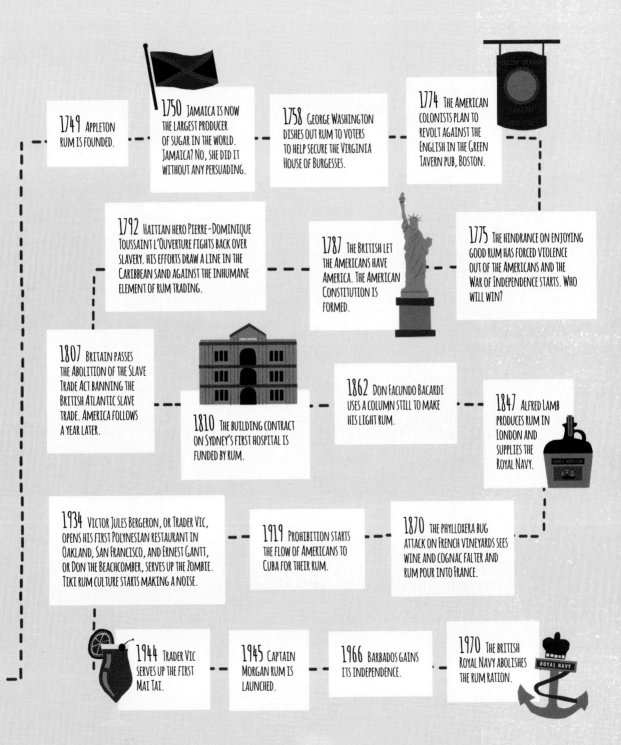

1749 APPLETON RUM IS FOUNDED.

1750 JAMAICA IS NOW THE LARGEST PRODUCER OF SUGAR IN THE WORLD. JAMAICA? NO, SHE DID IT WITHOUT ANY PERSUADING.

1758 GEORGE WASHINGTON DISHES OUT RUM TO VOTERS TO HELP SECURE THE VIRGINIA HOUSE OF BURGESSES.

1774 THE AMERICAN COLONISTS PLAN TO REVOLT AGAINST THE ENGLISH IN THE GREEN TAVERN PUB, BOSTON.

1792 HAITIAN HERO PIERRE-DOMINIQUE TOUSSAINT L'OUVERTURE FIGHTS BACK OVER SLAVERY. HIS EFFORTS DRAW A LINE IN THE CARIBBEAN SAND AGAINST THE INHUMANE ELEMENT OF RUM TRADING.

1787 THE BRITISH LET THE AMERICANS HAVE AMERICA. THE AMERICAN CONSTITUTION IS FORMED.

1775 THE HINDRANCE ON ENJOYING GOOD RUM HAS FORCED VIOLENCE OUT OF THE AMERICANS AND THE WAR OF INDEPENDENCE STARTS. WHO WILL WIN?

1807 BRITAIN PASSES THE ABOLITION OF THE SLAVE TRADE ACT BANNING THE BRITISH ATLANTIC SLAVE TRADE. AMERICA FOLLOWS A YEAR LATER.

1810 THE BUILDING CONTRACT ON SYDNEY'S FIRST HOSPITAL IS FUNDED BY RUM.

1862 DON FACUNDO BACARDI USES A COLUMN STILL TO MAKE HIS LIGHT RUM.

1847 ALFRED LAMB PRODUCES RUM IN LONDON AND SUPPLIES THE ROYAL NAVY.

1934 VICTOR JULES BERGERON, OR TRADER VIC, OPENS HIS FIRST POLYNESIAN RESTAURANT IN OAKLAND, SAN FRANCISCO, AND ERNEST GANTT, OR DON THE BEACHCOMBER, SERVES UP THE ZOMBIE. TIKI RUM CULTURE STARTS MAKING A NOISE.

1919 PROHIBITION STARTS THE FLOW OF AMERICANS TO CUBA FOR THEIR RUM.

1870 THE PHYLLOXERA BUG ATTACK ON FRENCH VINEYARDS SEES WINE AND COGNAC FALTER AND RUM POUR INTO FRANCE.

1944 TRADER VIC SERVES UP THE FIRST MAI TAI.

1945 CAPTAIN MORGAN RUM IS LAUNCHED.

1966 BARBADOS GAINS ITS INDEPENDENCE.

1970 THE BRITISH ROYAL NAVY ABOLISHES THE RUM RATION.

HEMINGWAY

It's a challenge to deliver a spiel on Hemingway that's anything except ernest. It was his name after all. Meanwhile, this legend's prose is lauded to the point where parody is impossible.

We will say this much: Hemingway was impatient. Renowned for his short. Lean. Pared. Back. Sentences. He didn't like to wait in life. Just ask his four wives.

He didn't have a lot of time for dying either, typing his own full stop by firing a shotgun at his head. Beyond that though (and despite the fact his mum dressed him as a girl), the man became an icon of virility, chiselled and carved while boxing at school or during early journalism stints at the *Kansas City Star* where he balanced drinking bouts with brilliant copy.

As an ambulance man in World War I Hemingway put neck and legs on the line when he suffered a serious shrapnel injury, picking up a medal of valour and a doomed love affair with his nurse along the way. This mix of merriment and machismo advanced his beefcake traits, but more importantly, influenced his work, with *The Sun Also Rises, A Farewell to Arms* and *Death in the Afternoon*, all put together with a drink on the go.

But as a rum hero we catch up with him in Cuba. In November 1932, Hemingway had scarpered from his newborn's nappies to join a friend on a two-week Cuban vacation. They were Havan... a great time, and, oblivious to parental obligations, Hemingway stayed for two months, fishing for marlin and knocking back rum at the Floridita bar in the evenings. He acquired a taste for Cuba and decided to stay for a further 20 years, becoming a rum-drinking regular at

Floridita and earning himself a life-size bronze statue at the bar. Unlike many other fleeting famous patrons, Hemingway really did drink there. A lot. His days and nights in Cuba were rum- soaked and barefoot, he bet on jai alai matches, indulged in game-fishing and shot pigeons at the Club de Cazadore, all while downing his trademark rum daiquiris.

The rum preserved Hemingway's courageous spirit and during World War II he rounded up a band of Nazi hunters and convinced the American Ambassador to finance upgrades to his own beloved fishing boat, the *Pilar*. Armed with bazookas, hand grenades and machine guns, he amassed a rum-addled crew comprising jai alai players, a salty sea dog nicknamed Sinbad, a Catholic priest, tramps and waiters from Floridita. He called it the Crook Factory. They searched for U-boats and didn't find any, but they did throw grenades at fish and Hemingway still managed to earn a medal for these exploits.

Hemingway didn't restrict himself to rum and would consume martinis mixed at a ratio of 15 gin to 1 vermouth. But certainly rum was a favourite. During his residency in Cuba, he wrote *The Old Man and the Sea* and won the highly prestigious Pulitzer Prize in 1954, proving he could stir a drink and yet still deliver. The Cuban revolution eventually forced Hemingway from his beloved Caribbean home, and shortly afterwards he commited suicide, but the words live on, as does his love affair with rum.

RUM

KENIA

Florida

New York

Ernest
Hemingway

RUM BORE BAR TIPS

SUGAR, OH HONEY HONEY

Sugar cane is a grass and in some places it is still harvested by men called cutters.

The cane is pressed to extract the water, then crushed to get the sugary juice. This cane juice can be fermented, but more commonly it is then boiled and treated to make sugar, the by-product being molasses, which is thick and black. The molasses is diluted, fermented and distilled to give you your rum.

LEGALS

Rum is any spirit made from sugar, either cane juice or molasses, and can be distilled anywhere. Famous in the Caribbean and South America, it is also produced in countries like India and Australia. When rum was first exported to Australia it was used as currency to finance buildings and catch criminals, and you could buy a wife with a gallon of the stuff. We don't know how much more you had to find to give her back, arf, arf.

IN THE NAVY

The British navy included a rum ration in the sailor's salary and rumour has it they would check its quality by pouring it over gunpowder. If the gunpowder successfully lit, it was proof the rum was alcoholic enough. It needed to be around the 57% mark to light, equating to the 100% proof term you still see on American bottles today. It also gave us the term Navy Strength.

BLUDFIRE

A naval term for rum in Nelson's blood. When transported back from his final battle at Trafalgar, Admiral Nelson was pickled in a potable. When he arrived in port the rum had disappeared, consumed by a rum thirsty crew. Was this true? We don't know, we weren't there.

GOT WOOD

Ageing is important in rum, it darkens the spirit, rounds and imparts flavour and usually happens in old bourbon casks. In tropical climates the pores of the wood open up so the spirit takes on more of the wood character over a shorter time compared to Scotland. Because wood is porous the spirit can evaporate and be lost. This is romantically often called the 'Angel's Share'.

WORD PLAY

The etymology of 'rum' is attributed to many sources; among the best are: an abbreviation from the Latin for sugar, *Saccharum*; rummage (an English ship's hold and what people did when they searched for cane spirit in their pockets); Brum, possibly after sugar cane fields in the Midlands (not true), but more likely after a drink Dutch sailors had in Malaya.

RHUM AGRICOLE

A very particular style that uses fermented cane juice

rather than molasses. The juice has to be used fresh and is harvested and crushed with rollers, giving this rum a very different taste from its molasses counterparts. It's an artisan product protected by an Appellation d'Origine Contrôlée.

DUNDER HEAD

Dunder is something used to enhance the esters that arrive in the most pungent rums. Dunder is a non-alcoholic residue left after distillation and is buried in the ground to attract bacteria. It's added during fermentation and raises the acidity to promote the esters, particularly in Jamaican pot still rum. Smells bad, makes the rum taste good.

ESTERS

Not a lovely little old lady with a name like Mabelle or Maude. No, these are the basic but all important flavour compounds that are created during the fermentation process. You'll find them in the most pungent rums where they contribute abundant banana and nail polish aromas.

STYLE IT OUT

You can select your rum according to some general styles:

❦

WHITE RUM: Colourless and usually not aged, although in some cases it has been aged then charcoal filtered to remove the colour. Sometimes light and usually crisp, they are blends and can also be pungent and aromatic.

❦

AGED RUM: Divided into two categories with nothing to officially determine each, but you'll see 'golden' and 'dark' as a general guideline. Golden rum has spent less time in oak but, as the name suggests, is golden. Dark will have spent more time in oak and quality examples will be rich and spicy.

❦

NAVY RUM: Part of the dark rum family and invariably a lighter column-still-style blended with pot still and heavier, sweet Demerara rum.

❦

SPICED RUM: From a golden rum base with a variety of spices added; brands like Kraken and Sailor Jerry are particularly popular.

❦

THE ANATOMY OF A RUM STILL

Here comes a science bit. Read it, or don't, up to you. Either way, deal with it, this book has 'thinking' in the title and you need to do some to understand how rum is made.

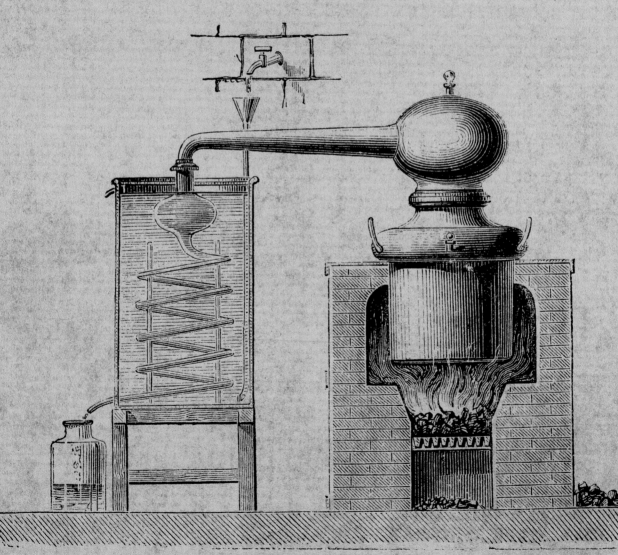

A distillate is made in a still that converts low alcohol to high, and there are two styles: pot still and column/continuous. Both are used for rum.

Fer-mental

Before we get to the pot, we need a fermented (alcoholic) liquid, which is low in alcohol content, much like beer (see Yeast page 24). In the case of rum the sugars come from cane juice or molasses. To distilling, this alcoholic is liquid boiled and the steam condensed, separating the alcohol compounds from the water and collected at a much higher alcohol by volume, or proof.

Pot

The pot still is the original distillation device, conceived in the ninth century by Arabic alchemist Abu Musa Jabir ibn Hayyan, or Gerber as he's known in the western world. This über clever clogs purposely wrote out his miraculous distillation methods in strange code, which the Europeans subsequently struggled to translate, and from 'Gerber' we arrived at the word 'gibberish'.

Today, Gerber's pot principles continue to apply roughly to whisky, brandy, bourbon, tequila and rum. Fermented liquid is heated and its constituent parts, alcohol and water, separate. Ethanol boils at 78.3°C (173°F), vaporising before water (boiling at 100°C/212°F). Vaporised alcoholic flavour compounds rise up the pot and start to condense into high-volume spirit. The most volatile compounds reach the top first, these are bad for us, so condense and are cut as the 'heads'. Then follow the safer of the lighter compounds, containing fresh fruit and floral aromatics. The heavier come last, and develop into flavours ranging from ripe fruit to leather. Finally, we hit the rank 'off notes'. The trick is to collect what you want, the 'heart', and cut off the rest, known as the 'tails'. All the way they interact with copper, which removes unwanted sulphur notes.

In most cases the condensed flavour compounds are captured, according to the style of spirit the distiller prefers, over two or possibly three runs. But for rum, distillers also use retorts. These are separate vessels and enable the distiller to further manipulate the compounds to exaggerate flavours. Rum distillers also use dunder at fermentation (see page 153) if they are looking to make high ester rums with big banana flavours.

Each distiller uses the stills differently, but if you're looking for great examples then Appleton in Jamaica is a heavy pot rum style, while R.L. Seale from Barbados is lighter.

Column Still

The column still was patented in 1830 by Aeneas Coffey (see page 72) and put to excellent use in rum in 1862 when Don Facundo Bacardi made his first spirit. Coffey used two columns, linked together, and his principles still apply.

The fermented alcohol is introduced at the top of a 'rectifier' column, which it passes through in a pipe and is heated – arriving at a second 'stripping' column as hot liquid. Steam is pumped into the bottom of this column. As the fermented liquid hits the steam, the alcohol boils off and the alcoholic compounds rise back into the bottom of the rectifier. As this steam rises, it heats the cool pipes carrying fermented liquid on its way down, and each time it hits one of a series of plates, it starts to condense again. The distiller takes the spirit from the plates he wants, being able to easily identify the heads, hearts and tails. The process allows the distiller to easily isolate lighter compounds to create a safe, highly rectified spirit.

Multiple stills include a hydro selection column to remove fuel oils and a de-methylising column to reduce methanol. Not all of the column-produced rums are light. If the spirit is pulled off the still at a lower strength, it will have more flavour.

CACHAÇA RUM & SPORT

Two of Brazil's natural expressions are football and the domestic sugar-cane spirit, and one man embodies them both: the phenomenal footballer Manuel Francisco dos Santos or 'Garrincha' – the 'little bird'.

Hard as it might be to believe, this book was compiled by two trained journalists. Bit of a shocker, eh? But it's true, we are actual journalists and everything. While honing our skills at real journalism college, we were ingrained with the understanding that every good news article must lead with the strongest element of the story – the crucial hook that draws the reader in during the opening paragraph of a tightly worded and interesting news piece.

So it is then, as we labour this introduction about a Brazilian sports star, having clearly learned very little, we juggle multiple nuggets and decide that, while we could celebrate his exquisite prowess on a football pitch, his penchant for a pint of cachaça or, indeed, his pooh-poohing of global celebrity in exchange for an undying devotion to his homeland, we would rather lead with the fact that Manuel Francisco dos Santos, or 'Garrincha', lost his virginity to a goat (or so it is claimed).

It is not our aim to undermine this football icon, far from it, since the World Cup winner's often peerless performances make him one of the best the sport has ever seen. Added to which he enjoyed cachaça, or Brazilian rum, making him a drinker who also achieved something. Even so, when we discovered in Ruy Castro's exceptional book *Garrincha*, that, aged 12, he bypassed the inconvenient disparity between adolescent lust and reciprocated female affection, by seeking sexy time with a goat, well, what could we do? Ignore it? Apparently it was common in his Pau Grande village. Even so. Who's he kidding?

OK, we'll leave that alone (which is what Garrincha might've done, since the genetic disposition for kicking makes the goat a

Manuel Francisco dos Santos, or Garrincha, the 'little bird', mugs off yet another defender.

dangerous bedfellow), let's not milk it... because the coming together of Brazil's football and its cachaça is what we'd rather dwell on.

Rarely appreciated outside its homeland, Brazil's cachaça derives from cane juice rather than molasses and is, remarkably, the second biggest selling spirit in the world. Its crowd-pleasing serve is the Caipirinha cocktail, a drink that, rightly or wrongly (wrongly), Garrincha poured for breakfast, having suggested to his wife he simply liked lime – and to be fair, there is a lot of vitamin C in the drink.

While Pelé might be football's most eminent Brazilian export, it is Garrincha who is prized by the purist. An extraordinary dribbler, he mesmerised defences, duping all and sundry with his trickery, and when Pele was injured ahead of the 1962 World Cup, it was Garrincha who dominated, collecting the Golden Boot for scoring the most goals and leading Brazil to victory.

The ball stuck to Garrincha like a man with molasses on his boot. He once weaved around an entire defence and a goalkeeper, and, facing an open goal, waited for a defender to return before he ghosted past him again and scored. This sense of humour endeared him to Brazilian fans.

Born with several almost crippling physical defects, Garrincha achieved sporting legend status despite having a right leg that bent inwards and was 15cm (6in) longer than the left one, which curved outwards. And his spine was deformed. Yet even this couldn't contain his sprightly skill.

Despite the plaudits he garnered, he rarely indulged in the celebrity that accompanied his talent and when courted by Real Madrid he refused to quit Brazilian club Botafogo, preferring to stay in his country of birth. Garrincha was happier heading home for Christmas to turn out for his former factory side, competing in a friendly each year against the factory owners. The prize was beer and cachaça, the winners drinking while the losers watched, and naturally Garrincha was always on the winning side.

Garrincha was a prolific scorer with the ladies too. The 'alleged' incident with the goat barely set him back and he subsequently fathered 14 children with five different women, including the celeb-rated Samba singer Elza Soares, doing much of his carousing with a drink in his hand.

Granted there was the tragic incident when he drove into a potato truck and killed his mother-in-law, so his life wasn't without its downs.

Meanwhile, despairing club officials lambasted Garrincha's cachaça-inducing calorific intake, his battle with the bulge being a constant misgiving. But in spite of this, he was twice a World Cup winner, and the way that he succeeded in spite of himself struck a chord with Brazilians who adored his artistry on the field and most of his antics off it. Thousands of people attended Garrincha's funeral, bringing the surrounding area to a standstill as fans abandoned cars on motorways to see his casket, carried by a fire engine to his grave in the village where he was born. The coffin proved too big for the hole, an irony for the "little bird" who could thread a ball through the legs of every single defender he faced.

Choosing Cachaca

If you fancy experimenting with cachaça then sample something aged. Beija Flor grows its own sugar cane and is a trusted brand, with its Pura aged for a year. Elsewhere, the Avuá Amburana Cachaça is matured for two years in the rare Brazilian hardwood amburana. And Armazem Vieira Terra takes things to the next level with a 12-year-old that spends two years in Brazilian grápia wood and 10 in Brazilian aribá wood.

RUM SWASHBUCKLERS
THE TOP SEAFARING RUM RASCALS

PIRATES LOVED RUM. THIS IS NOT NEWS. THEY LOVED SKULLS AND DUGGERY, PARROTS AND PEG LEGS, BOUNTY AND BOOTY, AND, THEY LOVED RUM. BUT FINDING A RUM-SOAKED PIRATE WHO EFFICIENTLY SHIVERED HIS OTHER PIRATE TIMBERS IS NOT SO STRAIGHTFORWARD. Take Bartholomew 'Black Bart' Roberts. Here is a sea-based scoundrel who captured 400 ships in three years, accrued a bounty worth £50 million in today's earnings, blew his foe down, and when he fought the Navy was shot through the throat and buried at sea. A true pirate. But then we discover that Roberts was a teetotaller – literally, as in he drank tea! That's no good. No good at all. So he's a rubbish pirate. Then you've got Howell Davis, an inspiration for Roberts and a squiffy swashbuckler whose dastardly deeds and yo-ho ho-ing haunted any legitimate high seas traveller. Alas, when trying to loot a Spanish vessel, Davis was so plastered on rum he needed 20 attempts at broadsiding the target. Embarrassing to say the least. Perhaps unsurprisingly, his affection for rum saw him quickly caught and killed in an ambush. Great rum drinker then, but not so proficient in the plundering.

These are the frustrations you face when searching for your favourite pirate, but worry ye not, because we have delved into the deep sea chest of pirate archives and pulled out the pick of the rum-drinking pirates. Here they are:

SIR FRANCIS DRAKE

PIRATE RANKING: 6
RUM RANKING: 8

A potential pioneer of the pirate pack. Except… Drake was actually a privateer, a man who was licensed to plunder, splitting his bounty with the Queen. He loses a lot of points there. Even so, Drake was a rule breaker and made a scurvy knave of himself, his one-man war against the Spanish ignored enough orders to qualify for skull-and-crossbones status. In 1579, commanding his ship the *Golden Hinde*, he attacked the Spanish craft *Cacafuego* (translating to 'fire shitter', apparently) and stole the largest bounty ever recorded, £100,000 million by today's pieces of eight. The Spanish called him El Draque, or the dragon, since he was always chasing them, and he was knighted for his efforts. Olé.

Drake recognised the medicinal value of a sip of spirit and encouraged the ritual among the crew. After a particularly blood-soaked battle in the Caribbean, shipmates reportedly licked wounds with rum, sugar, medicinal mint and lime, mixing up the first mojito. A tale as tall as Drake's mainsail, not least because, while they sipped a sugar-based spirit, 'rum' was not recorded in print for another 50 years. So on the one hand Drake's not a rum man but, on the other hook, he gave us one of the biggest cocktail bar calls in the world, and that's the hook we'll go with.

BLACKBEARD

PIRATE RANKING: 9
RUM RANKING: 10

SIR HENRY MORGAN

PIRATE RANKING: 7
RUM RANKING: 7

A Welsh buccaneer – not a privateer but not quite a pirate. Points dropped, although Morgan creatively focused his plundering on cities because the British government demanded that sea bounty be split, while spoils of land went entirely to the victor. Very piratey. Hugely successful, Morgan took Panama in 1670, which Drake couldn't manage, and his exploits eventually earned him a knighthood. Some accounts describe his bride as 'the daughter of his uncle'… so his cousin then. Dirty devil.

But was Morgan a true rum drinker? When he pillaged Puerto Principe in Cuba, he weighed anchor and sailed to Jamaica with a hearty 250,000 pesos for his troubles. His crew fritted away the loot on rum, while he bought land. Boring. That said, no other pirate has a rum brand named after him so points even out there.

Edward Teach, Thatch, or 'Blackbeard' was a pirate with a black beard – it was a remarkable coincidence. He wore belts with loads of guns attached and dangled flaming candles from his facial hair. If he suspected any crew of mutiny, he took them all below deck and randomly started shooting salty seamen in the dark. He sailed during the golden age of pirates, buried his treasure and was hunted and killed by the navy. And he achieved all this in two short years. He earns top marks for an an epic last stand in 1718 (see below), and only loses a point for not completely making it down to Davy Jones's locker – the navy kept his decapitated head as a trophy.

Blackbeard was a rum drinker and his crew fought like animals for him when loaded to the gunwales. When the ship ran dry, they got confused and plotted mutiny. The night before his final battle he heard the navy encroach, but drank through regardless. Then, as he sailed into close-quarter battle he demanded more rum as he attacked. It needed 20 hacks of a sword and five gunshots before he went down, so infused with rum was he. His decapitated head was later stolen and used as a rum punch bowl, ensuring that even after his death, his rum legacy lived on.

AROUND THE WORLD IN A SELECTION OF RUMS

Well, around the parts of the world that make quality rum. If you're trying to convince a doubting dinner guest to sample rum, then serve it with dessert. Or tell them to get out of your house for being so rude.

BARBADOS

The historic home of rum boasting 300 years of production. Expect proud pot-still rums here, chock full of depth and body. **Foursquare Distillery** embraces traditional values but injects modern panache with a wide range of brands, but try **Doorly's XO**, rich versus spicy, toffee and vanilla butting up to sultanas, nuts and bananas. Match with caramelised banana for a rich and rewarding sweet and toffeeish experience.

JAMAICA

Jamaican life presents an incongruously complex relationship – a slap in the face with one hand, an immediate all-is-forgiven stroke with the other. This combustible conundrum sums up the rum and **Appleton Estate** is an excellent exponent. Big, bold, pokey pot-still creations, intense but with sweet rich qualities. The VX tickles the tongue with voluptuous vanilla, toffee and banana before a spicy orange kick to the throat at the end. Match with Jamaican ginger cake. Seriously.

TRINIDAD

An industrial hub and home to one of the biggest carnival blowouts in the world. Trinidad's cultural blend of science and irreverence flows through its rum. The **Angostura** distillery plays both boffin and bon vivant, with sky-scraping column stills engineering note-perfect spirit primed for parties. Try the 1919: its white chocolate whines up front before oaky spice sambas through the centre, culminating in a light, moreish funky chicken finish. Match with a luxury light, milk chocolate. Or a cheap one.

MARTINIQUE

This French-owned island, part of the Antilles, does things a little differently with **Rhum Agricole** being the *style de maison*, using vesou or fresh sugar cane juice. The **Rhum J.M.** distillery is amongst the best, using volcanic soil. J.M. Blanc is an assertive example of raw product, rested for four months before bottling, it amuses then blasts the *bouche* with fiery pepper, fresh tropical fruits and a flippant earthy finish. Serve with cheese or after-dinner dancing.

HAITI

A country infamously off the hook, Haiti's rum is conversely high class. Famed for its French style, using vesou in the mix, **Barbancourt's Five Star** brand deserves its self-appointed status. Considerably more entertaining than a 1980s pop band, it revels in a heritage born from Cognac and is distilled in column and pot stills, then aged for eight years in Limousin oak, bestowing it with rich, ripe banana and an abundance of tropical fruit flavours. Serve with apricot and almond pudding.

GUATEMALA

Central America was primarily concerned with caffeine but joined the rum revolution in the 20th century. Today it is recognised for sweet, snappily dressed rums. In **Zacapa** they have one of the best in the world, with an average age of 23 years aged at 2330m (7645ft). Using a solera style technique used in sherry production, it delivers a dashing drop of cocoa. The chocolate hit on the rum is really quite extraordinary.

GUYANA

Geographically speaking South American but spiritually speaking Caribbean, Guyana doesn't suffer from confusion in its rum, with Demerara sugar steadfastly at its heart. Famous for the deep, soft rums in Navy styles, the **Diamond Distillery,** in particular, uses the sugar source to create righteous rums and perhaps more astoundingly does so with wooden stills. The column still here is the oldest operating Coffey still in the world. Try the **El Dorado 15-year-old,** an archetype for aged rums that is as sweet and sultry as you'd expect from Demerara, with rich, ripe banana and some citrus spice from the wood to balance. Serve it poured over chocolate brownies and ice cream.

161

RUM COCKTAILS

★ ★

MARY PICKFORD

An ode to the rum-drinking actress, a true leading lady.

GLASS: WINE OR MARTINI
50ml (1¾fl oz) rum
2 dashes maraschino liqueur
50ml (1¾fl oz) pineapple juice
1 tsp grenadine
ice cubes

Shake all the ingredients with ice and strain into a glass.

DAIQUIRI

Any seafarer worth his salt, or indeed sugar, would've added a sweetener and lime to a cane spirit on his travels. Dispute reigns over the best design for the Daiquiri.

DAIQUIRI NUM. 1

As taken from the Bar La Florida *Cocktails* recipe book (1935). In Cuba today it's ordered as a 'Natural Daiquiri', meaning not blended.

GLASS: MARTINI
60ml (2fl oz) white rum
1 tsp caster sugar
juice of half a lime
GARNISH: LIME WEDGE

Shake well on ice and strain into a cocktail glass. Garnish with lime.

DAIQUIRI HEMINGWAY/ PAPA DOBLE

Hemingway didn't muck about when it came to his Daiquiri. Since his daunting drinking prowess at Floridita, his signature drink has been tamed slightly but he was said to order plenty of rum and no sugar.

GLASS: MARTINI OR COUPE
90ml (3fl oz) white rum
6 dashes maraschino liqueur
juice of 2 limes
juice of half a grapefruit
shaved ice

Add all the ingredients to a blender, one-quarter full of shaved ice. Blend for a few seconds and pour into a glass.

MOJITO CUBAN-STYLE

As necessary to the diet as cigars, beans and revolutions, this Cuban staple is best when served up and enjoyed in the famous Bodeguita del Medio bar, Havana.

GLASS: HIGHBALL
Large lime wedge
60ml (2fl oz) rum
6 fresh mint leaves
1 tsp caster sugar
soda water and ice, to top
GARNISH: SPRIG OF MINT

Squeeze the juice from the wedge then add to glass. Add the rum, mint and sugar. Top with soda water and ice. Stir lightly and garnish with mint.

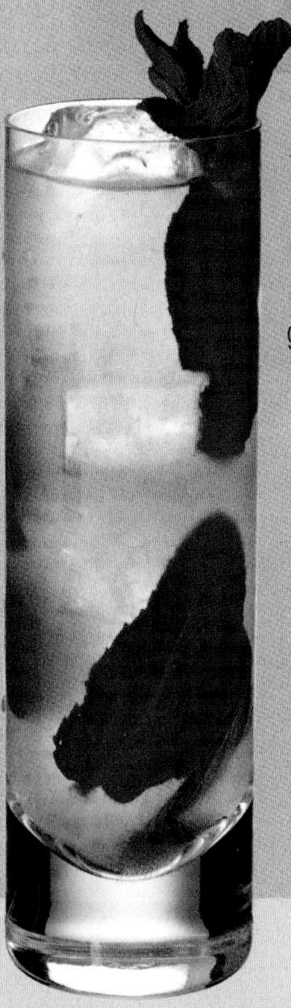

PLANTER'S PUNCH

A maritime mainstay – the name is taken from the hindi word *panch*, meaning five – this is a blend of spirit with temperers and vitamin C tonics that travelled back with 17th century seamen had probed the Indian Ocean. This particular serve of the drink became a mainstay at the Planter's Hotel in Charleston, South Carolina, during the 19th century.

GLASS: HIGHBALL
60ml (2fl oz) dark rum
dash aromatic bitters
4 tsp lemon juice
½ tsp sugar syrup
ice cubes
sparkling water, to top
GARNISH: DRIED PINEAPPLE SLICE

Shake the first four ingredients with ice, strain into a glass over fresh ice, top with sparkling water and stir once. Garnish with a dried pineapple slice and drink with a straw.

PINA COLADA

Vaguely attributed to Puerto Rican pirate Roberto Cofresi, who nailed his victims to the deck before kicking back with pineapple and rum. This cocktail gets its first mention in the *American Travel* magazine (1922), without coconut.

GLASS: HURRICANE
50ml (1¾fl oz) white rum
75ml (2½fl oz) pineapple juice
25ml (1fl oz) Coco Lopez cream
  of coconut
25ml (1fl oz) single cream
300ml (½ pint) cracked ice
GARNISH: PINEAPPLE CHUNK
  AND MARASCHINO CHERRY

Blend all the ingredients together with the cracked ice for several seconds. Pour into a glass. Garnish with a Maraschino cherry and a slice of pineapple.

GIN
Genever Juniper

Despite its Dutch history, gin is as quintessentially
British in origin as a packet of pork scratchings in a pub
garden. Brimming with botanicals, it's the garden that
grows on you and, with a burgeoning bevy of new gin styles
arriving on shop shelves, even the most cack-handed
horticulturists will find a herb and spice mix to cultivate.
So, continuing this garden analogy, why not
roll up your sleeves and dig into gin?

HISTORY & CULTURE

The drink of royalty, movie stars and literary legends, of bounders, braggarts and bon vivants, gin has, at times, been cast simultaneously both as hero and villain of the drinks cabinet – and even found itself labelled as a libation for little old ladies with blue hair.

Mercifully we're currently revelling in a gin renaissance. The spirit has recently established itself as the cool kid in the bar classroom, someone with an edge who does kissyface with the best-looking girls and earns an effortless A-grade. But its history is long, so it's unsurprising to learn gin has underperformed during past school terms, perhaps even earning an expulsion for seriously bad behaviour. Because gin has some roguish stories in its locker and it has been a long battle to get the botanical wonder back in the good books.

Gin's origins are intrinsically linked to juniper and it was originally used for medicinal purposes. Juniper has long been celebrated for its curative powers – it has been infused in liquids for thousands of years. Versatile in its application, it was prescribed to cure insomnia for Europeans, while the Native Americans gave it a Viagra-esque endorsement as an aphrodisiac –

the contradictory purposes might explain why the cultures didn't hit it off when they first met.

By the 13th century the Italians were recording juniper potions and the botanical quickly became synonymous with curing the ignoble occupational hazard of the nobles: indigestion. This medicinal benefit led them to blend the botanical into eaux de vies after banquets, a practice that then spread across the Lowlands and eventually into Holland.

The Dutch were the first to record recipes for these juniper tipples, thus we credit them with the official 'invention' of gin, or genever, as they called it. They subsequently introduced it to the British as they fought side by side during the Thirty Years War, and when Dutchman William of Orange took the British throne in 1690, Londoners went loopy for the stuff.

These opening credits for the gin adventure would unfortunately derail during the 18th century, when the 'gin craze' in London presented us with arguably the biggest train wreck in spirit history. London's streets in the 1720s and 30s were filled with bedraggled boozers, the scabrous scenes of which were eventually depicted by William Hogarth in his *Gin Lane* prints of 1751. But they say it takes a man to hit rock bottom before he can rise again, and that is exactly what gin achieved.

During the late 18th and early 19th centuries the great producers of gin emerged with more refined and discerning spirits. Thomas Dakin at Greenall's and an array of London distillers, such as the Booth family, Charles Tanqueray, Alexander Gordon and James Burrough of Beefeater – the list goes on – all endeavoured to improve methods and flavour.

The 19th century also saw the arrival of gin palaces in London, churches in which gin worshippers could pay their respects. Unfortunately, some patrons proved a little too fanatical and these palaces almost undid the gin reformation. German Max Schlesinger recounted the vast choice of gin available in his 1853 *Saunterings in and about London Town,* as he enjoyed honey, cream and cordial gins, but he also reminded the British they hadn't quite got a handle on responsible drinking. 'If your nerves are delicate, you had better not pass too close by the gin shops for as the doors opens – and these doors are always opening – you are overwhelmed with the pestilential fumes of gin.'

But, by this stage, gin wasn't the preserve of the European, it had cracked America too. The 1860s was the golden age of the cocktail, and America was in dashing form, dunking gin into mixed masterpieces like the Martinez and Martini. The nonsense of the noble experiment that was Prohibition put a dent in gin again as bathtub beverages poisoned punters, but even here gin can be heralded a hero. It contributed to cultural change as the likes of Dorothy Parker and her female peers proved women wanted a drink in the American bar. Gin stoked the feminist fervour and, instead of worrying about a suitable husband, women drank and danced with reckless abandon.

Prohibition proved to be a but a hiccup and the 20th century made the Martini an iconic serve. Humphrey Bogart and James Bond sipped it on screen, it oiled the wheels of world diplomacy and, thanks to the tax deductible Three Martini Lunches, it even inspired the kind of business deals our current bankers can only dream of. As the 20th century wore on, though, vodka became the fly in gin's ointment; indeed it proved to be a massive bluebottle that guzzled all of gin's profits. By the 1970s, the botanical belle of the ball was

Dorothy Parker drank gin. Sometimes it made her smile. But only sometimes.

sitting on a mouldy pumpkin wondering why its less attractive sister was getting so much action. Loitering on the dusty end of the shelf, gin found solace in the hands of the Queen Mother herself as well as elderly cream sherry sippers.

It took a blue bottle, in the form of Bombay Sapphire, to repair gin's split ends and turn it into a sexy black dress option for the 1980s generation. And by the 1990s a renewed interest in cocktail history among a batch of budding bartenders on both sides of the Atlantic led them to scour classic cocktail books and sweep gin off its feet again. Such enthusiasm sparked the launch of new brands, with brilliantly obscure, exotic botanicals making it onto the bill.

Today then gin is fresh, hip, cool, dope, sick, dench or whatever term those crazy kids use for something fashionable, ensuring that after a few centuries of ups and downs, gin is flying high.

From its Dutch genever roots to its contemporary place at the heart of cocktail culture, gin is now at the forefront of an artisan spirits revival that stretches from London to New York and beyond.

200 AD GREEK PHYSICIAN GALEN CLAIMS JUNIPER CAN CLEANSE THE LIVER AND KIDNEYS BUT MIXES IT WITH ALCOHOL, THEREBY UNDERMINING HIS 'HEALTHY' THEORY.

1055 MEDICAL SCHOLARS IN SALERNO, ITALY, WRITE DOWN JUNIPER HERBAL REMEDIES.

1266 DUTCHMAN JACOB VAN MAERLANT PUBLISHES DER NATUREN BLOEME AND REFERENCES A JUNIPER-FLAVOURED DRINK WITH MEDICINAL POWERS. IT IS ACTUALLY A TRANSLATION OF BELGIAN THOMAS VAN CANTIMPRE'S LIBER DE NATURA RERUM BUT PEOPLE MISSED IT FIRST TIME AROUND.

1340 JUNIPER IS BEING CARRIED AROUND WITH OTHER AROMATICS TO WARD OFF THE PLAGUE.

1663 PERENNIAL SICK BOY SAMUEL PEPYS DIARISES HIS ATTEMPTS TO CURE CONSTIPATION WITH STRONG JUNIPER WATERS.

1585 THE ENGLISH FIGHT WITH THE DUTCH AGAINST SPAIN AND ARE INTRODUCED TO JUNIPER SPIRITS.

1572 PROFESSOR SYLVIUS DE BOUVE CREATES A COMMERCIAL JUNIPER SPIRIT; IT IS BEING CALLED GENEVER.

1560 THE HUGENOTS IN FLANDERS ARE NOW MAKING JUNIPER DISTILLATES.

1689 DUTCHMAN WILLIAM OF ORANGE TAKES THE BRITISH THRONE AND JUNIPER SPIRITS BECOME FASHIONABLE.

1694 BEER IS HEAVILY TAXED, GIN BECOMES CHEAPER.

1702 QUEEN 'BRANDY NAN' ANNE (SO-CALLED BECAUSE SHE LIKES A DRINK) TAKES THE THRONE. SHE ENCOURAGES DISTILLATION ACROSS LONDON BUT THE QUALITY OF THE SUBSEQUENT SPIRITS HITTING THE CAPITAL DO NOT TICKLE HER FANCY.

1714 THE WORD 'GIN' APPEARS IN PRINT FOR THE FIRST TIME AND BRITAIN SEES AN ALARMING RISE IN PRODUCTION AND CONSUMPTION.

1720 THE START OF THE GIN CRAZE PROPER AND PRODUCTION OF GIN IS STARTING TO REACH DIZZYING HEIGHTS.

1734 JUDITH DEFOUR KILLS HER CHILD AND EXCHANGES THE BABY'S NEW CLOTHES FOR MONEY TO BUY GIN. THE TRIAL BECOMES A FULCRUM FOR GIN REFORM.

1729 THE FIRST GIN ACT. DUTY IS RAISED ON GIN, HELPING TO FUND THE BRITISH EMPIRE AT LEAST, BUT THE GOVERNMENT FAILS TO IMPOSE NEW LEGISLATION IN DISTILLATION.

1723 THE DEATH RATE IN LONDON EXCEEDS THE BIRTH RATE. GIN IS THE CULPRIT. WOMEN ARE THE BIGGEST FANS AND GIN IS GIVEN NAMES SUCH AS 'MOTHER'S RUIN'.

1736 11 MILLION GALLONS OF GIN ARE NOW BEING DISTILLED IN LONDON. A GIN ACT IS PASSED, THE PUBLIC RIOT AND HOLD FUNERALS FOR 'MOTHER GENEVA', BUT CONTINUE TO MAKE GIN ILLEGALLY.

1738 GIN ACTS RECRUIT INFORMERS TO UNCOVER THE UNLICENSED PRODUCERES OF GIN. INFORMERS ARE THEN, UNSURPRISINGLY, ATTACKED AND KILLED.

1743 MEN, WOMEN AND CHILDREN (YES, CHILDREN) IN LONDON ARE CONSUMING TWO PINTS OF GIN A WEEK.

1751 HOGARTH DOES A PAINTING AND THE GOVERNMENT ANNOUNCES AN 8TH GIN ACT, WHICH FINALLY STARTS MAKING AN IMPACT ON ILLICIT GIN PRODUCTION.

1830 CHARLES TANQUERAY OPENS HIS DISTILLERY.

1793 PLYMOUTH GIN BEGINS. IT IS THE ONLY BRITISH GIN STILL BEING MADE AT THE SAME DISTILLERY IT STARTED FROM.

1769 ALEXANDER GORDON OPENS GORDON AND COMPANY IN BERMONDSEY, SOUTH LONDON.

1761 GIN BECOMES MORE EXPENSIVE AND THE DISCERNING DISTILLERS GET A FOOTHOLD IN THE MARKET. THOMAS DAKIN OPENS HIS GREENALL'S GIN COMPANY IN WARRINGTON. IT CONTINUES TO OPERATE TODAY.

1757 A BAD HARVEST ENABLES THE GOVERNMENT TO BAN GRAIN DISTILLING.

1830 THE CREATION OF AENEAS COFFEY'S CONTINUOUS DISTILLATION METHOD MEANS THAT GIN INCLUDES HIGHLY RECTIFIED SPIRIT AND DRY GIN. LONDON DRY GIN IS SOON BORN.

1858 ERASMUS BOND LAUNCHES A TONIC WATER WITH QUININE TAKEN FROM THE BARK OF A CINCHONA TREE, A BITTER INGREDIENT WITH ANTI-MALARIAL PROPERTIES.

1870 SCHWEPPES LAUNCHES ITS INDIAN TONIC WATER. THE SUBTROPICS EXPATS ARE NOW GULPING GIN AND TONICS.

1876 BEEFEATER GIN IS LAUNCHED.

1898 GORDON'S AND TANQUERAY MERGE.

1920S GIN RETURNS TO AN ERA OF POOR PRODUCTION AS PROHIBITION AMERICA STARTS TO TURN OUT RETREATED INDUSTRIAL ALCOHOL, FLAVOURED WITH JUNIPER, OR BATHTUB GIN.

2000 TANQUERAY NO. TEN IS LAUNCHED. PREMIUM LUXURY GINS START TO EMERGE. BARTENDERS REDISCOVER CLASSIC GIN COCKTAILS. GIN ENJOYS A NEW BUT DISCERNING CRAZE.

1993 US TAX LAWS ARE CHANGED TO ALLOW ONLY 50 PER CENT OF 'LAVISH AND EXTRAVAGANT' ENTERTAINING TO BE DEDUCTED AS BUSINESS EXPENSES. THUS ENDS THE THREE-MARTINI LUNCH.

1988 BOMBAY SAPPHIRE IS LAUNCHED.

1970S GIN IS IN THE DOLDRUMS, VODKA IS THE WINNING SPIRIT IN THE WESTERN WORLD.

William of Orange

European pioneer, trade innovator, warrior, wearer of wigs, but, above all else, a Dutchman who gave the Brits a national tipple.

The Dutch gave gin to the the world. They also gave us top-shelf gentlemens' pamphlets and a reason to window shop, the Cruyff Turn and tulips, the Dutch oven and decent cigarettes. They gave us the word booze – a derivative of the medieval Dutch word *busen*, 'to drink heavily'. And they gave us guts – when the British fought with the Dutch they were served a shot of juniper spirit before battle to embolden them, coining the expression 'Dutch courage'. But most of all, the Dutch gave us gin, thanks largely to William of Orange.

William was sovereign Prince of Orange in the 1680s, chief magistrate of the United Provinces of the Netherlands and married to the English heir Mary II. Mary was actually his cousin, but no questions were asked; it was a different time. His wife gave him an in with the English, which proved particularly useful when the English kicked James II off his bejewelled beanbag and into France, inviting William to unify the two countries.

A Dutchman on the throne in Britain was controversial and Middle England tabloid hacks quickly stirred controversy over 'Johnny foreigner stealing our monarch's job'. But William appeased the masses by launching a blockade on French goods and while a ban on Boursin and baguettes caused a little initial consternation, the lack of brandy left a gap in the UK spirits market.

Under the guidance of land-owning parliamentarians, William supported a new distilling act to encourage entrepreneurs to produce spirits from corn, simultaneously alleviating farmers from a glut of grain. He then helped establish the Bank of England with a related Tonnage Act, enabling the country to raise tax on beer.

By 1694 then, the market was primed, distillers were operational and natural resources abundant, and all laws supported gin production. All the country needed was demand and with returning soldiers high on the same genever the new king was drinking, the national spirit gin was born.

William inspired gin's popularity by drinking plenty himself, sharing bottles of Holland Gin with friends of the palace. He also drank his fair share of Dutch courage himself and was lauded during the Battle of Landen when he rode into a massacre with musket shots piercing his hat and cloak. Gin also inspired his enlightened thinking as one of the first genuine Europeans, sharing the spirit with friend and fellow European pioneer Peter the Great of Russia. After his wife died, William of Orange overdid it a bit. One aide reported how on a hunting trip the King had forgotten bullets but was so sozzled he didn't even notice and assumed he was simply missing every time. And perhaps gin even led to his death. He fell off his horse, although said horse had tripped over a molehill…

Either way, William the Dutchman loved the stuff, and more than that, he gave the British gin. For that, we should thank him.

WILHELMUS DE DERDE
ONING VAN ENGELAND.

WILLIAM OF
ORANGE

GIN BOTANICALS

Whether it's the flavour or the provenance of gin that catches your interest, it's the botanicals that tell the story.

Botany is one of the oldest disciplines of scientific research in human history, and principally involves peering at plants. Centuries of scholars have inspected herbs, roots, fruits and spices in search of natural pharmaceuticals and flavours.

When we lobotonise gin, juniper is isolated as the most significant of the spirit's multifaceted botanical bill, and investigations into this particular ingredient date back multi-millennia. Archaeologists reveal Palaeolithic men (cavemen) used stones and bones to poke around for plants to cure empty bellies and ailments, and since juniper was knocking around 250 million years ago, we can only assume someone, somewhere ingested it. Sumerian society, meanwhile tickled their tongues and cured tummy trouble with juniper nearly 6000 years ago; there's actual evidence of that. Assyrian pharmacies definitely stocked it on shelves with anise and caraway, while Egyptians recorded its curative capabilities in their papyri (paper) along with dance moves, fancy coffins and pyramids.

Fast-forward to the 16th century and we discover that the medicinal investigations into juniper and distillation have collided, with the Dutch distilling their genever. From linctus to social lubricant, juniper became the star at the bar then, and today remains the dominant gin flavouring.

So what the hell *is* juniper? Well, it's not a spaceship, nor is it a bathroom accessory, and while it is definitely the surname of a woman in a Donovan song, here we refer to the tree or shrub. Rather than chuck an entire shrub into a still, gin producers are specifically interested in the things that grow on the shrub. Referred to as berries, they are actually cones and contain organic compounds called alpha-pinene, also found in rosemary, and myrcene, which is also present in hops and cannabis. Distillers are after the essential oils and it can take up to three years for the berries to mature before they are hand-harvested by fastidious farmers. Junipers are hardy bushes, and they grow wild around the world; the most prized for their berries grow on the mountains slopes of Macedonia and Tuscany.

Why are the berries important? Because they are, OK, just deal with it. They impart the pine aroma and bittersweet flavour profile that has become synonymous with gin. Indeed, such is their significance they are recognised as essential additives under EU law. If you smell basic gins, chances are what you can mostly smell is juniper.

But juniper is merely one of many botanicals infused in gin recipes today. With the arrival of column stills and highly rectified spirits, other botanicals appeared on the canvas during the 19th century – coriander first, then roots and citrus peels. Today you'll find an even wider, more exotic range, but here are some popular ingredients in current use for gin:

Juniper Berries

KEY INGREDIENTS

Liquorice

Angelica

LIQUORICE

The liquorice root imparts some subtle notes of the flavours you might expect; earthy notes are also relevant here, but they are not potent. Liquorice is more crucial for its glycyrrhizin, which carries sweet flavours across in distillation.

CUBEB BERRIES

Contains the piperine compound which brings a spicy pepper kick but combines it with limonene to balance that with citrus. Two very popular profiles in gin.

Cubeb Berries

ANGELICA ROOT

Brings an earthy quality to gin and marries other botanical ingredients. It's related to poisonous hemlock so needs careful sourcing.

CORIANDER

Specifically coriander seeds. The second most important ingredient for gin-makers. The essential oils impart earthy thyme, floral notes and, crucially, a citrus top note in gin.

Cardamom

CITRUS PEELS

Lemon and orange are both commonly used to flavour gin. The distiller looks to extract the more potent oils from the skin.

ORRIS ROOT

The light violet aroma aside, this ingredient is mostly used as a fixative, often employed in the perfume industry and a common allergen.

CARDAMOM

The third most expensive spice in the world and depending on the source it imparts either a higher spice note (Mysore) or a eucalyptus flavour (Malabar). Also adds a lavender or citrus note to gin.

Orris Root

GIN BAR BORE TIPS

JUNIPER VODKA

A highly simplistic interpretation of gin has seen some drinks enthusiasts deem it 'flavoured vodka'. At its base is rectified neutral grain spirit, or vodka, which is then flavoured with botanicals, the most important being juniper. So we take the point. But it undermines the art of handling the botanicals, so we definitely don't agree. It's like calling tea 'flavoured water'. Which it is. But we like tea.

LET'S GET TECHNICAL

To flavour the spirit, some gin producers macerate and re-distill in copper. Diluting 96% highly rectified spirit to 60% with water, they then add the botanicals for a spell before they start. Some distil immediately (Tanqueray), while others leave it for a period of time (Beefeater for 24 hours). Bombay and Hendrick's use carter head stills meaning they suspend the botanicals in the still using a basket and allow the alcohol vapours to pass through during distillation. Meanwhile, Ian Hart at Sacred gin adds another element of science by using the vacuum distilling technique.

LIMEYS

Surgeon James Lind's 1747 discovery that citrus combatted scurvy had encouraged the Navy to make lime juice standard issue by the 19th century. The Brits skulled the vitamin C booster and subsequently became known as limeys. A highly original nickname, up there with roast beef or frogs' legs or orange head, for that guy at our school who had an orange-shaped head. As an aside, in 1867 Lauchlin Rose created the world's first concentrated fruit drink in his Rose's Lime Cordial as he experimented with ways to preserve the lime juice he supplied to the Navy. This was a favourite with the officers and gave us the Gimlet cocktail.

DUCKS

During the mid-14th century the bubonic plague made a nuisance of itself. Men dressed up in masks with long beaks full of herbal combatants and burned juniper in a bid to ward off the disease. By the 18th century the word 'quacksalver' was being dished out, a disparaging term applied to faux physicians who embellished their medicinal know-how. There is a suggestion the insult was used during the plague, shouted at the beaky blokes. The etymology is contested by some historians and it does seem a convenient coincidence; quacks, beaks and all that. But we should point out, ducks are funny and it kind of fits the bill. Either way, it is now believed the burning juniper did actually offend the rats carrying the plague, suggesting these 'quacks' were more efficient than they were given credit for and that juniper really was providing some health benefits before it became fashionable as a gin ingredient.

A WEE DROP

During the height of the gin craze in the 18th century, gin tasted like piss. We can say this with some authority, due to accounts of the awful ingredients used to bulk it out. One being piss. Drinkers called it Piss-quick. Other customers complained of acid stomach for the first time, possibly because it was occasionally bulked up with sulphuric acid.

❧

GENEVER, OH

Genever, the Dutch juniper spirit that gave rise to gin, is still alive and well today. It is protected by geographic indication and is produced in the Netherlands, Belgium and France. Producers use low alcohol grain spirit *moutwijn* and highly rectified spirit. There are two classifications: *jonge*, which has a lower percentage of *moutwijn*, and *oude*, with higher. Both are worth trying.

STYLE IT OUT

Here are the key styles of gin

Gin: According to EU legislation, gin is made from 96% highly rectified spirit and must 'taste predominantly of juniper'. Taste is subjective, so this is a point that the purist's debate. Gin must also have a minimum of 37.5% ABV. Flavourings can be used.

Distilled gin: Importantly, this is made by re-distilling the 96% ABV highly rectified spirit using juniper berries and other natural ingredients. Flavourings can be added after this process but again it must taste predominantly of juniper and be 37.5% ABV or more.

London Gin: Goes a step further in that it is the same as distilled gin but no other flavourings or sweeteners can be thrown in after it's distilled. This is what designates it London Dry. It does not have to be made in the city of London, however.

Plymouth Gin: Plymouth Gin has a protected geographical indicator and it must be made in the Devonshire town of Plymouth, England. It is a distilled gin and production is limited to one distillery. The style is earthier, fruitier and sweeter than London Dry.

Old Tom: Old Tom is another style of gin popular before the highly rectified spirits from the column still arrived in the 19th century. A heavy dose of sugar was added to cover up the compounds created in rudimentary stills. It's a style that died out in the face of London Dry but it's enjoying reappraisal, albeit with more discerning recipes.

HOGARTH &
THE ART OF GIN

Art, eh? Nothing more than puffed-up, overpriced, archival snapshots from self-indulgent, (probably illiterate), time-rich, showoffs. Are we right, you guys? Are we right? Huh? Are we? Well, in the case of William Hogarth, yes, we are.*

Don't take our word for it, just have a look at his depiction of London in 1751. Go on, look at it. Titled *Gin Lane*, it's pompous, spurious nonsense. Hogarth seems to be blaming gin for London's ills. Gin? Do us a favour, you mug. Such narrow-minded misrepresentation surely endorses our claim. And it's pretty basic stuff, folks. While the French were embracing their demurely amorous *fêtes galantes*, going lavishly loco with Rococo, this sketcher was using a ballpoint to draw naughty women with their knockers out and babies guzzling booze.

OK so there's more to *Gin Lane* than this. Admittedly, at first glance it's easy to dismiss the drawings as crude propaganda, about as artful as an anti-alcohol advert, for Hogarth was a goody two-shoes with more interest in Presbyterianism than the pub. But on closer inspection, he possibly had a point...

In the 20 years after William of Orange had encouraged distillation, London had sunk itself into a gin craze. By the end of the 1720s, 75% of children under five were dying, the death rate exceeded births and any efforts at sexy time were thwarted by impotence-inducing alcohol. By the 1730s men, women and children (yes, children) were guzzling two pints of gin a week. Gin's pseudonyms alone tell the story of how degenerative this liquid was viewed - busthead, crank, strip-me-down-naked, blue ruin, strikefire – and other nasty names that put you off.

The battered masses were making bad life decisions and newspapers lapped up the misery, but one sob story really tickled the tabloids. In 1734, a poverty-stricken, gin-addicted Judith Defour murdered her baby and exchanged the infant's clothes for money to buy booze. The shocking crime and its subsequent trial coverage became a fulcrum for attempts at distillation reform, but government efforts fell on gin-drowned ears and by the 1740s, 11 million gallons of the spirit were being distilled in London.

The government was desperate. By 1751, seven Gin Acts had failed and the last throw of the dice, as so often is the case in national dire straits, was to commission a drawing. Up stepped the doyen of satirical sketches, Hogarth.

Hogarth's *Gin Lane* made an immediate impact. It directed a piercing light on the consumption of the spirit and he presented a London facing Armageddon with gin the nuclear bomb. At the centre of the image is Madame Genever or, indeed, Judith Defour, boobs on show as she lobs a baby into the doorway of a gin shop. Behind her a coffin is being filled with another woman (boobs on show again) and her child watches on, sipping a gin to commiserate/celebrate. To the right of the image, a woman adopts the perfect breastfeeding pose but force-feeds her child with, you've guessed it, gin. Buildings crumble, riots explode and starvation ensues. London is gin-soaked and down-and-out.

Hogarth's image was presented alongside another work called *Beer Street*. Here Hogarth shows how beer flows, industry flourishes and residents get fat. It is the joyful contrast to the jeopardy of gin. The images were printed in papers and the public took note. Just like that. Well, not exactly. The government got an eighth Gin Act through and a bad harvest denied the public of the precious grain to make gin. But the combination of circumstances abated gin abuse.

So gin was all bad, we get the point, but further investigation reveals that Hogarth had more up his sleeve than a big stick to beat gin with. His satire poked at a wider context. While history points a wagging finger at gin, Hogarth was identifying a brutal poverty that explained the public's escape into alcohol.

Aggressive urbanisation and a lack of space in London led to the rapid spread of disease; meanwhile prostitution, unemployment and neglect of children were commonplace, and as the oil ship of England tried to turn into a simple industrial revolution, it was daft to distil society's problems into a bottle labelled 'gin epidemic'. Gin takes the blame for London's downfall, and certainly it deserves some. But it became a government

Hogarth's *Gin Lane*, 1751. A very particular view of London at the time.

scapegoat in the face of more significant societal pressures. Was it a good piece of art? Well, it's in black and white, so a bit boring. And the baby is massive, not even nearly in proportion to the rest of the drawing.

But contrary to our opening comments, it does seem that Hogarth saw beyond the gin haze and took a valuable satirical bite out of the government's neglect of urban society. Perhaps art is important after all.

* Actually, we're not right.

OLD TOM GIN

The gin that sparked slightly sinister shenanigans on the streets of 18th-century London would've been very different from today's splendid spirit. Mixed and mashed with whatever was to hand, the murky liquid would've been stored in barrels and masked with flavourings like anise, and in many cases it proved to be poisonous.

Among the adjustments to conceal the disgusting nature of these early incarnations was the addition of sugar, an olden day vodka Redbull, if you like. There's nothing wrong with sugar, of course, in moderation. It remained an ingredient for some producers and was very likely the gin Americans used in their first cocktails.

The style still exists, in fact, and is now referred to as Old Tom, but the etymology is a point of conjecture amongst ginophiles. Added to which there's a cat fight over who first associated a feline with Old Tom, the animal that appears on the label. One of the characters stirred into the story of Old Tom's origins is Captain Dudley Bradstreet. An 18th-century Irish bounder, full to the brim with blarney, Bradstreet's role in gin is an infamous one, but whether he is responsible for the cat on Old Tom gins is debatable. Regardless, we celebrate his enterprise rather than his legitimacy.

Fortunately for everyone, Bradstreet chronicled his life's exploits in his hilarious *The life and Uncommon Adventures of Captain Dudley Bradstreet* which covers the ins and outs

of tutelage with pedantic schoolmasters, charming encounters with whores and his 'various vices, schemes and immoralities'.

The book also offers a fascinating insight into gin through his illegal stint as a spirits seller in London during 1739. The gin craze was coming to its peak when Bradstreet arrived in London but entrepreneurial gin traders were struggling as the government employed enforcers to cull the number of small retailers. Bradstreet recalls how anyone found selling the spirit in a quantity less than two gallons would need to cough up a £10 fine to an informer or face a spell in the big house. Despite the law, Bradstreet recognised the public were 'noisy and clamourous for want of their beloved liquor' and it soon occurred to him to 'venture upon that trade' himself in a business-savvy move.

Bradstreet discovered a loophole in the law and realised informers needed to know the name of anyone renting a house and selling gin. So he took on a property on the sly, put a sign of a cat on the building and ran a lead pipe from the inside, having a word in the ear of potential customers and alerting them to the whereabouts of his disreputable destination, before barricading himself inside. Customers would come to the house with the cat, paid Bradstreet for gin by placing a coin in the cat's mouth and then collected their prize as it poured through the pipe and out the cat's paw. 'Why the big paws?' they probably didn't say if they ever had to wait. The authorities were powerless to

Early posters for Old Tom gin date from the 1700s, although the gin is still in production today.

act and so successful was his business that others copied the cat, kicking off a series of Puss and Mew houses around the capital.

The relation of the cat to Bradstreet's enterprise has encouraged some historians to suggest he was the originator of the association, but, quite amazingly, it's still causing a lot of ill feline. Suppose nobody's purrfect, eh? Amongst our drinks historian peers to investigate is David T. Smith, who explores the 'Old Tom' etymology in his book *Forgotten Spirits & Long-Lost Liqueurs*. Smith delves into a legal case with Boord & Son v Huddart from 1903, which links the branding of a cat and a recipe for sweetened gin. He also references distiller Thomas Chamberlain who, in the 1830s, was also believed to be responsible for the connection to this gin style: Chamberlain's apprentice Thomas Norris, or Young Tom, opened a gin palace and bought gin from Chamberlain, and subsequently named the gin 'Old Tom' on his barrels.

Such are the mass debates that rage in the world of gin, but regardless of those responsible, the good news is that you can still find Old Tom in shops today. Amongst the best exponents are the historic Hayman's Old Tom, one of the first to re-acquaint nostalgic gin drinkers with the style when it launched in 2007. Using a family recipe from the 1860s, it's bold in the botanicals, with the sweetness carrying through in the citrus.

GIN LEGEND

SIR THEODORE DE MAYERNE

WE'VE OFTEN CONSIDERED THE PROFESSION OF GENERAL PRACTITIONER TO BE AN ODIOUS OCCUPATION. ONE DAY DIAGNOSING HALITOSIS THE NEXT HAEMORRHOIDS. BUT EVEN TODAY'S GP WOULD RECOIL AT THE SCENES SIR THEODORE DE MAYERNE WITNESSED.

De Mayerne is regarded as 'the father of English distilling', but his major contribution to history comes in the world of medicine, and he was highly regarded in his own lifetime and beyond for his marvellous methods of recording treatments. So revered was his regimen that he was eventually required to bestow his bedtime manner on royalty. Along the way though, he saw some serious shit, and that's not simply an excuse to drop a swearword. He once treated a Scottish boy who was excreting wool.

While de Mayerne was lauded for chronicling his treatments, the patient complaints and remedies he prescribed read like fiction. Take the man who came to him with an infection, for example. Sounds routine enough, but he was infected with a nest of worms and thought he was possessed. He probably wasn't possessed, but we're not sure what a nest of worms referred to, nor could we unearth de Mayerne's treatment for that one; perhaps he wriggled out of the case.

Then there's typhoid, certainly not unheard of but treatment ranged from bleeding, purges and enemas to the more modern application of pigeons to a shaven head. Breathing difficulties? Try a syrup comprising tortoise flesh, snails, animal lungs, crawfish and frogs. And talking of animals, which we just were, he even wandered through the vestibules of veterinarian centres, medicating epileptic horses with a mix of human excrement and white wine. He subsequently discovered the mix of horse dung with wine helped humans – helped them smell at least. For symptoms that seem more familiar to us, he still stirred up some strange concoctions. Impotence for example was dealt with by rubbing a powder of burned newt on the toe of the right foot. It doesn't work, trust us.

The status of some of de Mayerne's patient's meanwhile, made life doubly difficult. An early appointment for example was Cardinal Richelieu. He was the close advisor of King Louis XIII and the de facto second-in-command of the kingdom of France, so a bit of a big deal, and he was coming to de Mayerne to show off a nasty venereal disease. Naturally discretion was demanded in such cases and had de Mayerne squealed on his patients then his head would've been lopped off. Despite the danger and obvious pitfalls, de Mayerne was devoted to the work, and proved himself a sterling secret keeper because he went on to become Physician to Henry IV of France and then to James I and Charles I of England.

But crucially, and we'll get to the drinks point here, his experiments into medicine and alchemy led to a fascination with distillation, something fellow philosopher and physician Abū Mūsā Jābir ibn Hayyān had discovered in the Middle East during the 8th century. As well as undertaking a bit of espionage for the British monarch, and having interests in coal, lead and oyster beds, the entrepreneurial de Mayerne had a nice side line making alcohol, and such was his affection for this industry, he also helped regulate it.

De Mayerne had befriended Sir Thomas Cademan, a learned chap and a successful distiller who was frustrated by the lack of respect for his profession, which was dumped in with the Company of Apothecaries at the time and still regarded as medicinal practitioners. In 1638, de Mayerne took heed of Cademan's gripe and rounded up other distilling troops to petition for a new, independent 'Company of the Distillers of London'.

The Company was given the power to exercise a monopoly and regulate the distilling trade within 21 miles of the cities of London and Westminster. It also lobbied Parliament to defend the interest of distillers against unfair legislation. De Mayerne had used his influence with the royal family to get the patent through and it proved a crucial moment in the history of gin. It not only recognised the importance of distilling, it also laid down the foundation for rules and guidelines on making quality spirit. By liberating the distillers, de Mayerne had helped establish an environment in which gin would be able to prosper. The value of the organisation would be emphasised 50 years later when the monopoly was ended under William of Orange, enabling more people to distil in London. The impact of that decision led to the 18th-century Gin Craze (see page 176).

It is testament to de Mayerne that the Worshipful Company of Distillers still exists today. The Company promotes charitable endeavour and education in the world of drink, and also aims to 'bring together members of the livery and their guests in an atmosphere of good fellowship, in convivial surroundings'.

MEDICINAL GIN

ADDING A MEDICAL MAESTRO TO OUR CATALOGUE OF FELLOW THINKING DRINKERS IS NOT AS TENUOUS AS YOU MIGHT THINK, INDEED SPIRIT CONCEPTION WAS ORIGINALLY INSPIRED BY A PIOUS CURATIVE INTENT. When they weren't getting naked and wrestling, the Ancient Greeks dabbled with distillates and, perhaps more successfully, the alchemists of the Middle East around 700/800 AD experimented with boiling alcohol in a bid to address various ailments.

Between 1000 and 1300, the methods the Moors had tested filtered through Europe as scholars like Robert of Chester translated Arabic texts, while intrepid explorer Marco Polo spread the medical message. To improve the restorative effects of gin, it was mixed with other herbal ingredients and in 1712 Richard Stoughton lauched his Stoughton's Elixir or 'Stoughton's Bitters'; his blend of alcohol, herbs and spices was hailed as a medicinal marvel. Then, in 1786, Antonio Benedetto Carpano invented the vermouth.

The creative rights of the Martini have been attributed to many, and in more than one case incorrectly. The Martinez is one interpretation of its birth, its blend of sweet vermouth and Old Tom gin making it an obvious relation, the dashes of maraschino, sugar syrup and bitters keeping it on the right side of medicinal.

The Martinez: gin, vermouth, bitters, curaçao and sugar syrup.

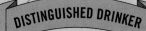

HUMPHREY BOGART

Bogart famously said 'I don't trust any bastard who doesn't drink.' Harsh perhaps, but Bogart's Martini consumption, acting skills and iconic status earn him a place in our book.

One of the most notorious anecdotal lines from the plethora of great drinkers in our book might be Bogart's deathbed rattle. Repenting, as many do, his last gasp was for a drink. Before he kicked the ice bucket and bounded up to the big bar in the sky, he told friends and family that his biggest regret was switching from Scotch to Martinis. Did he really say this? Certainly, Bogart had the sense of humour to deliver the line as he faded away, and certainly he loved a drink. But he was a martini man long before he faced his final curtain so there is certainly some myth stirred into this.

Bogart was an early adopter of gin and trained himself during the dark days of American temperance. Expelled from school, he enlisted in the navy, but a little late for World War I action, quickly returned to discover his father had blown the family fortune. He pinged through a series of professions that didn't really suit, and, out the door at five on the dot from each, spent his evenings in speakeasies. The notorious 21 bar was amongst his favourites along with Bleeck's Artist and Writers Bar, where hard drinkers included actress Tallulah Bankhead (whose last words were 'codine' and 'bourbon') and Dylan Thomas (last words: 'I have had 18 straight whiskies, I think that's the record'). In each Bogart was exposed to enough bathtub gin to forge formidable bar tabs. Indeed, Bogie's bills tended to stick around, becoming as infamous as his capacity to sink a Martini. He tried to claw back cash on the chess tables, but not quite a master and playing for a mere 50 cents a game, he heard more bar owners declare checkmate than he ever did.

Tired of dead-end jobs, Bogart, much like the Thinking Drinkers, identified Hollywood as a safe bet for financial security, so set his sights on the stage and, in spite of his hangovers, started finding roles on Broadway. Initially the drinking didn't abate, but Bogart learned early in his career that, as fond as he was of gin, he needed to put his professionalism first. In 1923, after a night on the martinis in speakeasy Chumley's, he rolled up to a performance of *Meet the Wife* and forgot his lines, using set parts to lean on as he struggled through. To his credit, he recognised the abject failure of this moment and subsequently refused to bomb on stage or set ever.

As Hollywood came calling, he moved to LA and held court at the Cock & Bull pub, site of the creation of the Moscow Mule cocktail, and at the Chateau Marmont. Meanwhile, drinking on set was standard. In Sahara in 1943 his wife brought a coffee flask to the set for him, to be used not for coffee but, of course, to keep his martinis ice-cold. His love of the stuff made it into movies. Consider one of the most iconic lines of movie history: 'Of all the gin joints in all the towns in all the world, she walks into mine.' Bogart's affection for gin didn't hinder his on-screen heroics, indeed it was a fuel for his creativity. He tried quitting drinking once but said 'it was the most miserable afternoon of my life'.

CASABLANCA

Humphrey BOGART
Ingrid BERGMAN
Paul HENREID

DRY GIN

Humphrey
Bogart

THE GIN PALACE v.
THE SPEAKEASY

Whether it's the slip of a heel and the slap of a handbag or a flailing fist and the thud of a falling face on the foot rail, everyone loves a bar fight. America and Britain enjoyed their own in the 18th century, their rum-fuelled rows causing such a stink they went to war. Allied these days, the two nations still snipe about less important issues like sport and culture, or foreign intervention, and occasionally debate who has the best bars in the world.

Both countries love their gin and both are responsible for styles of bars that shaped our drinking culture today: the gin palace and the speakeasy. The question is, which is better? Another question is, do you care? We think you should, so read this:

The Gin Palace

With a royal right hook, the heavyweight gin palace landed a venerable haymaker on the Victorian drinking scene. Cyclopean structures devoted to gin consumption, these establishments changed the face of English drinking. But despite an impressive stature, the palace was light on its feet, combining a heavy gin punch with the decorative bob and weave of an exhibitionist. In the 1820s, pioneering property developers shook a fist at shabby public houses and jabbed progressive feng shui into derelict buildings. Far from seeking tranquillity and neutral backdrops yah, intrepid interior designers bigged up the bling, poured a reviving bucket of water onto the faces of rundown buildings splayed out on the canvas, and refurbished big style, seriously sprucing up the nation's drinking experience. Intrigued and enthusiastic imbibers soon began to flood into these glorious palaces, dens of discerning gin drinking, and paid homage to the journeyman gin. The spirit had looked down-and-out in the 1750s during a spell of insane abuse (see page 176), giving it all the credibility of a boxer taking a dive, but these palaces initially restored gin-drinking dignity.

The Speakeasy

American drinkers found themselves on the ropes in 1919 when the daft government implemented the infamous and ill-fated Volstead Act, deeming alcohol a banned substance. Unfazed, New York's resilient drinkers ducked and dived their way through the red mist of legislative lunacy and weighed in with the speakeasy. A sneaky scrapper of a bar, often diminutive in size, these illegal drinking dens surprised everyone by going the distance, feinting and sucker-punching coppers throughout Prohibition. Illicit drinking became de rigueur, particularly in the Big Apple, where as many as 30,000 unlicensed bars served a thirsty public. Speakeasy gin provided crucial creative sustenance for writers and film stars who raised drinks like the Gin Martini to iconic status, and as jazz and countercultures emerged, the bar inspired a younger generation of arty types. Thanks to the speakeasy, rebellion reminded a cautious, conservative America that life without gin, simply wouldn't do.

Opposite: The gin palace provided huge barrels, perfect for leaning on.
Right: Meanwhile, over at the Speakeasy: 'Someone get this guy a gin, his coat is massive.'

FIGHT NIGHT

LET'S GET READY TO RUMBLE, SECONDS AWAY, DING, DING.

ROUND 1 — DECOR

When it comes to design, the cumbersome Gin House heavyweight proved it could also dance like a butterfly with graceful interior design. Fabulous French mahogany, beautiful balustrades, quality cornicing and sumptuous stucco rosettes dazzled like a diamanté-studded dressing gown. Elsewhere magnificent ornate mirrors and glazed interior windows with sparkly new gas lighting enabled light to bounce around the bar. These were colossal buildings and sturdy enough to see out the final seconds of the opening round.

The Speakeasy held its own with rough-and-ready exposed brickwork, dim lighting and basements settings. Often intimate, but basic and with low lighting and no frills, these bars were all about the drinking. The dressing gown a Walmart basic. Crafty and ready to back out of any corner, the Speakeasy was a resilient fighter and could open itself anywhere, its owners ready to scarper at a moment's notice to serve gin somewhere else.

DECISION: Points shared

ROUND 2 — LEGALITY

The Gin House was a law abider, strictly above the belt punches here. That said, they did serve children, not illegal then, but a little bit stupid. But the speakeasy was a law breaker. The 1919 Volstead Act and Prohibition said as much. Bar operators fingered by a gumshoe detective could dodge a spell in stir by forking up some green backs for Sergeant O'Hullahan, but it was still illegal. 'Why I oughta, dem's da breaks.'

DECISION: Too many illegal punches from the Speakeasy, round goes to the Gin House

ROUND 3 — GIN OFFERING

The Gin Palace unleashes its lengthy reach. Referred to as a 'flash of lightning', juniper-flavoured spirit came in the form of cordial gin, medicated gin, cream-gin and honey-gin. It was a time of Old Tom, a sweetened style, and as they enjoyed the arrival of the new column-still technology, they also saw servings of the rectified spirit that paved the way for London Dry.

The Speakeasy is on the ropes, since the gin itself is ropey. Bathtub gin made the headlines during Prohibition. Gin was easier to replicate than the aged spirits of whiskey and rum, and proletarian producers crawled into the hidden woodwork of their homes and came out stinking of juniper oils and industrial alcohol. You could actually buy one-gallon stills in New York during the 1920s, but you had to know how to use them. As well as poisoning people, amateurs caused the occasional explosion in apartment blocks, sometimes killing their neighbours.

DECISION: Round goes to the Gin Palace

ROUND 4 — AUDIENCE PARTICIPATION

Men women and even children inhabited the gin palaces, all of them proper palookas. Gin was served on its own or with ginger beer or in a

'Purl', or with tea in an 'English Martini'. Punters overindulged and staggered out looking for ropes to hold. So irresponsible were drinkers they even encouraged the government to tighten the screws of gin producers, who after the early 18th-century gin craze had just begun to drop their guard.

The Speakeasy, meanwhile, had actual boxers as customers. Al Capone, who ran thousands of speakeasies across America, also kept his hand in on boxing bets, and mixed gin with water when ringside with world champ Mickey Walker. When Harry Greb beat Walker in 1925, the two met by chance in LaHiff's Tavern. Here they drowned sorrows together over bathtub gin. Granted, that scene ended up in a bare-knuckle street fight, but they were great customers otherwise. Then there were the artists and the increasing number of women who were 'liberating' themselves in speakeasies, so to speak. It was a great crowd.

DECISION: Speakeasy wins the round

ROUND 5 LITERARY LIQUORISTS

The Gin House comes at this round with the punchy Charles Dickens. Dickens penned a loving ode to the gin palaces in *Sketches by Boz*, describing them as 'All is light and brilliancy… perfectly dazzling when contrasted with the dirt we have just left.'

The Speakeasy comes back firing with a litany of literary legends. Dorothy Parker was amongst the heroines of the scene, drinking with herculean efforts that put men to shame, and under the table. On a typical night, Parker could be found sipping a Tom Collins in Tony Soma's speakeasy with Pulitzer Prize winner Robert Sherwood and fellow gin fans Scott Fitzgerald and wife Zelda.

DECISION: Speakeasy win.

ROUND 6 ACCESSIBILITY

Gin palaces were absurdly abundant in London's West End, you couldn't miss the sparkling beacons of beverage worship. If you didn't know what it was, then you only had to note the number of people bustling around the place. And they were packed to the rafters every night, making it hard to reach the bar.

The Speakeasy, by contrast, goes hiding here. Its ambition was to be hard to find, and you often needed a password. The best also had the red rope of celebrity-only status. Obviously this was a necessary evil with the law. Even so, sometimes you just want a pub and a G&T without all that faff. However one got into a speakeasy was considered a win. If you had to wait a bit because it was busy, frankly, who cared?

DECISION: Points shared

ROUND 7 INFLUENCE ON BARS TODAY

Gin palaces changed the expectations of the British drinker. These epic churches of drinking devotion beat down-at heel beer houses hands down and encouraged wide-reaching renovation in pubs. They had stamina and can still be found today, poster boys of an authentic past pub experience. One of the best is the Princess Louise in London's Holborn.

The speakeasy inspired a style of drinking still celebrated in New York today. Seek out the real deal in some contemporary New York bars such as Please Don't Tell in the East Village.

DECISION: Points shared

So, if you actually look at the judges' scores, you'll see it's a draw. Both hold a special place in drinking history. We'll make gin the winner.

A PRESIDENTIAL COCKTAIL

We tend to rebuff any reprobates who, drinker or not, leave a more dubious stain on the inside leg of history. Our aim is to showcase the stain removers, the men and women who brightened the past. Occasionally, though, it's unavoidable. Sometimes one must cast an embarrassing glance at that stubborn teetotaller who smeared the contemptible idea of fascism on the fabric of our world, or pick at a crusty Russian leader whose affection for sauce almost heaved his country's hopes over his own shirt. Because, every now and then, you find an unavoidable doozy, a dirty protest that even bleach can't dislodge from the annals of time. And so we give you the mem-

bers of the 1917 American Congress. Now, these daft dimwits take some beating, because their stain was the 18th Amendment, which led to the 1919 Volstead Act and Prohibition.

Prohibition was daft. For a start it led to adulterated gin and sent inadvertent imbibers to the morgue. It created perfect conditions for crooks to organise crime. And it dehydrated a righteous revenue stream for the government. Some stains are accidents (we've all been there), and perhaps good intentions went awry with the temperance attempt, but we can't forgive this one, particularly as it required 13 years and a strong president to scrub Prohibition away.

It was the evening of December 5th, 1933, when a man stepped up to push through the 21st Amendment and repeal this abomination. That man was Franklin D Roosevelt, and he did it with a martini in his hand.

Roosevelt will be remembered for many things, not least digging his country out of the depths of the Depression, remaining steadfast during World War II and completing an unprecedented four terms in office, feats all accomplished while

Silver cocktail shaker and glasses from the Franklin D Roosevelt Presidential Library and Museum in Hyde Park, New York state.

he fought his way through a paralytic illness. But getting giggle juice back down the gobs of his countrymen is what brought him immortality. Seriously folks.

Gin Martinis were his drink of choice. Not only did he serve the drink pre-dinner at the White House, he mixed them himself. He set an hour aside in the day to indulge and even kept abstainers from his study so he indulged without criticism. True he was known to fall over at family get-togethers; yes he got amorous with his assistant, and OK, the chink of glass was occasionally followed by the clangour of his un-statesman-like singing. But peers maintain he was judicious with his juice, and publicly he insisted: 'A gentleman learns his capacity and tries not to exceed it.'

He also mixed Martinis in the political arena, serving them for King George and Queen Elizabeth during a visit and drinking them with Churchill as they helped end World War II. It earned Churchill's profound respect. The British Prime Minister claimed: 'Meeting Roosevelt was like uncorking your first bottle of champagne.' And crucially his championing of alcohol invigorated government and industry, helping recoup the billions of tax dollars lost in the previous decade. He carried a cocktail kit wherever he went, along with silver cups, now on display at the FDR Library in Hyde Park in New York. He liked martinis wet (heavy on the vermouth) which ticks today's flavour boxes and sometimes he even added absinthe. The man was a martini machine.

Why did he love the Martini? Probably because it's the greatest cocktail of all time: a careful blend of gin with vermouth, the slightest change in conditions affecting flavour, from the measure of vermouth to dilution from ice. It showcases gin in all its glory and while apple, espresso, pornstar and even vodka have subsequently been stirred in, here at Thinking Drinkers Towers, we are steadfastly proud Gin Martini men.

THE MARTINI
★ ★ ★ ★ ★ ★ ★ ★ ★ ★ ★ ★ ★ ★ ★

When you're asked if you'd like it wet or dry, the barman is referring to the amount of vermouth you prefer. Somewhere around 8 parts gin to 1 part vermouth is common, suggested as quite wet, but some go for the original 50:50 spec. Then the aim is to balance dilution and temperature. James Bond had his shaken, but if you stir it, you can control that process. You want it chilled, clear and not overly watery. And use a chilled glass.

GLASS: MARTINI
60ml (2fl oz) of gin/vodka
3 tsp vermouth
ice cubes
GARNISH: OLIVE OR LEMON ZEST TWIST

Stir the ingredients in a mixing glass with ice, and strain into a Martini glass. Garnish with an olive or a lemon zest twist.

GIN
RECOMMENDATIONS

*Some of these recommendations are familiar gins like Tanqueray No. Ten –
brilliant beverages and absurdly inexpensive. But others are gins that are
boutique in production with interesting botanicals and back stories.*

TANQUERAY NO. TEN 47.3% ABV

Tanqueray London Dry uses a minimalist but steely base of juniper, coriander, liquorice and angelica. Tanqueray No. Ten builds on this, ramping up the juniper and adding whole Florida oranges, Mexican limes, grapefruits and chamomile. The result is mellow and outstanding. Marvellous in a Martini.

HERNO JUNIPER 40.5% ABV

Amongst this Swedish spirit's bright light botanicals you'll find meadowsweet and lingonberries, but the significant story is the ageing process. The gin is rested in a special juniper wood cask for 30 days to make it resinous and spicy.

SACRED 40% ABV

Sacred are botanical pioneers and employ a careful vacuum distillation process that heightens flavour intensity. Added to which, distiller Ian Hart distils it in his living room, believe it or not, with pipes running around the bookcases. We're serious, it's utterly bonkers. Along with citrus, juniper and cardamom you'll find nutmeg and Hougari frankincense in his vibrant gin. This one is another excellent Martini bedfellow.

BERKELEY SQUARE 40% ABV

From the historic Greenall's distillery, this gin asks the question: how does your garden grow? If, like us, it's paved over, then try this gin. Botanicals include juniper, coriander, angelica plus basil, sage, French lavender, cubeb berries and Kaffir lime. Light but floral, herbal and soft, just like a garden, right?

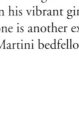

WHITLEY NEILL 42% ABV

Slightly smoother and sweeter, this gin retains juniper but also includes some interesting botanicals such as Cape gooseberry and the fruit of the Baobab tree. Boababs bear fruits called 'monkey bread'. Citrusy.

ST GEORGE TERROIR 45% ABV

Californian distiller St George specialises in authenticity of flavour and digs deep into the surrounding area to create a gin that hums of botanicals sat in the West Coast sun. Douglas fir, California bay laurel and coastal sage are all in there to back up the piny gin. Powerful stuff.

ADNAMS FIRST RATE 48% ABV

Notable for its boutique grain base, Adnams distillery uses the fermentables from malted barley, wheat and oats in its neighbouring brewery. Add botanicals including juniper, cassia bark, vanilla pods, angelica root, caraway seeds, fennel seeds and thyme, and you discover a spirit full of crisp botanical bursts.

BURROUGH'S RESERVE 43% ABV

Beefeater London Dry is celebrated for its citrus notes, original distiller James Burroughs a stickler for selecting the very best peels. This gin is faithful to his 1860s nine botanical recipe, has been distilled in 19th century copper pot still and then rested in Jean de Lillet oak casks. Oak-aged gin is a new direction for the category and this exponent is something you can easily chill and drink neat, like a Martini.

PLYMOUTH NAVY STRENGTH 57% ABV

If there's any chance you're going to sprinkle your gin over gunpowder, then Lord knows you want the stuff to light again after. You'll get in a right pickle otherwise. So it was that Coates & Co. distilled a 'proof' gin for the British Royal Navy that remained flammable when Martinis were spilled during 19th-century cannon capers. This incarnation comes in at 57% ABV and is bursting with blistering barnacles of botanicals to keep salty seamen happy on the high seas. Big and bold with pine, sage, coriander and citrus on nose and palate.

SIPSMITH SLOE 29% ABV

Sipsmith introduced London to the first copper still in the city for nearly 200 years when it launched in 2009. It makes a host of heroic spirits, including a super-duper London Dry. Stretch your horizons by sampling the sloe. These chaps have done wonders using wild, hand-picked sloes to deliver tart, cherry berry up front and a pepper gin crack at the back.

GIN COCKTAILS

★ ★

AVIATION

Created by Hugo Ensslin at the Hotel Wallick, Times Square, New York in the early 1900s.

GLASS: MARTINI
60ml (2fl oz) gin
3 tsp lemon juice
3 tsp maraschino liqueur
1 tsp crème de violette
ice cubes

GARNISH: A FRESH CHERRY

Shake the first four ingredients with ice cubes and fine strain into a glass. Squeeze the oil from the lemon zest over the surface of the drink and discard. Garnish with a fresh cherry.

TOM COLLINS

A mixed marvel that tickled fancies in gin palaces during the early 1800s. Thought to have first been served at the Coffee House bar at the Limmer's Hotel, London.

GLASS: HIGHBALL
60ml (2fl oz) gin
30ml (1fl oz) lemon juice
4 tsp sugar syrup
sparkling water, to top
ice cubes

GARNISH: SLICE OF LEMON

Shake the ingredients with ice and strain into a highball over fresh ice. Top with sparkling water and garnish with a slice of lemon.

SINGAPORE SLING

Invented in 1914 in the Long Bar at the Raffles Hotel, Singapore.

GLASS: HIGHBALL OR HURRICANE
30ml (1fl oz) gin
3 tsp lime juice
3 tsp cherry brandy
1½ tsp Cointreau
1½ tsp Benedictine
120ml (4fl oz) pineapple juice
2 tsp grenadine
dash of Angostura bitters
ice cubes

GARNISH: PINEAPPLE AND CHERRY

Shake the ingredients with ice and strain into a glass. Garnish with a slice of pineapple and a cherry.

CORPSE REVIVER NO. 2

Designed to raise the dead. It won't. This recipe was made famous by Harry Craddock in the 1930 *Savoy Cocktail Book*.

GLASS: MARTINI
25ml (1fl oz) gin
25ml (1fl oz) Cointreau
25ml (1fl oz) Lillet Blanc
25ml (1fl oz) fresh lemon juice
dash of absinthe
ice cubes

GARNISH: MARASCHINO CHERRY

Shake the ingredients well with ice and strain into a glass. Garnish with a maraschino cherry.

GIMLET

In 1867 Lachlin Rose launched a preserved lime juice (Rose's) to combat scurvy suffered by sailors. It was mixed with gin by a naval officer and gave rise to this classic cocktail.

GLASS: ROCKS
60ml (2fl oz) gin
4 tsp lime cordial
dash of soda water
ice cubes

GARNISH: LIME ZEST OR WEDGE

Stir the ingredients in a mixing glass with ice and strain into a rocks glass over fresh ice. Top with soda water and garnish with a wedge of lime or some zest.

PEGU CLUB

Created at the Pegu Club in Burma and adapted from Harry Craddock's classic 1930 *Savoy Cocktail Book*.

GLASS: MARTINI
50ml (1¾fl oz) gin
25ml (1fl oz) orange curaçao
3 tsp lime juice
dash of Angostura bitters
dash of orange bitters
ice cubes

GARNISH: FRESH RASPBERRY

Shake the ingredients with ice and strain into a glass. Garnish with a raspberry.

APERITIFS, DIGESTIFS & NIGHTCAPS
A Complete Drinks Cabinet

*So, as the sun sets on this Thinking Drinker tome, let us slide
into our leather armchair, cigar in one hand and a snifter in
the other, and embrace those illustrious alcoholic innovations
that are so deserving of appreciation from even the most
discriminating of dipsomaniacs. From the fabulous fortified
wines of Portugal and Spain to absinthe, armagnac, cognac
and campari, these are the drinks that at some
time, somewhere, really made a difference.*

HISTORY & CULTURE

The most disappointing kind of discerning drinker is a monogamous one. While monogamy is to be applauded in one's love life, those blindly loyal to just one life-enriching liquid are living in a fool's paradise.

Our lives are too short and too blessed with intoxicating opportunity to deny ourselves the undoubted pleasures of promiscuity. To misquote an anonymous witticism often ascribed to Oscar Wilde, you should 'try anything once except incest, Morris dancing and Advocaat'.

Chastity is particularly cheap in the land of liqueurs, even the celibate monks that distilled and created some of the earliest examples will tell you that (assuming they're not the ones in a silent order, of course).

Liqueurs are a broad church of bottles, sweetened and flavoured with eclectic ingredients. While some are sweeter than a penguin in a tuxedo, others deliver all the dry bitterness of a cuckolded sand dune. They can be creamy, fruity, nutty or herbal; they can vary in strength, they come in various colours or no colour at all, and many use spirits such as whisky, rum or brandy at their base.

Brandy Alexander, a liqueur-based cocktail that everyone needs to try at some point.

The word 'liqueur' has its roots in the Latin term *liquefacere*, meaning to 'dissolve or melt', and dates back to the Middle Ages when it was discovered that pretty much anything can be dissolved if you distil it.

Initially, ingredients were herbs and plants boasting supposed medicinal benefits and these elixirs were called *eau-de-vie* – 'water of life' which could cure everything from syphilis and gout to stomach ache and liver twang. Of course, none of them did this but, as they tasted nice and tended to lift life's load, if only temporarily, people persisted with them purely for pleasure, experimenting with anything they could get their hands on – fruits, roots, spices, herbs, plants, vegetables and even meat (in Renaissance England, distilled spirit was made using egg yolk, scorpions, worms and chickens. It must have tasted fowl).

The laws surrounding liqueurs are a bit looser than they used to be but, still, there aren't any solid stipulations. What separates them from 'straight' spirits is that they're sweetened with something, most often sugar. Often found dwelling on the back bar or on the drinks trolley, picked up to play cameo roles in cocktails, liqueurs are the drinks that turn up and discreetly let you know why they're so thoroughly deserving of distinction.

That such grandeur has faded in recent times owes much to the decline of two classic imbibing occasions that, sadly, no longer regularly enrich our busy modern lives – namely the aperitif and the digestif.

The word 'aperitif' comes from the Latin *aperire*, meaning 'to open'. An aperitif's job is to 'open', or stimulate, one's appetite and, to do this, it should ideally express dry, bitter or herbal elements, as bitterness activates the hunger hormone, ghrelin.

While the Egyptians, Ancient Greeks and Romans were big on bitter herbal beverages, a big *merci* and *grazie* must go to the French and the Italians for making the idea of leaving work early to have a drink a sign of sophistication.

While the Italian *aperitivo* revolves around vermouths, the French are famous for their *quinquinas* (Dubonnet, Suze, Pernod) which contain quinine – great at getting the gastric juices into gear and a well-known antimalarial too. Many rose in popularity in the 19th century when French troops were fighting both the men and the mosquitoes of Algeria.

Liqueurs are also the driving force behind the after-dinner digestif. As well as herbal liqueurs made with mint, liquorice, ginger, caraway, cumin and other stomach-settling succours; other drinks that counter the ill effects of excess consumption include the fruit-based liqueurs Limoncello and Poire William, bitters such as Underberg and Becherovka; cream liqueurs such as Kahlúa; and nutty affairs such as Disaronno (almonds) and Frangelico (hazelnuts).

The doyenne of the digestif, however, is most definitely brandy. As Samuel Johnson once said: 'Claret is the liquor for boys; port for men; but he who aspires to be a hero must drink brandy.'

Brandy is the oldest established spirit in the world, first made by the Moors who, having come up with the idea of distillation, invaded Spain in 711 AD and began distilling the local wine.

When the Moors left and the alembics were left in the hands of the monasteries, distilled wine became a massive medicinal money-maker, and 'burned wine' was soon giving the Romans enormous revenues in tax. It was the Dutch, in the 14th century, who discovered brandy's true

The Connaught Bar in London's Mayfair, an extremely dapper drinking destination, boasts a beautiful back-bar.

beauty. Until they began shipping it all over Europe, 'burned wine' was feisty firewater – a grapey concentrate that was cheaper to transport and was watered down to make wine.

But as the brandy bobbed up and down in the ships, its barrels acting as ballast, it took on the character of the oak and the harsh moonshine mellowed into something a lot smoother.

They began making 'brandy wine' (as the English called it) all over Europe but, by the 16th century, the most esteemed area for brandy distillation was in Cognac, France. Not only was it ideally situated on the coast, it also grew grapes that were heinous in wine yet heavenly when distilled and aged in oak.

Whether your tipple is brandy, absinthe or a banana-based liqueur, now is the time to put the wheels back on the after-dinner drinks trolley, now is the time to open your mind and your mouth to the aperitif and now is the time to let all good liqueurs into your life.

> "*The decline of the aperitif may well be one of the most depressing phenomena of our time*"
>
> ~ LUIS BUÑUEL ~

1411 WINE IS DISTILLED IN GASCONY, FRANCE, NEAR THE SPANISH BORDER, AND 'ARMAGNAC' IS BORN.

1525 A YOUNG TAVERN OWNER GIVES A LOCAL PAINTER IN SARONNO A BOTTLE OF HER HOMEMADE ALMOND LIQUEUR.

1531 A DANISH LORD CALLED ESKE BILLE SENDS A BOTTLE OF AQUAVIT TO OLAV ENGELBREKTS-SON, THE LAST ROMAN CATHOLIC ARCHBISHOP OF NORWAY, AND ACCOMPANIES IT WITH THE FIRST WRITTEN REFERENCE TO 'AQUA VITAE' – 'WHICH HELPS AGAINST ALL KINDS OF INTERNAL DISEASES'.

1631 QUININE IS FIRST USED BY ROMANS TO CURE MALARIA.

1605 MARSHALL FRANÇOIS HANNIBAL D'ESTRÉES, WHO WAS CLOSE TO KING HENRY IV OF FRANCE, HANDS OVER AN ANCIENT MANUSCRIPT ENTITLED 'AN ELIXIR OF LONG LIFE' TO THE MONKS OF A CARTHUSIAN MONASTERY IN VEUVERT, FRANCE.

1575 THE BOLS FAMILY ARRIVE IN AMSTERDAM AND BEGIN TO DISTIL LIQUEURS AND, BY 1664, A DUTCH GIN CALLED GENEVER, WHICH WAS ORIGINALLY RETAILED AS A REMEDY FOR MUSCULAR PAIN.

1715 JERSEY-BORN JEAN MARTELL CREATES A COGNAC BUSINESS BEARING HIS NAME.

1724 REMY MARTIN FIRES UP ITS STILLS IN COGNAC, FRANCE.

1737 CARTHUSIAN MONKS IN THE FRENCH ALPS DISTIL A NEW MEDICINAL LIQUEUR CALLED CHARTREUSE.

1765 IRISH EXILE RICHARD HENNESSY STARTS UP A COGNAC-BASED BUSINESS EXPORTING SPIRITS.

1805 HORATIO NELSON DIES IN THE BATTLE OF TRAFALGAR AND HIS BODY IS PRESERVED, SO IT SAYS HERE, IN A BARREL OF BRANDY WHICH IS DRUNK IN HIS HONOUR BY SAILORS ON THE SEA VOYAGE HOME.

1794 JOSEF VITUS BECHER (1769–1840) BLENDS HERBS AND SPICES TOGETHER AT HIS CZECH STILL-HOUSE AND BECHEROVKA IS BORN.

1792 THE ORIGINAL ABSINTHE LIQUEUR IS CREATED BY DR PIERRE ORDINAIRE IN THE SWISS TOWN OF COUVET.

1805 HENRI-LOUIS PERNOD ESTABLISHES PONTARLIER, FRANCE, AS THE EPICENTRE OF ABSINTHE PRODUCTION.

1817 GEORGE IV WRITES TO HENNESSY ORDERING A 'VERY SUPERIOR OLD PALE' (VSOP).

1818 PETER HEERING STARTS SELLING A CHERRY LIQUEUR FROM HIS COPENHAGEN GROCERY STORE.

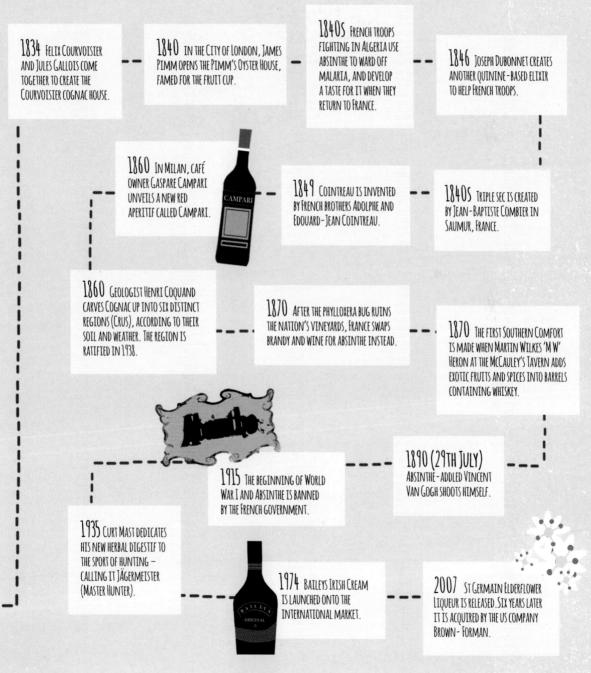

1834 Felix Courvoisier and Jules Gallois come together to create the Courvoisier cognac house.

1840 In the City of London, James Pimm opens the Pimm's Oyster House, famed for the fruit cup.

1840s French troops fighting in Algeria use absinthe to ward off malaria, and develop a taste for it when they return to France.

1846 Joseph Dubonnet creates another quinine-based elixir to help French troops.

1860 In Milan, café owner Gaspare Campari unveils a new red aperitif called Campari.

1849 Cointreau is invented by French brothers Adolphe and Edouard-Jean Cointreau.

1840s Triple sec is created by Jean-Baptiste Combier in Saumur, France.

1860 Geologist Henri Coquand carves Cognac up into six distinct regions (crus), according to their soil and weather. The region is ratified in 1938.

1870 After the phylloxera bug ruins the nation's vineyards, France swaps brandy and wine for absinthe instead.

1870 The first Southern Comfort is made when Martin Wilkes 'M W' Heron at the McCauley's Tavern adds exotic fruits and spices into barrels containing whiskey.

1890 (29th July) Absinthe-addled Vincent Van Gogh shoots himself.

1915 The beginning of World War I and Absinthe is banned by the French government.

1935 Curt Mast dedicates his new herbal digestif to the sport of hunting – calling it Jägermeister (Master Hunter).

1974 Baileys Irish Cream is launched onto the international market.

2007 St Germain Elderflower Liqueur is released. Six years later it is acquired by the US company Brown-Forman.

VAN GOGH

Toulouse-Lautrec walks into a Parisian bar and sees Vincent van Gogh sitting in the corner, having a drink and doing some painting. 'Bonjour Vincent,' says Lautrec. 'How you doing?'

'Things aren't great if I'm honest Henri,' says van Gogh. 'I've been tortured by acute anxiety from an early age which has rendered me an obstinate recluse, social situations have always terrified me, my only true friend during my sorrowful life has been loneliness and there's an indescribable darkness deep down inside that, every day, snags on my soul. And another thing. I've not made a single centime from these paintings that I do – knowing my luck, they'll fetch up to $82.5m long after I kill myself with a shotgun.'

'Oh', says Lautrec, shuffling awkwardly on his cane. 'Sorry to hear that Vinny. How about I buy you an absinthe?' 'That's very kind of you Henri but that won't be necessary,' replies Van Gogh, raising a glass filled with green liquid. 'I've got one 'ere.' Dyageddit? Do you? Oh.

· The most fascinating and famous artist of the absinthe era, Vincent van Gogh endured a desperately tragic life that didn't begin particularly well… and then got worse. A delicate, distant child who seldom socialised with others, his behaviour as a young boy baffled his strict Calvinist parents whose own emotional detachment made him even more of a recluse. While Vincent drew comfort from his interest in art, he never fully managed to brush away his demons; any periods with psychological stability were infrequent and short-lived. Cantankerous, incredibly intense and, by all accounts, a little odd, van Gogh struggled to hold down employment. Relieved of his first

job as an art dealer, van Gogh turned to a career in the church – but his missionary work was criticised for 'an excess of zeal bordering on the scandalous' while a short stab at evangelism was seriously undermined by him 'lacking a talent for speaking'.

Forming friendships wasn't his forte either. No oil painting in the looks department, van Gogh was particularly calamitous in love, forever falling for inappropriate women whose feelings for him ranged from utter disinterest to acute fear.

His incessant pursuit of a widowed cousin proved the nadir in a wretched love life. He asked her to marry him and she said no. Undeterred and increasingly obsessed, he continued to pester her, forcing her to seek refuge at her parents' house in Amsterdam.

Rather than play it cool, Vincent played it 'scalding' – he turned up at the house, plunged his hand into the flames of a burning lamp and pledged to keep it there until she saw him. Amid the stench of burning skin, he then fainted.

There is, however, a notoriously thin line between madness and heightened creative genius and whatever was going on inside van Gogh's famously frail psyche, it saw and perceived things that the minds of otheres simply didn't.

During van Gogh's time in Paris with his brother Theo, his early paintings were dismissed as 'impudent monstrosities' by critics. But his art improved as he spent more time with

ABSINTH

Vincent van Gogh

Impressionist artists who, like himself, had been derided by the established art scene.

This also happened to be the period when van Gogh first became enchanted with the 'Green Fairy'. When van Gogh would meet with the likes of Camille Pissarro, Claude Monet, Edgar Degas and Auguste Renoir and others in the cafés of Paris, it was absinthe that would decorate the mahogany.

Absinthe was the ultimate alcoholic aesthete in that, unlike other inebriates, it furnished its drinkers with an intoxication that was neither fuzzy nor blurred. It was exalted among artists for the clarity of vision that it induced. It gave colours extra vibrancy, it sharpened light; it opened up the eyes and endowed the mind with an imaginative wanderlust in a way that other drinks simply didn't. And, importantly for impoverished artists, it was considerably cheaper than wine.

Absinthe increased its influence on van Gogh's art when he moved from Paris to Arles, in southern France, where there was more natural sunlight and where, rather worryingly, absinthe consumption happened to be four times greater than the national average.

In Arles, absinthe proved a particularly powerful muse for van Gogh, an artist captivated by the communicative power of colour. Reluctant to merely reflect reality as the Impressionists had, he was encouraged by absinthe to introduce a distorted dimension to his art, which ultimately opened the door to Expressionism.

Absinthe's effect is acutely evident in *Night Café* – a sinister, contorted depiction of his local drinking den in Arles. Several different shades of green, the colour of absinthe, and yellow, the shade when water is added, are swathed in thick paint against a brooding, despairing, dark red backdrop. 'I have tried to express the idea that the café is a place where one can ruin oneself, go mad or commit a crime,' wrote van Gogh the day after. 'I have tried to express, as it were, the powers of darkness in a low public house, by soft Louis XV green and malachite, contrasting with yellow-green and harsh blue-greens, and all this in an atmosphere like a devil's furnace, of pale sulphur.' It's an ominous insight into van Gogh's increasingly absinthe-addled mind. He used absinthe to anaesthetise his anxiety. He would drink himself numb, reaching for absinthe when the 'storm within gets too loud.'

Eventually the storm became deafening and, in the vast quantities that van Gogh was drinking it, absinthe began to exacerbate rather than allay his mental illnesses and he was dogged by delirium tremens. Van Gogh's increasingly bizarre behaviour earned him the local nickname *Fou Roux* (the Red Madman) and when he cut off his own ear and took it to his favourite brothel, after a night drinking with Paul Gauguin, he was sectioned.

Despite sustained periods of mental stability under the supervision of French physician Dr Gachet, van Gogh shot himself on 27 July 1890 but, in typically tragic fashion, he took two long days to die.

Van Gogh's association with absinthe continued beyond his death. When he was buried in a local cemetery, Dr Gachet planted an ornamental tree next to van Gogh's grave. The tree was a thuja which, unbeknown to Gachet, was a rich source of thujone – the chemical that supposedly provides absinthe with its hallucinogenic powers.

Fifteen years after his death, when they went to move van Gogh's coffin so he could be next to Theo, they discovered that the roots of the tree had tightly coiled themselves around the artist's casket 'as though', said one onlooker, 'they held him in a strong embrace'.

What is Wormwood

At the centre of absinthe's whole hallucinogenic hullabaloo is wormwood (*Artemisia Absinthium*). Unbearably bitter, it's defined in the Oxford English Dictionary as 'an emblem of what is bitter and grievous to the soul'. While the Slavic word for wormwood is, rather ominously, *Chernobyl*.

Hailed historically for its healing properties, wormwood earned its name from curing ringworm in the Middle Ages; Hippocrates used it to cure flatulence; Pythagoras used it to ease childbirth; and virgins took it to rid them of 'the scab'.

Many, however, cite wormwood's most active ingredient, thujone, as the cause of absinthe's anarchic and artistic side. A menthol-like terpene classified as a convulsant poison, it's been blamed for hallucinations, convulsions, excitability and unconsciousness when consumed in moderate quantities, while larger doses can, it's claimed, be fatal.

But analysis of 19th-century absinthe has revealed very little evidence of thujone and, modern day absinthe barely contains any thujone at all. So what gave the drink its delusional dimension? While biochemists have pointed to terpenes found in other herbs used in absinthe (star anise, fennel, coriander and sage among them) its alcoholic potency remains the main culprit, with a key co-conspirator being the mind-expanding reputation that has always gone before it.

The Ritual

1. Pour one measure (25ml/1tbsp) of absinthe into a glass.

2. Rest a perforated absinthe spoon on the glass.

3. Place one sugar cube on the spoon.

4. Take very fresh water and, drop by drop, drip it on the sugar cube so it dissolves and disintegrates, dropping into the absinthe with the water.

5. With every drip, the translucent green liquid turns from a transparent green liqueur into a milky whitish colour. This is called the louche effect and, for Lautrec and Verlaine, it was an integral part of the absinthe drinking ritual.

*The dictionary definition of **louche** is 'disreputable or sordid in a rakish or appealing way'.*

THE GREEN MONSTER

PAUL VERLAINE

PAUL VERLAINE EMBODIED 'THE GREEN CURSE' AT ITS MOST OMINOUS AND MENACING. HIS LIFE WAS DOWNRIGHT DREADFUL, AND WHENEVER TROUBLE TURNED UP, WHICH WAS ALMOST ALL OF THE TIME, ABSINTHE WAS RARELY ABSENT.

Unlike van Gogh, Verlaine was no absinthe apologist and, shortly before he died, wrote a damning assessment of absinthe in his *Confessions*. Firmly attributing the 'absurdities' of his existence to that 'horrible drink', he wrote, "the source of folly and crime, idiocy and shame, which governments should tax heavily if they do not surpress it altogether. Absinthe.'

In absinthe's defence, however, one can call an acutely odd upbringing to the stand. Verlaine's childhood was anything but normal. His mother, the well-to-do Elisa Dehée, doted after Verlaine having earlier suffered three miscarried pregnancies. Peversely, though, she preserved the small foetuses in alcohol, storing them in glass jars in the pantry – there for Verlaine to see whenever he was feeling peckish. Some years later, Verlaine demolished the jars in an absinthe-fuelled rage.

Long before he encountered the charms of the Green Fairy, Verlaine drank heavily during his teenage years and early twenties, only adopting absinthe as his emotional crutch in 1863 when he became part of Paris's Parnassian school of poets, which was known for its precise, emotionally detached verse.

While marriage to Mathilde Mauté de Fleurville ushered in a few months of absinthe abstention, Verlaine returned to the Green Fairy with gusto on meeting a certain Arthur Rimbaud, a 16-year-old poet enamoured of Verlaine's poetry.

Verlaine and Rimbaud's relationship was debauched, depraved and drenched in the green stuff. They'd consume copious amounts of absinthe, sleep together, then attack each other with knives while, curiously, writing some of their most powerful poetry.

Their time together became increasingly tempestuous and when Rimbaud announced once again that he was leaving, Verlaine shot him twice with a revolver. Verlaine was arrested, charged with attempted murder and sentenced to five years in jail.

Unlike those of the Latin Quarter, the bars of prison protected Verlaine from his absinthe addiction, and incarceration inspired some of his greatest writing. But after serving only 18 months,

Verlaine was released and it wasn't long before he was once again being given the green glad-eye.

He was soon back in jail, serving a month's sentence for attacking his mother, and after she passed away in 1886, Verlaine's life slouched into its final years of despair. While his work was finding widespread critical acclaim, Verlaine would be seen arched angrily over an absinthe in the bars of the Left Bank when he wasn't in brothels, institutions or hospitals.

His voracious appetite for sex and absinthe manifested itself in cirrhosis of the liver and syphilis. During the last months of his life as he lay in hospital, Verlaine's friends would visit him and surreptitiously slip some 'bottled madness' under his pillow. He drank until the end, but a year before his death in 1896, Verlaine lamented his dalliances with the 'green and terrible drink.'

TOULOUSE-LAUTREC

HE MAY NOT HAVE BEEN VERY BIG, BUT HENRI DE TOULOUSE-LAUTREC WAS AWFULLY CLEVER AT CAPTURING DECADENT PARISIAN LIFE ON A COLOURFUL CANVAS.

A 19th-century painting paparazzo, he was at one with Montmarte's literary and artistic set and a permanent fixture at the Moulin Rouge where he would furiously sketch his surroundings, often exposing their 'squalor and ugliness'.

He was an adventurous imbiber of alcoholic beverages too, especially absinthe. He would mix it with cognac in a '*tremblement de terre*' (earthquake) and would store several measures in his cane, as if it were not only a physical crutch but an emotional one too.

Painting Parisian nightlife meant absinthe was a prominent feature in several of his paintings, most notably '*The Absinthe Drinker*' (1888), '*At Genelle, Absinthe Drinker*' (1886) and, of course,

his 1887 depiction of van Gogh sipping the Green Fairy in a café.

Like van Gogh, Toulouse-Lautrec died at the age of 37 and his death, occurring shortly after leaving a sanatorium, is widely attributed to absinthe addiction. More than 50 years later, both men were held up as examples of dangerous addicts by W R Bett in a scathing address to the Medical Society of London.

'When day is done and night is a lyric ecstasy with a million stars; when the lust for life flames like red wine in the heart of man; when out of the torturous darkness temptation strides with fawning hips and painted face, do you remember Vincent van Gogh, [and] the satyric figure of a dwarf with enormous head, huge fleshy nose, repulsive scarlet lips, black bushy beard, myopic malevolent eyes?

'He [Toulouse-Lautrec] leans for support on a tiny cane. He stands by a dust bin polluting the night with its hideousness-symbol of filth and putrescence. He sits down at a marble table, eagerly welcomed by those who have wasted life, and now life wastes them: drinking absinthe with hopeless hopefulness. The fairy with the green eyes has enslaved their brains and has also stolen their souls.'

THE CLASSIC DRINKS CABINET

Beyond the stable spirits, the classic drinks cabinet should show-case alcohol at its most eclectic and esoteric. It is the engine room of an erudite imbibing existence, a sanctuary for liqueurs that add an extra, invaluable dimension to one's discerning drinking.

AMARETTO DISARONNO 28% ABV

Italian, almondy and instantly recognisable in its dappled oblong decanter, Disaronno dates back to the Renaissance when, in 1525, a beautiful widowed innkeeper posed for a pupil of Leonardo da Vinci in Saronno. Flattered to be a muse for his painting of the Madonna at the Chapel of Santa Maria delle Grazie (which can still be seen), she gave him a bottle of her home-made almond liqueur.

How to drink it? Amaretto Sour.

BAILEYS 17% ABV

According to research recently undertaken by the Thinking Drinkers, around half the people in the world are actually women. Remarkable. Further research reveals that, apart from chocolate and shoes, many of these women people (OK, and some men) like a nice glass of Baileys over ice. The Irish-whiskey based liqueur is to some what catnip is to cute little kittens (and we do know men who like those, too.)

How to drink it? While watching *Sex and the City* wearing silk pyjamas.

BENEDICTINE 40% ABV

Don't be mistaken by the monastic moni-ker, this brandy-based blend of 56 different herbs and spices is not a genuine piece of monky business. It was the idea of Alexan-der Le Grand, an industrial entrepreneur who tweaked a 16th-century formula found in a book belonging to a French Benedictine monastery. During World War I, soldiers drank it with hot water to keep warm in the trenches.

How to drink it? Bene 'n' Hot.

CAMPARI 25% ABV

Known for its starring role in the Negroni, that most alpha-male of aperitifs, Campari was invented in 1860 by Gaspare Cam-pari in the basement of his eponymous Milanese bar.

His son, Davide, gave it internation-al appeal by selling it into bars while chasing a rather attractive opera singer all over Europe and America. While none of the 68 herbs, fruits and spices have been changed over the years, vegetarians will be pleased to know that it no longer gets its striking red colour from carmine dye, sourced from the crushing of cochineal insects. Less creepy-crawly ingredients now produce the same colour.

How to drink it? Equal parts gin, campari and vermouth over ice. Stir.

CHAMBORD BLACKBERRY LIQUEUR 16.5% ABV

Named after Chateau Chambord in the Loire Valley, this liqueur was served up to Louis XIV in the 17th century but didn't achieve fame until the 1980s when an American named Sky Norton rediscovered the recipe and unleashed it on to the US market. There's all manner of intriguing ingredients in the distinctive orb-shaped bottle – including blackberries and raspberries, honey, vanilla and citrus peel as well as cognac.

How to drink it? In a French Martini: vodka and pineapple juice.

CHARTREUSE VERTE 54% ABV

Unlike Benedictine, this glorious green gift from the Gods is still made by monks (Carthusian this time) up in the mountains near Grenoble. The Chartreuse recipe rests in the hands of just three monks and each one only knows two-thirds of a formula that contains 130 herbs and spices. Thrice macerated in alcohol, they are distilled four times and, after the addition of honey and golden syrup, aged in giant oak casks for between three and five years. Most commonly consumed chilled over ice as a digestif, Chartreuse's most illustrious imbibers include Hunter S Thompson, Jon Bon Jovi and Charles de Gaulle. Used by local farmers to cure flatulence in cows,

it was also enjoyed by the Queen Mother when at the Ascot races – but for different reasons.

How to drink it? In the Blenheim, created by Joe Gilmore, head barman at the Savoy, London, to commemorate Churchill's 90th birthday.

DRAMBUIE 40% ABV

After defeat at the Battle of Culloden in 1746, Bonnie Prince Charlie went into hiding on the Isle of Skye. As the Isle is situated too far north for trees to grow, Charlie had nothing to hide behind but help was at hand from the McKinnon clan, who gave him sanctuary. To reward their kindness, Charlie gave them the recipe for a *dram buidheach*, a 'drink that satisfies' that was made with whisky sweetened with heather honey.

How to drink it? In a Rusty Nail cocktail, along with whisky.

DUBONNET 15% ABV

The Queen Mum also greatly admired this iconic quinine aperitif made from the wines of Langudeoc-Roussillon, deliberately designed by Joseph Dubonnet in 1846 to help French legionnaires fight off malaria in North Africa. To balance quinine's intense bitterness, other ingredients include orange peel, elderflower, cocoa beans, Colombian coffee, cinnamon and chamomile. The 'Dubonnet Man' was the first advert designed by French graphic artist Cassandre, complete with the slogan 'Dubo, Dubon, Dubonnet.'

How to drink it? In a Queen Mother, so-called because she would have two before lunch. One part gin, two parts Dubonnet, plus a twist of lemon or orange if you must. But no more.

GALLIANO 42.3% ABV

One of the biggest battles in Italy's ill-fated military incursion into Ethiopia occurred in 1895, when Mayor Giuseppe Galliano and his Italian troops, outnumbered 36 to 1, put up an impressive fight for 44 days against 80,000 Ethiopians at Fort Edna. They were defeated, but the courage of Galliano and his men was praised back home and Arturo Vaccari, who owned a distillery in Tuscany, invented a liqueur in honour of the gallant Galliano, who died in a battle shortly after. As usual, the recipe remains a closely guarded secret but, rest assured, there's plenty in that towering totem bottle – star anise, Bulgarian coriander, yarrow, cardamom, sage, mugwort and vanilla.

How to drink it? In a naughty Harvey Wallbanger cocktail.

GRAND MARNIER 40% ABV

Grand Marnier was the lovechild of two French drink dynasties that came together in 1876. When Louis Alexandre Marnier, the son of a wine-making family, wed the granddaughter of Jean-Baptiste Lapostolle, famed for his fruit liqueurs, the result was 'Curaçao Marnier', a blend of cognacs flavoured with essence of dried orange peels from the Caribbean. Hailed by famed hotelier César Ritz as 'Grand Marnier!', it became synonymous with the Cosmopolitan – a cocktail created by Dale DeGroff in New York and which famously starred in *Sex and the City*. The liqueur was also known to be served on the RMS *Titanic*.

How to drink it? It goes down well with a big chunk of ice.

HEERING CHERRY LIQUEUR 24% ABV

The original cherry liqueur first sold in 1818 by Peter Heering, who, on taking over Mrs Cartensen's grocery shop in Copenhagen, inherited her recipe that remains the same today. Its distinctive almond edge, gained from crushing the stones as well as the fruit, is mellowed by oak maturation and the addition of extra herbs and spices. Fifteen years after it was first served in the Singapore Sling, it appeared in the famous *Savoy Cocktail Book* as an essential ingredient in Blood & Sand, named after a silent film starring Latin lothario Rudolph Valentino as a matador.

How to drink it? It was famously added into the Singapore Sling, created by Ngiam Tong Boon.

JAGERMEISTER 35% ABV

While Jägermeister has become famous for its kinship with a certain carbonated energy drink, it was certainly not caffeine-fuelled hedonism that Curt Mast had in mind when, in 1935, he meticulously milled, mixed and macerated 56 different herbs, roots and spices in neutral spirit to produce Jägermeister. Meaning 'Master Hunter', it was drunk as a much-needed digestif after a hard day hunting deer and then eating them. The moody looking stag on the front is St Hubertus, the patron saint of hunting, while the poem on the back is taken from *Hunter's Salute* by Oskar Von Riesenthal.

How to drink it? Responsibly. Chilled. Ideally not with an energy drink.

KING'S GINGER 41% ABV

King Edward VII made the most of his privileged position. Much to the chagrin of his mother Queen Victoria, he was a playboy prince who eschewed kissing babies and shaking hands in favour of playing golf, shooting animals, bedding mistresses, smoking cigars and living the good life dressed in tweed. As King, he also liked driving around his open-top Daimler which, much to the concern of his Royal Physician, exposed Edward to the elements. King Edward's cockles needed warming and, at the physician's behest, the wine and spirit merchants Berry Bros & Rudd created the King's Ginger – a lavish liqueur laced with spicy ginger root and a little bit of lemon peel too.

How to drink it? In King & Tonic, with tonic water and Angostura bitters.

LILLET 17% ABV

When he wasn't sipping Chianti with fava beans and a slice of human liver, Hannibal Lecter loved a Lillet. An iconic, oak-aged aromatised wine made from a blend of Bordeaux wines (85%) and citrus liqueurs (15%), it was created in 1872 by the Lillet brothers, Paul & Raymond. The French drink it like Dr Lecter, 'with a slice of orange over ice' but its most iconic serve is the Vesper Martini, first ordered by James Bond in Ian Fleming's 1953 novel *Casino Royale*. Although back then it was called Kina Lillet and contained more of the bitter quinine – so add a dash of Angostura bitters for the authentic Bond experience.

How to drink it? In a Vesper Martini.

MANDARINE NAPOLEON 38% ABV

Short in stature, ambitious in millinery and forever picking fights with pretty much any European country that looked at him a bit funny, Napoleon Bonaparte wasn't a particularly enthusiastic drinker. But he did inspire this marvellous mandarin liqueur, created for him in the late 1700s by Antoine-François de Fourcroy. A chemist and amateur distiller who was close to Napoleon, Fourcroy mixed aged cognacs and some new-fangled mandarin oranges sourced from Napoleon's native Corsica. Fourcroy's recipe was discovered some years later by Louis Schmidt, a Belgian chemist who then released it commercially in 1892, some 71 years after Napoleon had popped his modestly-sized clogs, aged just 51, while living in exile on the island of St Helena.

How to drink it? Short. Alongside a double espresso.

MENTZENDORFF KUMMEL LIQUEUR 38% ABV

Distilled using principally caraway seeds, but also cumin, anise, lemon and orange peel, Kümmel is a delicious yet distinctive tasting digestif that's been dividing opinion in Europe since the 16th century.

Mentzendorff is a magnificent kummel, first distilled in the Latvian town of Riga back in 1823 yet now done so in the Loire Valley using old copper stills. While often overlooked by the French, Mentzendorff Kummel is big on the golf courses of Britain where, flowing from a hip flask, it successfully settles both an upset stomach and the hands.

How to Drink it? On the first tee. 'Don't drink and drive. Don't even putt.'

PIMM'S 25% ABV

More quintessentially English than a sexually-repressed Morris dancer, Pimm's No.1 Cup has long been the exclusive preserve of the fictional British summertime. Many point to James Pimm, a London shellfish seller, who opened the Pimm's Oyster House in the City back in 1840.

But while the Pimm's bottle proudly states 1840 on the label, many name Samuel Morley, Pimm's successor, as the true Pimm's pioneer. For it was Morley who, in 1860, secured the bar's first liquor licence which allowed Pimms's to be served to the patrons in special tankard-style 'cups'.

As well as the original Pimm's Cup, No.1, which is gin-based and seasoned with numerous botanicals (one of which was, of course, quinine), other lesser-known Pimm's variants include No.2 (scotch), No.3 (brandy), No.4 (rum), No.5 (rye whiskey) and No.6 (vodka).

How to drink it? With lemonade, fruit and cucumber. Undercooked BBQ sausages optional.

RICARD 25% ABV

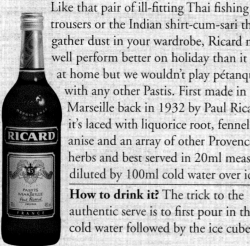

Like that pair of ill-fitting Thai fishing trousers or the Indian shirt-cum-sari that gather dust in your wardrobe, Ricard may well perform better on holiday than it does at home but we wouldn't play pétanque with any other Pastis. First made in Marseille back in 1932 by Paul Ricard, it's laced with liquorice root, fennel, star anise and an array of other Provencal herbs and best served in 20ml measures diluted by 100ml cold water over ice.

How to drink it? The trick to the authentic serve is to first pour in the cold water followed by the ice cubes.

ST. GERMAIN ELDERFLOWER LIQUEUR 20% ABV

Within that sexy looking bottle lies an equally sensual elderflower liqueur made from petals picked in the shadow of the French Alps. Having harvested it by hand, the producers quickly macerate the evocative elderflower in an eau-de-vie made from a blend of Chardonnay and Gamay grapes before sweetening with a smidgeon of Caribbean cane sugar. It's 'trés bon' as they say in France.

How to drink it? Topped up with either soda water (over ice) or champagne.

SOUTHERN COMFORT 20% ABV

During the 1870s, the American whiskey served straight from the cask in the bars of New Orleans bore little resemblance to the smooth-sipping bourbons drunk today. At McCauley's Tavern, situated in the French Quarter, an Irish bartender named Martin Wilkes 'M.W' Heron began bunging exotic fruits and spices into barrels containing the scratchier spirits. Having first bottled the bourbon under the name 'Cuffs & Buttons', Heron rechristened his whiskey-based liqueur Southern Comfort after a bar he'd opened in St Louis. Post-Prohibition, the Fowler family breathed life back into the brand and in 1939 sales soared on the coat-tails of the Scarlett O'Hara cocktail, named after the heroine in *Gone with the Wind*.

More recently, the brand's marketing has focused on a bronzed fat man strolling down the beach in nothing but a pair of tight 'budgie smuggling' swimming trunks.

How to drink it? in a Scarlett O'Hara cocktail.

TAYLOR'S VELVET VALERNUM
11% ABV

Many believe Malibu to be the sexiest sugar-cane-laced liqueur to come from the Caribbean island of Barbados. We're here to tell you that these people are wrong. An acquired taste well worth acquiring, it was described by Charles Dickens in 1892 as 'a curious liqueur composed from rum and lime-juice' in his Victorian periodical *All the Year Round* – Falernum is a sweet, syrupy coming together of cloves, almonds and a bunch of other botanicals that the Bajans won't tell us about. A must-stock if you're partial to Polynesian-style Tiki drinks and other tropical-fruit-laden cocktails.

How to drink it? We slip it into our Rum Swizzle – to give it a cheeky lift.

TOUSSAINT 30% ABV

Smoother than a cashmere codpiece and made with Arabica coffee beans infused in three year-old Caribbean rum, Toussaint (pronounced too-sun) is a coffee-based liqueur named after François-Dominique Toussaint L'Ouverture, a military mastermind who was the leader of the 1804 Haitian Revolution. In emancipating his people and giving Haiti independence, the Black Napoleon kicked the dastardly slave trade right in the swingers – a blow from which it thankfully never recovered. Toussaint's testicles, however, were terrific and he fathered 16 children before being remembered in the words of Wordsworth and the music of Santana, Steel Pulse and er…Wyclef Jean.

How to drink it? In an Espresso Martini (instead of the Kahlúa).

Churchill's Cabinet

'Good cognac is like a woman. Do not assault it. Coddle and warm it in your hands before you sip it.'
WINSTON CHURCHILL

Winston Churchill had an insatiable appetite for exquisite and exotic brandies – not just cognac (Hine was his favourite) but also cases of Armenian brandy sent to him every year by Stalin. Old brandy, along with hot baths, cold peas and cold champagne, were the essentials of life.

Lord Richard Butler, a contemporary of Churchill, wrote: 'I had no less than eight gargantuan dinners with him alone… the dinners being followed by libations of brandy so ample that I felt it prudent on more than one occasion to tip the liquid into the side of my shoe.'

Churchill would sip a snifter at lunch and it was also his preferred after-dinner digestif, a muse for some of his most vital military decision-making. In 1945, with World War II won, he freely admitted that he'd consumed enough brandy 'to fill three railway carriages'.

As he approached his eighties, doctors requested he tone down his drinking – which he did by dropping brandy from his repertoire. Only to replace it with Cointreau.

10 THINGS YOU NEED TO KNOW ABOUT PORT & SHERRY

01 Francis Fisticuffs
England's historical appetite for sherry can be attributed to the serious swashbucking antics of Sir Francis Drake. At the height of maritime fisticuffs between England and Spain in 1587, Drake waltzed into the port of Cádiz and, catching the Spanish unaware, lit a match to the Spanish Armada and also relieved Philip II of around 3000 barrels of sherry. Back at the British court, sherry thereafter became a fabulously fashionable fortified wine among England's rich and poor.

02 Hailing from Jerez
Sherry was the first Spanish product to be granted the Denomination of Origin status meaning that it must be made from grapes grown in a certain area – incorporating the Andalusian Sanlúcar de Barrameda, El Puerto de Santa Maria and Jerez de la Frontera.

03 Back in Black
Each sherry barrel is deliberately painted black to make it easier to spot leakages, as seeping sherry shines bright upon the matt surface of the cask.

04 You're Bard

Sherry appears in Shakespeare's *King Henry IV Part II* when Sir John Falstaff sings its praises: 'A good sherris-sack,' he says, 'ascends me into the brain; dries me there all the foolish and dull and crudy vapours which environ it; makes it apprehensive, quick, forgetive, full of nimble fiery and delectable shapes; which, deliver'd o'er to the voice, the tongue, which is the birth, becomes excellent wit. The second property of your excellent sherris is, the warming of the blood; which, before cold and settled, left the liver white and pale, which is the badge of pusillanimity and cowardice: but the sherris warms it and makes it course from the inwards to the parts extreme. It illumineth the face, which, as a beacon, gives warning to all the rest of this little kingdom.'

05 Shipshape Sherry

Bountiful barrels of sherry accompanied Christopher Columbus on his expedition to America and it was the first wine to travel around the world when Ferdinand Magellan fuelled his circumnavigation with the famed Spanish fortified wine.

06 Moors Magic

Sherry's history dates from 1100 BC when vines from Lebanon were taken to Xera by the Phoeni-cians. When Arab Moors took control of much of Spain and Portugal in the 8th century, grape-growing was 'justified' by Islamic authorities as nutrition for soldiers. In 1264, when the Christians took Jerez, the Moors left behind alembic stills, so allowing them to fortify wine.

07 I Like Big Butts and I Cannot Lie

Unlike wine, sherry doesn't do years. Instead it uses the 19th-century solera system that improves consistency. Barrels holding wines of different ages are ranked in tiers and when a small amount of wine is taken from the oldest barrel at the bottom, that barrel is then topped up with younger wine taken from a barrel above and so on until the top tier is filled with fresh wines.

08 Pass It To The Left Hand Side

According to Debrett's, the 'trusted source on British social skills, etiquette and style', port should always be passed to the left and should be served after pudding with the coffee course. 'If the port passes you by without your glass being filled, don't ask for the port, thereby making it change direction,' it says. 'Instead send your glass after the decanter and ask for it to be filled.'

09 Norwich Know-how

Should the decanter elude you, don't directly demand it. Instead, ask the person nearest the decanter: 'Do you know the Bishop of Norwich?' If they are well informed in the ways of port, the decanter will swiftly reach you. If they do not admit to knowing the Bishop, you must add 'he's a terribly good chap, but he always forgets to pass the port.'

10 Vintage Port

The ultimate port is vintage port, a wine from a single and particularly strong year using wines from a house's finest vineyards. It's bottled early, when it's about two years old, full of youthful exuberance and taut with tannins. Having not aged in oak, it requires a lot of maturation in the bottle and seldom reaches its peak before its twentieth year. It develops a heavy sediment, so always decant it.

PORT & SHERRY
RECOMMENDATIONS

Fortified wines are not just for Christmas, they're for life – a life too short for shabby sherries and poor ports. Here are ten tips to suit all seasons.

AMONTILLADO NAPOLEON
HIDALGO BODEGAS 16% ABV

Aged longer than a Fino, Amontillado has lost its film of flor. Fortified to 16-18% ABV, oxidisation doesn't take place too quickly, making it darker and fuller in body than Fino. Distinctively dry and packing a pungent punch, this family-owned bodega comes out with plenty of nutty tang.

LA GUITA MANZANILLA
15% ABV

Manzanilla hails from the coastal town of San-lúcar, where the maritime climate, more humid than Jerez, creates a thicker layer of flor, producing wines that are lighter and fresher than fino. A hugely popular Man-zanilla, this epitome of the style actually smells of the seaside with an evocative salty tang and a brisk, refreshing bite.

PEDRO'S ALMACENISTA SELECTION FINO
15% ABV

Fino is the world's most popular style of sherry and really does more for a phenomenal aperitif – ideal with a bowl of almonds and a warm Andalusian evening. Or, as we have done, with a packet of Monster Munch in our office in Kings Cross, London – it still tastes great. Protected from oxidisation by a layer of flor during the entire ageing process, Fino wines are pale and refreshing and produced by using the more elegant casks of Palomino grapes. This is a really great value Fino and is a little fuller than most, courtesy of taking 20% of the blend from a solera that boasts an average age of 15-20 years. It's bracing and zesty with a touch of pistachio in there too. Serve chilled.

OLOROSO RIO VIEJO
LUSTAU 19% ABV

Oloroso sherries mature for several years in the barrel without the protective layer of flor. Acutely oxidised and more highly fortified, oloroso tends to be darker and richer with enough character to deal with big, meaty dishes. A delicate example of the style from a widely revered producer, this mahogany-hued sherry comes from a solera dating back nearly a hundred years. A mellow blend of coffee, autumnal fruit, nuts and toffee – it's got legs, length and a lovely lingering light finale.

PX CARDENAL CISNEROS

18% ABV

A sweet style of sherry made with dried Pedro Ximenez grapes (hence the PX), its fermentation is halted with the addition of spirit. An unctuous, opaque after-dinner affair to rival port and cognac, it's aged for more than 15 years in the solera system. Espresso, Christmas cake, chocolate-coloured raisins and a touch of tobacco.

SÁNCHEZ ROMATE, CAYETANO DEL PINO PALO CORTADO

21% ABV

Palo Cortado bridges the gap between Oloroso and Amontillado. Beginning life as a Fino and then an Amontillado, it's aged for longer once the flor has disappeared and oxidisation works its magic. Championed by smaller producers, it offers great value for money – especially this deep, dry smoky sherry from a historic, family-owned bodega who have supplied the Vatican.

WARRE'S OTIMA

10 YEAR TAWNY PORT 20% ABV

A terrific tawny port that blows the cobwebs from Port's clichéd persona. Golden brown and made up of wines aged in oak for an average of 10 years, Warre's is a well-balanced and rounded port with a light acidity mellowed by sweet, honeyed tones and a nice nutty backbone. Best served chilled with olives or a slice of cheesecake.

GRAHAM'S LBV 2008

20% ABV

Using grapes from a single year's harvest, this Late Bottled Vintage ruby port is aged for between four and six years. Graham's works with the finest quintas in the Upper Duoro valley and the quality comes through in this elegant, inky drop – black cherry, liquorice, dark chocolate and there's a bit of rum and raisin in there.

TAYLOR'S CHIP DRY WHITE PORT

20% ABV

Less mahogany-clad gentleman's club and more summer terrace, White Port is called white port because it's made using white grapes such as Malvasia Fina, Códega, Gouveio and Donzelinho Branco. It's barely aged before bottling and is best served chilled, over-ice or as a long drink with tonic. It's also perfect accompanied by a pint of prawns.

NIEPOORT RUBY DUM NV PORT

20% ABV

Vibrant, fresh and fruity with a touch of tannin as well too, this example of the most popular type of port is made using grapes from the Cima Corgo region in the Douro valley of Portugal. It's aged in large wooden casks for an average of three years and goes spectacularly well with a chunk of quality milk chocolate or a wedge of ripe, robust Roquefort. Or maybe even both.

5 THINGS YOU NEED TO KNOW ABOUT BRANDY

01 Devil Drink
The idea of double-distillation, key to the production of Cognac, came to a 16th-century Knight in a hellish dream. Legend has it that Jacques de la Croix-Maron endured a nightmare in which Satan attempted to boil him in order to get hold of his soul, but was, at least initially, unsuccessful. With typical demon derring-do, Satan tried to boil him a second time. When Croix-Maron suddenly awoke from his nightmare, he realised Beelzebub was trying to tell him something about his brandy: distil the wine a second time and its soul will reveal itself.

02 Nelson's Blood
In 1805, during the Battle of Trafalgar, Britain showed the French and Spanish who was boss when it came to battleships. Yet the gloss was taken off the 22 ships to nil victory by the untimely death of Admiral Lord Nelson, hit in his heavily-medalled chest by a French musket ball aboard HMS *Victory*.

To halt decomposition of his body during the trip back to Gibraltar, Nelson was sub-merged in a barrel of French brandy which, if you believe the legend, was then tapped open and, in honour of Horatio, drained empty by sailors using straws.

'Tapping The Admiral' or 'Sucking the Monkey' are sailors' terms for the secret and surreptitious consumption of barrelled spirits using a straw.

03 Swiss Swindle

If you happen to find yourself shivering on the side of a Swiss mountain and in desperate need of a snifter-sized slug of brandy to warm you up, then don't expect a St Bernard dog to help you out – it's all a myth. An 1820 Edwin Landseer painting first depicted the dogs danglin tiny casks of brandy from their collars but we have to confirm that the monks of the St Bernard Hospice have only ever armed their canine companions with brandy for tourist photographs.

04 Cognac Regions

In 1860, a French geologist called Henri Coquand carved Cognac up into six distinct regions (crus) according to their soil and weather.

In order of excellence, the six key cognac regions of France are:

I. *Fine Grande Champagne*
Only cognacs made with 100% Grande Champagne eaux-de-vie can be called 'Fine Grande Champagne'.

II. *Petite Champagne* is situated to the south of Grande Champagne where the *eaux-de-vies*, while still elegant, show a slightly heavier touch. When blended 50/50 with cognac wines, Fine Champagne Cognacs are produced.

III. *Borderies* is the smallest of the crus and, with a greater wealth of woodland, it's also the sweatiest, producing a 'nutty' and 'violet' nose. Borderies mature more quickly and elegantly than Champagne crus.

IV. *Fins Bois*, meaning fine woods, is the biggest cru and it envelops both the Champagne and the Borderies. Lends itself to younger blends.

V. *Bons Bois* translates as 'good woods' but its *eau-de-vie* –rustic, robust and earthy – is not considered as good as the superior Cognac houses.

VI. *Bois Ordinaires wines*
Fast-ageing wines that do lack some finesse. Set on sandy soil with a salty, wind-swept character.

05 Cognac Code

Cognac producers have a highly complicated age classification system.

VS or Three Star: VS stands for 'very special'. The youngest eaux-de-vie has to be at least two and a half years old – from the date the grapes were picked.

VSOP *'Very Superior Old Pale'* cognac was first referred to by George IV in a letter to Hennessy in 1817. The youngest *eaux-de-vie* has to be aged for at least four and a half years. The 'S' can mean *'superior'* here as well as *'special'*.

Napoleon: Napoleon was given a bottle by Courvoisier in 1811 when in exile. The youngest *eaux-de-vie* has to be at least six and a half years old.

XO: Extra Old cognac is very swanky. From 2018, it must be blended using *eaux-de-vie* that is at least 10 years old. Until then, it has to be at least six years old but usually older.

Vintage Cognac: The *eaux-de-vie* in vintage cognacs are all taken from a single year as specified on the bottle. These examples are rare and expensive. We suggest them for special occasions only.

Château de Bordeneuve, where Thomas Guasch grows Ugni Blanc and Baceo grapes and distils his award-winning Baron de Sigognac Bas Armagnac.

ARMAGNAC

You've got to admire the sheer Gallic gall of it. The French have been fooling the rest of the world for centuries, fobbing us off with their so-called 'very superior' cognac while keeping Armagnac, the oldest, finest French brandy, all to themselves.

Just 2.5% of the 150 million bottles of cognac consumed worldwide are done so in France, while less than half of all the Armagnac sold every year, around six million bottles, is enjoyed abroad.

Sourced as Armagnac is, from the land of musketeers, you'd be forgiven for attributing its relative global obscurity to a cloak-and-dagger conspiracy but more convincing is Cognac's convenient location on the coast.

Armagnac is the spirit of Gascony, an inland area of idyllic uplifting isolation situated in the south-west of France, where there are no autoroutes, ducks outnumber people by 20 to one and the biggest town, Condom (stop it), boasts a seriously small population of just 7,000 people.

Cognac's less ostentatious, older cousin (dating back to 1411), Armagnac is 'La France Profonde' in liquid form. It's ramshackle, rural and rustic and, in stark contrast to the manicured maisons that control Cognac, it's steadfastly remained in the delightfully disorganised hands of more than 800 growers.

The Armagnacais are mostly made up of smaller growers boasting no more than a few hectares of vines who seldom own their own still. Late every autumn, as the countryside glows a glorious amber and gold, tractors trundle around Armagnac's rolling hills, taking tall copper stills from farm to farm and firing them up in what locals call 'La Flamme.'

Fiercely individual and fabulously French, Armagnac's producers have never agreed on one way of distilling their spirit – but therein lies its bucolic beauty. Its grapes are grown on vines that endure colder winters than Cognac, furnishing hardier fruit and a more robust character.

Unlike as with cognac, which must use a pot still, Armagnacais can use two different kinds of still (continuous and pot) and while their northern counterparts double-distil, the Armagnacais tend to have only one go at it – resulting in a spirit that is either brimming with rustic charm or just a bit rough – with much depending on whether you live above or below Bordeaux.

Armagnac drinks darker, deeper and stronger than the softer more delicate cognac, it's more supple in body with more fire in its belly and more hairs on its chest. Cognac is to Armagnac as silk is to velvet; it's the Mezcal to cognac's Tequila, feisty in youth, earthy in old age and, often, also features a funky farmyard finish.

It's a spirit that lends itself to the local cuisine. Gascony is the go-to place if you want to get gout yet Armagnac serves as a fine foil to *foie gras* and cuts through *confit de canard* with consummate ease. Pour it over prunes, another local delicacy, and everything should flow just fine. But we digress...

Armagnac doesn't bling up its bottles, it doesn't lend its name to lavish horse races and, if you asked an Armagnac producer about hip-hop, he'd probably mutter something about a medical procedure in the pelvic area.

With less money spent on the dark arts of commercial marketing, Armagnac tends to deliver a better brandy for your buck. If you spend the same amount of money on a cognac of the same age then don't be surprised to discover, beneath cognac's fur coat of refinement, a distinct lack of underwear.

It may come as a shock to the business folk of Shanghai, and don't tell Busta Rhymes, or indeed his heavily armed entourage, but Cognac may not be the best brandy in the world. In fact, there are some (including us) who that would say that it's not even the very best brandy in France.

Armagnac is obtained from the distillation of white wines produced from the grapes Ugni Blanc, Baco and, for a lesser part, Colombard and Folle Blanche. Also authorized are Clairette de Gascogne, Plant de Graisse, Jurançon Blanc, Mauzac Blanc and Rosé and Meslier Saint-François. None of them make particularly good wines, we are told.

Interpreting an Armagnac Bottle

The age indicated on the bottle always corresponds to the minimum ageing in oak barrels of the youngest *eau-de-vie* in the blend (see page 217). However, in practice, the blends are often of an average age well above the legal requirement.

VS, ***
1 year of ageing in wood, stands for very special

VSOP
4 years of ageing in wood

Napoléon, XO
6 years of ageing in wood

Hors d'Age
10 years of ageing in wood

What about vintages?
The vintage corresponds exclusively to the year of one particular harvest. They rarely reduce the alcohol. The *eaux-de-vie* are often sold at their natural alcohol strength, which is generally between 40% and 48% ABV.

BRANDY
RECOMMENDATIONS

The French are brilliant at transforming fruit into spirits. Whether made with grapes or apples, distilled in the north or south, here are some beautiful brandies.

DARROZE DOMAINE DE LASSERADE 1945 BAS ARMAGNAC 45.7% ABV

Darroze means that all the brandy in the bottle comes only from small domains in the Bas Armagnac region. What's more, you can rest assured that no additives have been used either. This is uncut Armagnac at its finest. Matured in new local wood, lasting between two and five years, before being placed into old wood.

CALVADOS PAYS D'AUGE
6-YEAR-OLD 40% ABV

A classy, classic French Normandy Calvados, from one of the region's most esteemed calvados producers, the Camut family. Their organic Calvados has not changed since the 1800s. More than two dozen apple varieties are double-distilled in its patented Charentais stills made from local apple wood.

ARMAGNAC DELORD
25-YEAR-OLD 40% ABV

'L'Authentique' is a traditional, authentic Bas-Armagnac blend from Maison Delord, a small French family Armagnac producer in Lannepax, Gers. A cask-strength blend of seven different vintages delivers Delord's renowned rounded richness. Rich fruit and a long finish.

HINE HOMAGE GRAND CRU 40% ABV
EARLY LANDED COGNAC

Hine is held in high regard by the cognac *cognoscenti* and is well-known for its celebrated Vintage Grande Champagne and 'early-landed' cognacs aged in Bristol, England, where the climate is cooler than in Jarnac in Cognac itself.

MARTELL V. S.
VS COGNAC 40% ABV

The oldest of the 'big four', Martell was founded on the banks of the Charente back in 1715 by Jean Martell, an entrepreneurial intermediary from Jersey who had dealt in everything from coal and butter to flowers and goat skins. At its height, it was the cognac served on Concorde and the Orient Express – and it starred in the opening scene of *Apocalypse Now*, when Martin Sheen, going stir-crazy within the walls of a Saigon hotel room, swigged it before smashing his hand through a mirror (don't try this at home). Using only Troncais oak, whose tighter grain offers softer oak tannins, Martell's house style is known as a delicate drop and its Cordon Bleu, launched in 1912, brings together eaux-de-vie from the Borderies area – reminiscent of orange peel, blossom and a pecan nut finish.

TARIQUET XO
12-YEAR-OLD 40% ABV

Before the family-owners of Tariquet turned to making excellent Armagnac (and, more recently, some decent white wines too), they earned a living from taming wild bears in the region. Aged for between 12 and 15 years, this ugni-blanc-inspired XO Bas Armagnac offers notes of hazelnuts, tobacco, vanilla and baked prunes – not to mention tremendous value for money.

TESSERON 40% ABV
LOT NO.53 XO PERFECTION

Tesseron tends to offer top-notch cognacs at prices that won't worry your wallet in quite the same way as the region's more recognised houses. When swirled in a snifter, this quixotic coming together of Grande Champagne cognacs serves up cedar and cigar on the nose with some smooth spicy notes in the mouth and a clean, cocoa finish.

DELAMAIN VESPER 40% ABV
GRANDE CHAMPAGNE COGNAC

Dating back to 1759, this family-owned Cognac house, founded by James Delamain, doesn't muddy its mains with cognacs that don't come from the Grande Champagne region and has dealt with the same independent producers for a number of generations. The Vesper is a mesmeric 35 year-old marriage, deep copper in hue, intensely aromatic on the nose with a woody palate that doesn't overdo the opulent oak. Not cheap but rather special.

COURVOISIER VSOP EXCLUSIF
MIXED COGNAC 40% ABV

From the preferred cognac house of Napoleon I and Busta Rhymes, this cognac was initially aimed at the Asian market but one that has come to be used in cocktails. Taking approximately 50 different eaux-de-vie from all of the four key cognac regions, it belies its average age of seven years with an impressive complexity. Plump and peppery, there's plenty of fruit and floral finesse on the finish – in fact, there's no reason why you couldn't drink it neat.

RÉMY MARTIN COEUR DE COGNAC
FINE CHAMPAGNE COGNAC 40% ABV

One of the classic cognacs, VSOP is the brandy on which the remarkable Rémy Martin tumultuous story has been built. Rémy represents one in every three bottles of VSOP sold worldwide. It boasts a hugely strong following in America, where it's heralded by the hip-hop crowd, including Jay Z and Ludacris, who no doubt appreciate Rémy Martin's policy of extended maturation in new wood during wet-weather years. Smooth and soothing; you pick up a little leather satchel on the nose, cinnamon and figs, with strokes of vanilla on the finish.

INDEX

Figures in *italics* refer to captions.

BIBLIOGRAPHY

BOOKS

Alcoholica Esoterica, Ian Lendler, Penguin Books 2005

Alexander the Great: The Invisible Enemy, John Maxwell O'Brien, Routledge 1994

Blackbeard: The Real Pirate of the Caribbean, Dan Parry, National Maritime Museum 2006

Bogart: A Life in Hollywood, Jeffrey Meyers, André Deutsch 1997

Bogart, A M Sperber and Eric Lax, William Morrow and Co 1998

Cinemachismo: Masculinities and Sexuality in Mexican Film, Sergio de la Mora, University of Texas Press 2006

Emilio Fernández: Pictures in the Margins, Dolores Tierney, Manchester University Press 2012

Europe's Physician: The Life of Theodore de Mayerne, Hugh Trevor-Roper, Yale University Press 2006

Grogan's Companion to Drink, Pete Grogan. Virgin Books 2010

Hemingway: A Biography, Jeffrey Meyers, Da Capo 1999

Ernest Hemingway: A Life, Carlos Baker, Penguin Books 1972

Hemingway: His Life and Work, Kenneth S Lynn, Harvard University Press 1995

The History of Pirates, Angus Konstam, Mercury Books 2005

A History of Vodka, William Pokhlebkin, Verso 1992

The Life of Graham Greene, Norman Sherry, Jonathan Cape 1989

Peter the Great, M S Anderson, Routledge 2000

Pursued by Furies: A life of Malcolm Lowry, Gordon Bowker, Flamingo, 1994

Saloons of the Old West, Richard Erdoes, Random House 1997

Scotch on the Rocks: The True Story of the Whisky Galore, Arthur Swinson, Luath Press 2005

Shackleton, Roland Huntford, Abacus 1989

Tequila: A Natural and Cultural History, Ana Guadalupe Valenzuela-Zapata and Gary Paul Nabhan, University of Arizona Press 2004

Thomas Jefferson on Wine, John Hailman, University Press of Mississippi 2009

Tough without a Gun: The Extraordinary Life of Humphrey Bogart, Stefan Kanfer, Alfred A Knopf 2011

Vodka Politics: Alcohol, Autocracy, and the Secret History of the Russian State, Mark Lawrence Schrad, Oxford University Press 2014

William III and the Godly Revolution, Tony Claydon, Cambridge University Press 2004

JOURNALS

The Biblical Archaeology Review, September/October Issue 2010

PICTURE CREDITS

Page 2-3 Rob Lawson/Jacqui Small; **6** Rob Lawson; **12-3 background** Shutterstock; **13** The Print Collection/Alamy; **18-19 background** Shutterstock; 18 Moviestore collection Ltd/Alamy; **19** SuperStock/Alamy; **20** Beers of Europe; **21** Glasshouse Images/Alamy; **22** Zvonimir Atletić/Alamy; **23** Alamy; **24** Geoffrey Kidd/Alamy; **25** Big Tom/Alamy; **26 top** North Wind Picture Archives/Alamy; **27** Ben McFarland; **30-31 background** Shutterstock; **32 background** Les Polders/ Alamy; **34-5** Bill Bradshaw/Jacqui Small; **38-39** Shutterstock; **39 top** Hemis/Alamy; **45 background** Shutterstock, Eric Anthony Johnson /Alamy; **46-8 background** Shutterstock **49 map** Shawshots/Alamy; **50** GL Archive/Alamy; **51** Mary Evans Picture Library/Alamy; **52** Mary Evans Picture Library/Alamy; **53** Classic Image/Alamy; **54-5 background** Shutterstock; **54** Domaine Leflaive; **55 top and bottom** Château de Tigne; **56** Shawshots/Alamy; **57** Wine stain: Shutterstock **left** Moviestore collection Ltd/Alamy, **right** AF archive/Alamy; **58** Shawshots/Alamy; **64** Jamesons; **65** 20th Century Advertising/Alamy; **64-5 background** Shutterstock **68-9** Simon Murrell/Jacqui Small; **72 top** Classic Images/Alamy, **below** Adnams; **73** Classic Images/Alamy, **background** Shutterstock; **74** Lordprice Collection/Alamy; **77 bottom** Simon Murrell/Jacqui Small; **78-9 background** Shutterstock; **85** Mary Evans Picture Library /Alamy; **88-9 background** Shutterstock; **91** Glasshouse Images/Alamy, **background** Shutterstock; **92** Shutterstock; **95** AF Archive/Alamy, **background** Shutterstock; **102-3 background** Shutterstock; **108-9 background** Shutterstock; **110** Hemis/Alamy; **112** Classic image/Alamy; **113** Robert Harding Picture Library/Alamy, **background** Shutterstock; **115 top** MARKA/Alamy, **115 bottom** Photos 12/Alamy; **118 background** Steve Hamlin/Alamy **120 Margarita and Paloma:** Rob Lawson/Jacqui Small; **121 Bandera** Christian Draghici/Alamy; **124 background** Incamerastock/Alamy; **Tommy's Margarita** Tomas Estes & Phil Bayly; **121 Batanga** Rob Lawson; **125** ITAR-TASS Photo Agency/Alamy; **130-1 background** Shutterstock; **132-133 background** Shutterstock;**133** Glasshouse Images/Alamy; **134** United Archives GmbH/Alamy; **135** Gabe Palmer/Alamy; **136** Allstar Picture Library/Alamy; **137 top** Keystone Pictures USA/Alamy, **middle** Everett Collections Historical/Alamy **bottom**

David Cole/Alamy; **143** Cosmopolitan cocktail: D Hurst/Alamy; **146-147 background** Shutterstock **top** BROKER/Alamy **bottom** Rob Lawson/Jacqui Small; **154** Shutterstock; **156-7 background** Zoonar GmbH/Alamy; **158 background** Helga/Alamy; **top** GL Archive/Alamy; **159 left** Henry Morgan: Mary Evans Picture Library/Alamy, **right** Everett Collection Historical/Alamy; **162-3** Rob Lawson/Jacqui Small; **166-7 background** Shutterstock; **167** Everett Collection Historical/Alamy; **172-3 background** Shutterstock; **172** Patrick Guenette/Alamy; **173** Angelica: Quagga Media/Alamy; **176 background** Falkensteinfoto/Alamy; **177** Mary Evans Picture Library/Alamy; **178 left** Boord & Son, **right** Hayman's; **180-1 background** Shutterstock; **181** Rob Lawson/Jacqui Small; **184** Mary Evans Picture Library/Alamy; **185** INTERFOTO/Alamy; **186-7 background** MARKA/Alamy; **188 top** Alliance Images/Alamy, **bottom** GL Archive/Alamy; **189** Rob Lawson/Jacqui Small; **192-7** Rob Lawson/Jacqui Small; **196-197 background** Shutterstock; **203** Rob Lawson/Jacqui Small; **204-205 background** Shutterstock; **204** Mary Evans Picture Library/Alamy; **205** Classic Image/Alamy; **206-11 backgrounds** Shutterstock; **206** Zoffoli **211** David Cole/Alamy; **212-3 background** Shutterstock; **216-218 background** Shutterstock.

ILLUSTRATIONS

Chapter openers, pages 10-11, 36-7, 62-3, 100-1, 122-3, 144-5, 164-5, 194-5: Andrew Bannecker/www.ba-reps.com; **Timelines, pages** 14-15, 40-1, 66-7, 104-5, 126-7, 148-9,168-9, 198-9: Nicholas Saunders/folioart.co.uk; **Distinguished Drinkers: pages** 16-17, 42-5, 68-9, 86-7, 105-6, 128-9, 150-1, 182-3, 170-1, 200-3, pages 1, 4-5, **Endpapers:** Martin Haake/www.centralillustration.com

PUBLISHER'S ACKNOWLEDGMENTS

The publisher wishes to thank the many drinks companies around the world who kindly provided images for this book. Thanks also to Berry Bros & Rudd, Simon Murrell and Amanda Skinner.

AUTHORS' ACKNOWLEDGMENTS

Tom would like to thank… My beautiful wife Claire, who supports and never questions the absurdity of my career. And son Joseph, a marvellous little fellow who provides me with plenty of awake time to think about words. To family: Mum and Dad, sister Ellen, brother Edward and Nikki for coming to the show and ceaselessly drinking Hobo beer! And to Rob, Janet, Stuart, Tracy, Harry and Rory – you can read it when you're 18, boys. One of the big regrets of projects like this is the time it consumes, hopefully I'll see more of you all now it's done. To extended family Nuala, Joe, Colin and the Irish contingent and to Seamus, Steve, Liam, Alex, Ant, Tait and Waitey, your humour works its way into some of these words.

Ben would like to thank… First and foremost, Mrs Sophie McFarland for simply being such a lovely, loving and utterly wonderful wife. To all my family for being brilliant – to my magnificent Mum for all her help, to Dad and Nicola for their unwavering support, and to my most ridiculously excellent big brother Barnaby. Thanks to Jacques, Alison, Tessa and Louis 'Superhoop' Le Bars as well as Mike & Ania, Tom, Alice & Zosia for all your love, sustenance and support. The following friends also deserve a special thank you – Tom, Hattie, Ned, Esther and Ely; Matthew & Sonya, Eddie & Zoe, Wheatley & Fleur, James & Diane, Katie & Jack, Shep and Harriet, Toby & Adela, Sophie & James; Flo & Russ; Tom & Kate; Miles, Adam Slate, Anja, the chaps behind Hobo Beer and, of course, Queens Park Rangers Football Club – you all know what to buy everyone this Christmas...it's what Jesus would have wanted.

Massive thanks to theatre darlings and impresarios Sal and Mal for helping make the Thinking Drinkers show such a success. Come out for a second bow.

Thanks to the Drinks industry and all who serve it. 'Drink Less. Drink Better.'

The British Library, an unbelievable free resource with an obscenely over-priced café.

To everyone at Jacqui Small – especially the incredibly patient Jo Copestick, Fritha Saunders, Rachel Cross, Alexandra Labbe-Thompson, Jacqui Small and all the illustrators. Thanks for all your help throughout.